Trade Unions in West Africa

Trade Unions Past, Present and Future

EDITED BY CRAIG PHELAN

Volume 7

PETER LANG
Oxford • Bern • Berlin • Bruxelles • Frankfurt am Main • New York • Wien

Trade Unions in West Africa

Historical and Contemporary Perspectives

Craig Phelan (ed.)

PETER LANG
Oxford • Bern • Berlin • Bruxelles • Frankfurt am Main • New York • Wien

Bibliographic information published by Die Deutsche Nationalbibliothek.
Die Deutsche Nationalbibliothek lists this publication in the Deutsche Nationalbibliografie; detailed bibliographic data is available on the Internet at http://dnb.d-nb.de.

A catalogue record for this book is available from the British Library.

Library of Congress Cataloging-in-Publication Data:

Trade unions in West Africa : historical and contemporary perspectives / Craig Phelan (ed).
p. cm. -- (Trade unions past, present and future ; v. 7)
Includes bibliographical references and index.
ISBN 978-3-0343-0117-6 (alk. paper)
1. Labor unions--Africa, West. 2. Labor unions--Africa, West--History--20th century. I. Phelan, Craig, 1958-
HD6880.T73 2011
331.880966--dc23

2011026713

ISSN 1662-7784
ISBN 978-3-0343-0117-6

Hochfeldstrasse 32, CH-3012 Bern, Switzerland
info@peterlang.com, www.peterlang.com, www.peterlang.net

Printed in Germany

Contents

CRAIG PHELAN

West African Trade Unionism Past and Present

This book is a collaborative investigation of trade unionism in Africa's most populous regional economic zone. With a population of 261 million in 2006, the fifteen countries that presently comprise the Economic Community of West African States (ECOWAS) represent approximately 34 per cent of the total sub Saharan African population. With the exception of the former British colonies of Nigeria and Ghana, however, surprisingly little has been written in English to describe and analyse the trade union movements that have played such pivotal roles in the histories of the these countries before and since independence: Benin, Burkina Faso, Cape Verde, Côte d'Ivoire, The Gambia, Guinea, Guinea Bissau, Liberia, Mali, Niger, Senegal, Sierra Leone and Togo. Eight of the fifteen ECOWAS states are officially Francophone and two are Lusophone, and their trade union histories have rarely been written in (or even translated into) English. Nor is there much literature on trade unionism in the smaller Anglophone West African states such as The Gambia, Sierra Leone or Liberia. This collection begins to fill the void in the literature by bringing together scholarship on the remarkably varied and undeniably important histories and contemporary dilemmas faced by trade unions across the region.

African industrial relations and trade union history is experiencing a renaissance of sorts in recent years. In the late 1950s and 1960s, following the success of African independence movements, a spate of broad ranging, multi-country studies appeared in both French and English on African trade union movements. These books were testimony to trade unionism's importance in the independence struggles and also to the grand debate over the 'labour question' in the new nations.[1] From the mid 1970s until the early 1990s, scholarly interest in African trade unionism was to some extent in retreat, as one-party regimes stifled or co-opted independent trade unions and as African economic development failed to meet expectations.[2] Only in the last ten to fifteen years has academic interest once again peaked. The role of trade unions in ending apartheid in South Africa, their presence in the dynamic movements for meaningful democracy in other African countries, and their resistance to the harsh social costs of structural adjustment programmes – these have provided much of the impetus for renewed interest in the subject.

Given its standing as the most economically advanced country on the continent, with the most developed trade union movement and industrial relations system, it is hardly surprising that most recent literature on African trade unionism focuses on South Africa.[3] There are also a growing number of studies that offer continent wide perspectives.[4] On trade unionism, the best of the recent collections are Gérard Kester and Ousmane Oumarou Sidibé (eds) (1997) *Trade Unions and Sustainable Democracy in Africa*,

1 Meynaud and Saleh-Bey (1963), *Le Syndicalisme Africain*, Roberts (1964), *Labour in the Tropical Territories of the Commonwealth*, and Davies (1966), *African Trade Unions* were three of the better known studies.

2 Important monographs and multi-country studies did appear in these years, to be sure, including Damachi et al (eds) (1979), *Industrial Relations in Africa*; Gutkind et al (eds) (1978), *African Labor History*; Sandbrook and Cohen (eds) (1975), *The Development of an African Working Class*; Fashoyin (1992), *Industrial Relations and African Development*; Copans et al (eds) (1987), *Classes ouvrières d'Afrique Noire*; and Thiam (1991), *Histoire du Mouvement Syndicale en Afrique, 1790–1929*.

3 There are numerous important collections on South African trade unionism, among them Adler and Webster (eds) (2000), *Trade Unions and Democratization in South Africa*, Bramble and Barchiesi (eds) (2003), *Rethinking the Labour Movement in the 'New South Africa'*, and Buhlungu (ed.) (2006), *Trade Unions and Democracy: COSATU Workers' Political Attitudes in South Africa*.

4 Kamoche et al (eds) (2003), *Managing Human Resources in Africa* contains little on trade unionism, yet it is a fascinating account of HR practices in eleven countries. Wood and Brewster (eds) (2007), *Industrial Relations in Africa* is an excellent resource, providing mostly contemporary descriptions of the industrial relations systems in fifteen countries.

a superior study of ten countries in which trade unions played a role in the process of democratisation in the late 1980s and early 1990s, and Jon Kraus (ed.) *Trade Unions and the Coming of Democracy in Africa* (2007), which brings the story of trade unions' struggle for political democracy up to 2007 in seven countries. In 2007 Gérard Kester published a monograph (*Trade Unions and Workplace Democracy in Africa*) that updates the findings of his 1997 edited collection, and Gérard Fonteneau, *Histoire du Syndicalisme en Afrique* (2004), offers a brief but wide ranging introduction to the subject for French readers.

To date, there is no single book that addresses the history and present condition of trade unionism in West Africa. There have been numerous country studies of trade unionism in Ghana and Nigeria, occasional studies of trade unionism in other individual West African countries, and several dated chapters on French West African trade unions, such as those by Elliot Berg (1959) in Walter Galenson (ed.) *Labor and Economic Development* and George Martens (1979) in Ukandi Damachi et al (eds) *Industrial Relations in Africa*. András November, *L'Évolution du Mouvement Syndical en Afrique Occidentale* (1965) also emphasises Francophone West Africa but, unfortunately, is unavailable in English. Frederick Cooper, *Decolonization and African Society: The Labor Question in French and British Africa* (1996) is a landmark study that contains much on West African trade unions in the 1940s and 1950s, although its geographical and thematic scope is much wider. *Trade Unions in West Africa* is not only the first comprehensive study of trade unionism in West Africa from its roots until the present, but also as the first regional study in the growing field of African trade union and industrial relations scholarship.

It is an understatement to say that West Africa represents an inhospitable environment for healthy trade union development.[5] In the political sphere the region passed from an era of colonial domination to decades

5 Useful overviews of West Africa include Crowder (1968), *West Africa under Colonial Rule*; Asiwaju (2001), *West African Transformations: Comparative Impacts of French and British Colonialism*; Olukoshi (2001), *West Africa's Political Economy in the Next Millennium: Retrospect and Prospect*; and Laurijssen (2010), *Trade Union Pluralism and Proliferation in French-speaking Africa*.

of political instability characterised by repeated coups d'état, one-party states and military rule; only in the past twenty years has pluralist democracy taken root in most of the region's countries, and even today such democracy remains extremely fragile. Economically, the size of the wage labour force has always been a minority in a region where industrialisation based on import-substitution largely failed, and which remains dominated by agricultural activity (in the form of small-holder peasant households rather than large-scale commercial farming). Gripping poverty and severe balance of payments problems led to the extensive involvement of the International Monetary Fund (IMF) and World Bank in the region as early as the late 1970s, and their structural adjustment programmes led to wrenching cutbacks in employment in the civil service and state-run enterprises, where the bulk of the wage labour force is concentrated. One result of structural adjustment has been the rapid expansion of the informal sector, which, as we shall see, is notoriously difficult for trade unions to organise. Another impediment to trade union growth has been the region's remarkable ethnic, religious and linguistic diversity. West Africa comprises hundreds of distinct ethnic groups, and only in a few countries does one group comprise a majority of the population. At least 250 ethnic groups exist in Nigeria alone, and ethnic lines cut across national borders. Various versions of Islam, Christianity and traditional religions compete across the region. Unresolved social conflict and the incapacity of the various states to provide adequate social provision for all citizens ensures that ethnic and religious strife remains constant and at times volatile in many parts of the region.

Remarkably, despite such an uncongenial environment, West African trade unionism has played an undeniably important role in the history of the region. Although numerically weak, and although often politically hamstrung, the various trade union movements of the region have frequently been at the forefront of West Africa's vibrant civil society and have exercised real influence on the course of events during key periods of transformation. Usually such influence has been exercised in coalition with other civil society actors, making West Africa a laboratory for the study of social movement unionism. A social movement approach to West African trade unionism would concentrate on those moments of transition in which trade unions were part of larger movements of resistance and change. The first such moment was the long push for independence, when trade unions joined hands with intellectuals and burgeoning nationalist political parties in a complex interplay of people and forces that eventually led to the elimination of the British and French colonial presence. A second moment was the equally long struggle to define labour's role in the newly independent states, as trade unions and other groups engaged in countless acts of resistance to political oppression and authoritarianism. A third moment of transition involved trade union responses to structural adjustment and the rapid growth of the informal sector, which involved alliances with NGOs and community activists who resisted the widespread impact of austerity measures and sought creatively to organise market traders and others who operated outside the formal sector. And a fourth moment was the wave of democratic transition that swept across the region beginning at the end of the 1980s; strike action and other forms of trade union activity were often the backdrop to broad based movements seeking a shift from authoritarianism to pluralist democracy.

The remainder of this introduction will examine these moments of transition in greater detail, in an effort to provide a sense of both the strictures and opportunities facing West African trade unions from the 1940s onwards.

Trade Unions and Independence Struggles

Sometimes referred to as the 'white man's grave' due to rampant malaria, yellow fever and other diseases, West Africa, unlike South Africa, Zimbabwe, Mozambique, Kenya, the Belgian Congo and elsewhere on the continent, did not experience extensive white settlement during the years of colonial domination. Disease, tribal wars and especially the ravages of the slave trade also kept the black population of the region in check, and thus the optimal use of the existing labour supply was always at the forefront of colonial thought. Both the British and French used taxation as a push to induce village populations to become a workforce for the coffee, cocoa and peanut plantations, and to provide the manpower to construct and maintain the basic infrastructures. Much more effective in creating a colonial labour force were systems of forced labour. In general, the system of direct taxation in French West Africa was heavier than in British West African colonies, and certainly the French made more extensive use of forced labour than did the British. The French also conscripted far more Africans to fight in the world wars than did the British, and the French system of arbitrary authority (the indigénat) help explain why, in the first half of the twentieth century, there was extensive migration from French controlled areas such as Côte d'Ivoire and Upper Volta (Burkina Faso) to the Gold Coast (Ghana). It has been argued that these migrations should be considered the first wave of labour protest in response to colonial rule.[6]

Labour needs in both British and French West Africa tore the fabric of village life, yet the number of wage workers remained relatively small throughout the colonial period. Even with relatively large scale investment from the colonial powers and rapid urbanisation, wage labour in manufacturing, mining, transport, commerce, education, and the colonial administration remained a small percentage of the total population. It has been estimated that in 1957 in French West Africa, only 4.6 per cent of the total population worked for wages. Europeans dominated the managerial and supervisory positions, while Africans assumed the less skilled places.[7] Yet it was here, among the bank clerks and railroad workers, teachers and especially colonial civil servants, that modern West African trade unionism took root.

While one can find evidence of early trade unions and industrial strife long before World War II in West Africa, it was only with the conclusion of that war that sustained labour movements emerged. Industrial relations practices, labour law and trade union development were very

6 Asiwaju (1976), 'Migrations as Revolt'; Deniel (1974), 'Mesures gouvernementales et/ou intérêts divergents'.

7 Martens (1979), 22; Berg (1959), 199–202.

heavily influenced by the colonial environment in which it took place. In essence, what took root in West Africa beginning in the late 1940s was imported trade unionism and industrial relations. In French West Africa, a decree of 7 August 1944 eliminated most of the impediments to the widespread creation of trade unions in the colonies, and in 1952 the French implemented the Overseas Labour Code, which imposed industrial relations practices based on those existing in France. The three dominant French trade union confederations competed with each other in recruiting Africans. Until the late 1950s, the largest trade union presence in French West Africa was the Confédération Générale du Travail (CGT), France's communist dominated confederation. Anne-Catherine Wagner's chapter in this volume investigates the CGT's efforts to organise West African wage workers from the 1930s onwards. Even today, much of the industrial relations systems found in former French colonies contain elements of the labour codes imposed by France in the colonial period, although these systems have withered and are now largely ineffectual. Trade union movements in former British colonies likewise bear the imprint of British law and trade union traditions. The 1938 Trade Union Ordinance provided the legal basis for union formation in Nigeria, and the Nigerian Trades Union Congress, created in 1943, was fashioned after the British TUC. Similarly, a 1941 Trade Union Ordinance paved the way for the creation in 1945 of a British-modelled Ghanaian Trades Union Congress. Both David Perfect, in his chapter on The Gambia, and Kwamina Panford, in his chapter on Ghana, demonstrate how industrial relations in Anglophone West Africa reflected its British origins.

West Africans also drew upon their own traditions when erecting trade union movements. The kingdoms and empires that dominated the region until the nineteenth century represented some of the most sophisticated pre-colonial efforts at nation building in Africa. This heritage of nation building and the relative absence of white setter colonialism, some scholars suggest, provided fertile ground for the potent intellectual and political currents that fuelled anti-colonial sentiment and trade union development. Cheikh Anta Diop's 'Egyptology', Léopold Sédar Senghor's 'Negritude', Kwame Nkrumah's 'Pan-Africanism' and other trends captured the imagination of West African politicians and trade union leaders. James Jones's chapter will explore the growing confidence and idealism of trade unions as they conducted lengthy strikes on the major railroad lines in the late 1940s. By 1956 approximately 35 per cent of wage earners in West Africa were trade union members, and in 1957, the French West African trade unions agreed to form a single federation – the Union Générale des Travailleurs de l'Afrique Noire (UGTAN) – and sever their ties with French unions. While short lived, UGTAN represented a giant step toward West African independence by signalling the emergence of a Pan-African agenda and a growing readiness to cut institutional links to the metropole.[8]

Political parties and trade unions established alliances in their confrontations with colonial authorities. In the 1950s progressive African political parties and trade unions shared a general commonality of purpose, although their partnership in states with more cautious parties was often contentious. In 1958, for instance, trade unionists in Benin toppled the colonial administration because of differing attitudes toward independence. Many of the strikes in this period were politically motivated and often supported by progressive parties as efforts to destabilise colonial regimes; strikes and other trade union activities were often quite successful in undermining both the French and British presence. In 1957 Ghana became the first black African state to gain independence. Trade unions were an important element of Kwame Nkrumah's Convention People's Party (CPP), and they were at the forefront of the CPP's campaign of civil disobedience, non-cooperation, boycotts and strikes during the 1950s that ultimately led the British to withdraw. Inspired by Nkrumah, Sékou Touré, a staunch trade unionist himself who was then president of UGTAN, encouraged Guineans to vote 'no' in a 1958 referendum on de Gaulle's Fifth Republic constitution. Guinea's famous 'no' vote led to the establishment of the first independent Francophone West African state. Elizabeth Schmidt's chapter explores the in detail the central role of trade unions in Sékou Touré's independence movement. By 1960 all French West African counties were independent, and in 1965 the last of the British colonies in the region, The Gambia, became an independent state.

8 Cooper (1997), 'UGTAN, the Loi-cadre and the Breakup of l'AOF'.

Trade Unions and One-Party States

A second major theme of the book is the fate of trade unionism in the midst of chronic political instability, one-party rule and militarism. Among the former British colonies, only The Gambia maintained the British parliamentary system for any length of time. Nigeria established a federal system, while the other states opted for centralised rule. Whatever their original choice of government, all former British colonies have experienced high levels of political violence and extensive militarism. Only one former French colony, Benin, established a multiparty government, and its first twelve years of independence were marked by intense political volatility. Senegal was exceptional in its stability. Léopold Sédar Senghor was president of Senegal from 1960 until 1980, when he handed power to Abdou Diouf, who ruled until 2000. The majority of independent West African countries proved far more combustible, and political succession was, at least until the democratic breakthroughs of the late 1980s and early 1990s, usually unconstitutional and accompanied by violence. Indeed, West Africa became known as the 'coup d'état belt' of Africa. Since 1963, when the Togolese army assassinated President Sylvanus Olympio, every country in West Africa with the exception of Senegal has experienced coups d'état and direct military rule. It has been estimated that since the early 1960s, each of the ECOWAS countries has experienced an average of three coups d'état and countless attempted coups.[9]

With independence, the alliances between trade unions and dominant political parties quickly broke down. There was no longer an obvious commonality of purpose. The desire to seek political legitimacy and popular support for modernisation programmes encouraged dominant parties to speak in the name of all citizens, the vast majority of whom (eighty to ninety per cent) were peasant farmers. States also inherited a large and expensive civil service, which diverted precious resources from other projects. Above all, political leaders were intent to harness all social

9 Olukoshi (2001), *West Africa's Political Economy in the Next Millennium*.

and economic energies to build political unity and promote economic advancement. Trade unions, on the other hand, represented the relatively privileged four to five per cent of the population who worked for wages. They were heavily concentrated in the civil service and the new state-led enterprises. Gains won for these workers, politicians often argued, no longer came at the expense of Britain and France but rather at the expense of the new nation. Having seen the capacity of unions to foment discord against colonial administrations, African political leaders also worried that trade unions could serve as the vanguard of opposition to their own regimes, especially in the urban areas.

For more than a decade after independence, infighting was rampant between established trade unions and the new regimes in West Africa, contributing to the region's political instability. In most countries, strenuous political efforts were made first to unify the multiple trade union confederations into a single national body, and then to control or absorb that unified confederation into the party apparatus, where they would become 'transmission belts' of party propaganda at the workplace and play a largely cosmetic role in corporatist industrial relations systems. General strikes, which had caused such disruption during the colonial period, were outlawed, legal restrictions on other traditional trade union activity became commonplace, political leaders often made unilateral decisions during collective bargaining negotiations, and leading trade union activists were seduced by the offer of political posts. Emphasis was placed on engineering a shift from 'selfish' to 'responsible' unionism, by which was meant that trade unions were expected to modify their agenda and embrace national goals rather than simply advance the interests of their members. Union opposition to these profound changes was often emphatic. In some one-party states, such as Ghana, Guinea and Côte d'Ivoire, the struggle between parties and trade unions was brief. Single union confederations were quickly created that were closely linked to the dominant parties. Burkina Faso and Benin, however, witnessed trade union-led coups d'états, while Mali, Senegal and other countries experienced intense conflict for many years, involving illegal strikes and bloodshed, between trade unions and ruling parties.[10]

By the mid 1970s, the grand debate over the labour question in West Africa had largely been resolved in favour of the ruling parties. Many states had established unified trade union confederations that pursued 'responsible' practices as defined by the parties. In Togo, for example, the one-party state that was established in 1969 after years of political instability, interfered incessantly with the affairs of individual unions and the two national federations. In 1972 the party dissolved the national federations and in 1973 replaced them with the new Confédération Nationale des Travailleurs du Togo (CNTT), which was integrated into the party structure. CNTT representatives took part in policy making bodies, and the state at first rewarded their responsible behaviour with limited wage increases for the membership, but official trade unionism had lost its oppositional voice and had assumed a largely productionist role. Similarly, in Benin, the pluralist and militant trade union movement that had played such a pivotal role in the first twelve years of that country's independence, was eventually incorporated by the state after the successful 1972 coup d'état led by Mathieu Kérékou. Kérékou's Marxist-Leninist regime, initially welcomed by workers and trade unions, disbanded the various trade union federations and in 1974 created the Union Nationale des Syndicats des Travailleurs du Bénin (UNSTB) as an appendage to the state. In his chapter, Azizou Chabi Imorou shows how individual unions resisted this party-controlled style of unionism. The unions of teachers and others challenged the Kérékou government despite heavy repression, so that the spirit if not the structure of independent unionism remained, and thus workers and their unions were able to play a leading role in the pro-democracy movement that eventually toppled the Kérékou regime in 1989. In his chapter on Guinea, Mohamed Saliou Camara assesses how Sékou Touré, arguably the most important trade union leader in French West Africa during the colonial period, suppressed independent trade unionism once Guinea declared its independence and Touré was installed as president. Touré moved quickly and decisively to

10 Martens (1994), 'French-speaking Africa'.

incorporate all popular movements into his one-party Marxist state, and as early as 1960 he unified the labour movement under a new confederation, the Confédération National des Travailleurs Guinéens (CNTG). Only the teachers' union challenged the move, and its leaders were sentenced to lengthy prison terms. Touré, perhaps more effectively than other West African leaders, maintained close control over trade union affairs and stifled independent trade union activity for decades.

Not all previously independent trade union movements shared the same fate. Senegal's period of trade union unity lasted only a few years, and while Mali's trade unions were unified, the confederation resisted efforts to absorb it fully into the party structure. In his chapter, Ousmane Oumarou Sidibé chronicles the oppositional role played by the Union Nationale des Travailleurs du Mali (UNTM). In the wake of the 1968 coup d'état, which the UNTM had vociferously condemned, the new one-party state shut down the labour federation and imprisoned many of its leaders. The UNTM was re-established as an appendage of the state but it defiantly continued to criticise the government and call for an end to one-party rule and the protection of civil liberties, leading to arrests and constant harassment of UNTM officials. The UNTM not only survived, but maintained its oppositional role through the tumultuous events of 1991, when a successful civil society push for democracy finally ended one-party rule.[11] Burkina Faso is the best example of a trade union movement that resisted incorporation and retained its pluralism. Through strikes and the spearheading of popular demonstrations, the trade unions of Burkina Faso showed the strength of united action, creating the unrest that toppled governments in 1966 and 1974. A well coordinated general strike in 1975 paved the way for the adoption of a new constitution enshrining the principle of multiparty elections.[12]

11 See also Sidibé, Sissoko and Coulibaly (1997), 'Mali, Evolution: An Unlikely Outcome'.

12 Silga (1997), 'Burkina Faso: The Land of Incorruptible Men'.

Trade Unions, Poverty and Debt

A third dominant theme of the book is the role of trade unionism in the midst of poverty. All West African countries emerged from colonial rule with the intent to promote rapid industrialisation as a key part of their economic development programmes. All pursued income-substitution policies and most adopted measures to attract foreign investment in manufacturing. In all West African countries, and especially in the Francophone areas, the state played a highly interventionist role. Much of the import-substitution strategy was concentrated on the production of light consumer goods geared toward the domestic market, which until the mid 1970s met with some success. From the early 1960s until the mid 1970s, the overall GDP rate for West Africa grew at a higher rate than the population. One result was that the size of the urban population grew at an astonishing rate, from 14 to 40 per cent of the population between 1960 and 1990. When states experienced balance of payment problems in the late 1970s and early 1980s, however, they were no longer in a position to finance manufacturing. Many factories closed their doors, while others scaled back their activities. The virtual impossibility of establishing a flourishing manufacturing enterprise under structural adjustment programmes set up in the 1980s and 1990s has meant that few new factories have replaced those that have foundered.

The balance of payments problem in West Africa that has caused such widespread misery dates to the 1970s, when OPEC quadrupled oil prices. With the exception of Nigeria, Africa's leading oil producer and a member of OPEC, all West African countries are net importers of oil. Coupled with falling prices for agricultural and mineral exports, and inflationary fiscal policies, high oil prices led West African states to enter into various international loan arrangements beginning in the late 1970s, accumulating debts that became increasingly difficult to service by the early 1980s. (When world oil prices collapsed in the 1980s, even Nigeria fell heavily into debt.) In every country in the region, external debt represents at least fifty per cent of its GDP, and in seven West African countries it represents more than 100 per cent of GDP. Efforts to service this debt entailed such expenditure that, according to the United Nations Development Programme's surveys in the 1980s and 1990s, West Africa included some of the world's poorest nations: Sierra Leone, Liberia, Niger, The Gambia, Benin, Guinea, Burkina Faso and Mali. Remarkably, despite its vast mineral resources, Nigeria was later added to this list. The consequent weakening of health and educational services threatened to undermine the entire region's modernisation process.

The burden of debt, and the structural adjustment policies of the World Bank and International Monetary Fund, has had enduring implications for many trade union movements in West Africa by shaping the economic and political environment in which they operate. The 'lost decade' of the 1980s represented a stark demarcation between an era of state-led development based on import substitution and one of neo-liberal policies. West African states increasingly opened their economies to foreign competition, slashed social welfare budgets, privatised many state-owned companies, and imposed labour market flexibility. Resulting labour unrest in reaction to those policies is often regarded by elites as a threat to economic stability and foreign direct investment, and thus it often provokes renewed efforts to liberalise labour relations. In many ways, structural adjustment programmes, public sector retrenchment, and high debt burdens further restrict the possibilities for trade unions to struggle for improved wages and working conditions. The evidence is clear that structural adjustment programmes have had a deleterious impact on West African trade unions. Public sector layoffs and new private sector labour laws have led to heavy membership losses and depleted trade union treasuries. Despite often heroic efforts to combat structural adjustment, trade union resistance has generally proved ineffectual. Mounting job insecurity and a falling off of real wages has forced many trade unionists into the informal labour market, thus leading some commentators to lament the virtual elimination of the wage earning class as a distinct entity.

The crises that today beset trade union movements in West Africa, and the urgent need to find the means to organise the informal sector, are explored in the chapter on Ghana by Akua Britwum. The Ghana Trades Union Congress (GTUC) has a long history of involvement in the informal sector, and beginning in the late 1990s, GTUC and its constituent unions made a sustained and concerted effort to organise informal sector workers. Britwum details the numerous geographical, legal, financial and organisational challenges faced by trade unions organising in this sector, even where the will to do so is strong. She argues that in Ghana, informal sector workers have demonstrated a keen interest in union organisation and representation, and she shows how the GTUC and its affiliate unions have achieved a remarkable level of success. The larger problem, according to Britwum, is how to keep informal sector workers in the trade unions once they have been organised; providing 'meaningful' union membership to these workers, she argues, requires unions to continuously rethink their goals, structures and strategies.

Trade Unions and Democratic Transition

A fourth theme of the book is the role of trade unions in bringing a measure of democracy to the region. In spite of its pervasive militarism, and in spite of the desire of one-party states to co-opt or silence independent trade unionism, West Africa is well known for the vibrancy of its civil society, in which trade unions often play the vanguard role. West African trade unions were at the forefront of movements that ended colonial domination, they were the most strident voices of opposition during the years when post-colonial authoritarian rule was being established, and thus it should come as little surprise that it was coalitions of trade unions, student unions and other civil society actors in the forefront of movements for political liberalisation in the late 1980s and early 1990s. A pro-democracy wave swept across sub-Saharan Africa twenty years ago, first appearing in Benin in 1989, then spreading to other Francophone countries and finally to Anglophone countries. While some commentators suggest that the fall of the Berlin Wall provided the impetus for African civil society to challenge authoritarian regimes on their own soil, the underlying causes of the democratic wave were the privations created by years of austerity under IMF sponsored structural adjustment and the loss of legitimacy experienced by authoritarian regimes after years of repression, corruption and dismal economic performance.

Benin, one of the world's poorest countries, had been ruled by Mathieu Kérékou's authoritarian regime since 1972. Despite Kérékou's Marxist-Leninist pretensions, Benin accepted structural adjustment in the 1980s and implemented, albeit half-heartedly, the neo-liberal programme of privitisations and retrenchment demanded in return for the IMF loans it received. Unemployment and underemployment increased dramatically, yet Benin's debts continued to mount and its economy continued to stagnate. As Azizou Chabi Imorou reveals in his chapter on teachers' unions in Benin, strike action against layoffs, wage freezes and non-payment of civil service wages became increasingly frequent from the mid 1980s, and trade unions joined hands with students and other critics of the regime in displays of public unrest. Such activity would have been met with effective state repression and mass arrests just a few years earlier, yet financial constraints on the regime coincided with the outpouring of public disenchantment, leading to political paralysis and a crisis of legitimacy for Kérékou. Widespread strikes and street demonstrations took place in 1989, forcing Kérékou to accept the popular call for a 'national conference' to which representatives from various sectors would be able to speak freely about the dilemmas facing the country. Trade unionists had helped pave the way for the national conference and were allowed to send delegates to it. When the national conference met, it went far beyond its original remit, declared itself vested with sovereign power, and declared multi-party elections that meant the end of Kérékou's regime.[13]

Events in Benin were quickly replicated elsewhere. In his chapter, Ousmane Oumarou Sidibé describes how the state-controlled labour federation in Mali, the UNTM, although officially committed to 'responsible particpation' in the one-party military regime of Moussa Traoré, surprised everyone by throwing its weight behind democratic reform. In 1990 it declared a forty-eight hour general strike in support of pro-labour

13 See also Heilbrunn (1994), 'Authority, Property, and Politics in Benin and Togo'.

legislation and pay demands. Although that strike failed to meet its objectives, it did pave the way for widespread civil unrest in Mali throughout 1990 among trade unions and student and youth groups. The bloody repression of unrest by Traoré led the UNTM to call another, far more successful general strike in 1991. In response, the army chose to side with the opposition; Traoré was arrested, paving the way for multi-party democracy and far greater trade union freedom of action.

Not all West African nations were involved in the wave of democracy, and not all efforts to secure democracy were successful. In Togo, for example, the one-party system led by Gnassingbé Eyadéma had been in power since 1967. Despite Eyadéma's frequent resort to repression in the face of unrest, economic weakness and the mass misery inflicted as a result of structural adjustment meant that a groundswell of opposition had developed in Togo by the end of the 1980s just as it had in Benin. Eyadéma relented and agreed to a national conference in 1991, although he denied the conference any semblance of sovereign authority. At the national conference the state-controlled trade union confederation, the Confédération Nationale des Travailleurs du Togo (CNTT), was roundly denounced, and in the wake of the national conference numerous trade unions disaffiliated and new independent unions were created. These unions joined hands in 1992 to engage in a lengthy general strike seeking to undermine Eyadéma. Unlike Kérékou, however, Eyadéma retained control of the military, which brutally repressed the strike, allowing Eyadéma to retian power until his death in 2005, whereupon the military declared Eyadéma's son to be the new president.[14]

Kwamina Panford, in his chapter on Ghana, investigates the role of trade unions during and after what is often regarded as West Africa's 'best example' of a successful shift from military rule to democratic governance. After ten years of authoritarian rule under Provisional National Defence Council (PNDC), Ghana in 1992 made a dramatic shift toward democracy by holding multi-party elections for president. When the charismatic Jerry Rawlings came to power through a coup in late 1981 and established

14 Ibid.

the PNDC, his populist rhetoric and his support for price controls were greeted enthusiastically by working people and trade unions. Yet when the PNDC accepted structural adjustment and vigorously pursued austerity measures imposed by the IMF, enthusiasm vanished. Some 90,000 public and civil service workers were laid off between 1985 an 1990, collective bargaining agreements were routinely ignored, and force or the threat of it was used to settle industrial disputes. The GTUC, Panford shows, played a significant role in the transition away from military rule by successfully negotiating with the PNDC as it prepared for elections, and when the new elected government met in 1992, freedom of association for workers was enshrined in the new constitution.

Trade Unions and the Future of West Africa

George Minet, who as a representative of the International Labour Organisation spent many years in West Africa, offers an insightful look at the promise and the unresolved problems facing trade unions in the region in his chapter on social partnership. Democratic reform has undermined state-controlled trade union unity and given rise to pluralism. New governments are more willing to set up tripartite bodies, including trade unions, to design and implement policy. Regional bodies (most notably ECOWAS) and outside agencies, including NGOs and the ILO, are more active than ever in Africa seeking to include workers' rights in any discussion of West Africa's future. Yet, Minet cautions, trade union pluralism, while on the whole a positive development, can and has served to weaken trade unions as bargaining agents and it has not yet yielded significant increases in membership. While new governments often include trade union representatives on tripartite policymaking bodies, these bodies are seldom used as originally designed. ECOWAS and the push for regionalism are relatively weak, and the push for national self-determination remains strong even though it is generally recognised that problems faced by countries in the region are often the same. The continuous call for workers' rights coming from the ILO and NGOs is offset by business interests and government leaders who call with equal vigour for industrial competitiveness, privatisation and continued retrenchment of government expenditures. Social dialogue is one path forward for West African trade unions, but, as Minet concludes, it will only become viable if all social partners are healthy and equally matched.

The future of West African trade unionism is as uncertain as is the future of the region itself. On the one hand, the host of problems that continue to plague the region leaves some commentators with a profound sense of pessimism. There has been a general failure to industrialise, with some 60 per cent of the region's workforce still engaged in agricultural pursuits, and many of the countries remain mired in desperate poverty. Thirteen of the fifteen countries who comprise ECOWAS were named in the UNDP's 1997 list of the world's poorest fifty countries. Nigeria and Côte d'Ivoire were the two exceptions, and the latter country's recent political catastrophe has had dire economic consequences. The problems that trade unions face today, once could argue, are perhaps even more profound than any they have encountered. Public sector retrenchment and the hollowing out of the wage earning labour force, and the continuing oppressive burden of external debt and structural adjustment programmes that eliminate alternative paths to development still confront West African unions. Social cohesion remains immensely problematic, as continued economic dislocation keeps alive ethnic and religious divisions. Despite the remarkable efforts of the Ghana Trades Union Congress, the large and ever growing informal sector remains largely unorganised. And democracy across the region remains in its infancy and extremely fragile. New governments continue to interfere in trade union activity, and even when new laws are passed, the implementation of those laws in never assured.

On the other hand, the retreat of authoritarianism has given rise to optimism among other commentators. By playing such a central role in the coming of democracy, trade unions have become more confident and assertive. Trade union rights have become codified in law if not always in practice. The dilemmas have not disappeared, but trade unions are now facing them as independent representatives of the working people, and they are approaching their problems with creativity and dynamism. The political role of many trade union movements has been enhanced, and as a result of the pro-democracy movements, the fighting spirit of the rank and file has been liberated, and many trade unions themselves have become much more democratic in their internal affairs. As weak as they are, tripartite policy-making bodies force trade unions to jettison the role of simply decrying neo-liberal policy decisions; independent trade unions need to articulate credible stances on questions of national economic interest. The environment for trade unionism in West Africa remains intensely hostile, but it has improved according to the optimists.

One thing is certain: the future of West African trade unionism will mirror its past. Unless and until enormous strides are made to organise informal workers across the region, trade union membership in the region for the foreseeable future will remain concentrated among public and civil service workers fortunate enough to keep their jobs, and well situated enough to bargain for wage increases that maintain its members' standing as a relatively privileged minority. In future moments of transition, these same trade unions will continue to serve as the vanguard of movements for progressive social change. It is clear that, as they have so often in the past, trade unions will continue to join hands with students, youth movements, intellectuals and community groups to contest authoritarian rule and austerity. In 2008 and again in 2010, for example, trade unions in Senegal, Niger, Côte d'Ivoire and Burkina Faso joined hands with numerous other groups in widespread demonstrations against the high cost of living in West African urban centres.[15] As numerous authors have commented, one of the brightest hopes for the continent is the strength of its civil society, and in West Africa, trade unionism has long been in the forefront of civil society efforts to make a difference. There is no reason to believe that trade unions are too weak to continue playing that role.

15 Maccatory, Oumarou and Poncelet (2010), 'West African Social Movements against the High Cost of Living'.

References

Asiwaju, A.I. (1976) 'Migrations as Revolt: The Example of the Ivory Coast and the Upper Volta before 1945', *The Journal of African History* 17(4): 577–594.

Berg, E. (1959) 'French West Africa, in W. Galenson (ed.), *Labor and Economic Development*, New York: John Wiley.

Cooper (1997) 'UGTAN, the Loi-cadre and the Breakup of l'AOF' in C. Becker, S. Mbaye and I. Thioub (eds), *AOF: Réalités et Héritages; sociétés oust-africain et ordre colonial*, volume 2, Paris and Dakar: Archives du Sénégal.

Cooper, F. (1996) *Decolonization and African Society: The Labor Question in French and British Africa*, Cambridge: Cambridge University Press.

Copans, J. et al (eds) (1987), *Classes ouvrières d'Afrique noire*, Paris: Kathala.

Damachi, U. et al (eds) (1979), *Industrial Relations in Africa*, London: Macmillan.

Davies, I. (1966), *African Trade Unions*. Baltimore: Penguin.

Deniel, R. (1974), 'Mesures gouvernementales et/ou intérêts divergents des pays exportateurs de main d'œuvre et des pays h6tes: Haute Volta et Cote d'Ivoire', in Samir Amin (ed.), *Modern Migrations in Western Africa*, Oxford: Oxford University Press.

Dioh. A. (2002) *Les syndicats de travailleurs au Sénégal*, Paris: l'Harmattan.

Fashoyin, T. (1992) *Industrial Relations and African Development*. New Delhi: South Asian Publishers.

Fonteneau, G. et al (2004) *Histoire du Syndicalisme en Afrique*, Paris: Karthala.

Gutkind, P. et al (eds) (1978) *African Labor History*, Beverly Hills: Sage.

Heilbrunn, J.R. (1994) 'Authority, Property, and Politics in Benin and Togo', unpublished PhD thesis, University of California, Los Angeles.

Kester, G. and Sidibé, O.O. (eds) (1997) *Trade Unions and Sustainable Democracy in Africa*, Aldershot: Ashgate.

Kester, G. (2007) *Trade Unions and Workplace Democracy in Africa*, Aldershot: Ashgate.

Kraus, J. (ed.) (2007) *Trade Unions and the Coming of Democracy in Africa*, Basingstoke: Palgrave Macmillan.

Laurijssen, E. (2010) *Trade Union Pluralism and Proliferation in French-speaking Africa*, Geneva: ILO.

Maccatory, B., Oumarou, M.B. and Poncelet, M. (2010) 'West African social movements against the high cost of living: from the economic to the political, from the global to the national', *Review of African Political Economy* 37(125): 345–359.

Martens, G. (1979) 'Industrial Relations and Trade Unionism in French-speaking West Africa', in U. Damachi et al (eds), *Industrial Relations in Africa*, London: Macmillan.

Martens, G. (1994) 'French-speaking Africa', in A. Trebilcock et al (eds), *Towards Social Dialogue: Tripartite Cooperation in National Economic and Social Policy-making*. Geneva: ILO.

Meynaud J. and Saleh-Bey, A. (1963) *Le Syndicalisme Africain: Evolution et Perspectives*, Paris: Payot.

Muase, C.K. (1989) *Syndicalisme et démocratie en Afrique noire: l'expérience du Burkina Faso*, Paris: Karthala.

November, A. (1965) *L'Évolution du Mouvement Syndical en Afrique Occidentale*, Paris: Mouton.

Olukoshi, A. (2001) *West Africa's Political Economy in the Next Millennium: Retrospect and Prospect*, Dakar: CODESRIA.

Roberts, B.C. (1964) *Labour in the Tropical Territories of the Commonwealth*, Bell and Sons: London.

Sandbrook, R. and Cohen, R. (eds) (1975) *The Development of an African Working Class: Studies in Class Formation and Action*, London: Longman.

Sidibé, O.O., Sissoko, S.M. and Coulibaly, M. (1997) 'Mali, Evolution: An Unlikely Outcome', in G. Kester and O.O. Sidibé (eds), *Trade Unions and Sustainable Democracy in Africa*, Aldershot: Ashgate.

Silga, G. (1997) 'Burkina Faso: The Land of Incorruptible Men', in G. Kester and O.O. Sidibé (eds), *Trade Unions and Sustainable Democracy in Africa*, Aldershot: Ashgate.

Thiam, I.D. (1991) *Histoire du Mouvement Syndicale en Afrique, 1790–1929*, Paris: Editions L'Harmattan.

ANNE-CATHERINE WAGNER

The *Confédération Générale du Travail* (CGT) in West Africa: The Difficulties of Constructing Trade Union Internationalism

Globalization generates new forms of inequality and domination: it widens the gap between those who master the new rules of the game and those who have to accept them. Africa appears as the archetype of a dominated continent, being more and more dependent on donors and international financial institutions. The share of sub Saharan Africa in world exports decreased from 6 per cent in 1980 to less than 3 per cent in 2008: in 2008, the stock of foreign direct investment throughout Africa represented only 3.4 per cent of world FDI.

Nevertheless, there are other modes of international relations which have arisen to counter economic domination. The nurturing of international socialist organisations were the first responses of the labour movement to the internationalization of capitalism. The labour movement got involved early on in the struggle against colonialism, in the name of 'brotherhood with the working class of the colonies'. French unions, especially the CGT (Confédération Générale du Travail)[1] played a central role in the establishment and in the consolidation of African trade unions during the colonial period and after independence.

1 The CGT is one of the major French trade union confederations. It has long maintained close ties with the French Communist Party. Founded in 1895, the CGT split in 1921 to create the revolutionary CGTU (*Confédération Générale du Travail Unitaire*), to which the current CGT traces its origins. In 1936, the unions reunified. In 1947 a new split occurred due to the departure of the minority that refused ties with the Communist Party, and which supported the Marshall Plan and then created the CGT-FO confederation.

What has happened to these internationalist traditions since then? The integration of African trade unions into international organisations has brought them political, economic and symbolic resources which allow them to play a role in the current process of social transformation in Africa.[2] At the same time, cooperation between trade unions is marred by contradictions and tensions, partly due to the legacy of colonisation. Since the early 1990s, such cooperation has also had to deal with the end of the political model inherited from the Cold War, as well as the internal transformations of African unionism.

In its founding principles, labour internationalism defends workers' interests, which are considered as 'independent of nationality, throughout the proletariat'.[3] But relationships between French and African trade unions illustrate the extreme heterogeneity of the working classes in France and in African countries. The notion of unionisation always involves national specificities. But the differences between industrialized and Third World countries are so important, that it is difficult to identify 'common interests' or common claims.

This chapter seeks to analyze the issues, social uses and ambiguities of these international links. It is based on a survey of trade unionists who are committed (or have been committed) to cooperation between France and countries in sub Saharan Africa.[4] After recalling the historical framework of union relations, it addresses their current challenges and ends by examining the renewal of these links.

2 Kester and Sidibé (eds) (1997), *Syndicats africains*.

3 Marx and Engels (1848).

4 The survey is based on work in archives and interviews with unionists engaged in relations with Africa. Interviews were conducted in two stages. A first set of interviews was conducted in 1999 and 2000. A second set, focusing on the militants of the CGT, was conducted in 2008 and 2009. The survey has also benefited from interviews conducted by Bénédicte Bretonnière, author of a Master's dissertation in political sciences, at the University of Paris 1, entitled 'La coopération syndicale franco-africaine. Inertie et dynamique d'une solidarité ouvrière', directed by J. Siméant (2009). I thank her warmly.

The Burden of History: Union Colonialism or Internationalism?

The shared history of French and African unions has forged the framework of their current relations. Thus, French involvement in Africa focuses on the countries of former French West Africa (Afrique occidentale française, AOF). Even the South African trade union movement is mentioned little by French trade unionists, in spite of its dynamism and its importance in pan-African networks. Relations with English-speaking countries are limited, due to the 'language barrier' and to differences in organisational structures, modes of action and ideological references in countries where unionism was built on the French model.

The role of the CGT in the fostering African trade unionism

In French-speaking Africa, the colonial past has forged close links between French and African trade unions. It has also been a source of ambiguities and contradictions that continue to be felt. Since its creation, at the Congress of Limoges of 1895, the CGT has aimed to bring together all workers of France and the colonies. Early on, it criticised the colonial system. The Red International of Labour Unions (Profintern), created in 1921 by Lenin in Moscow, supported national movements of colonised peoples. In France, the CGTU (affiliated with the Profintern) took a stance against imperialist wars in Syria and Morocco and called for a general strike against the Riff War in 1926. In 1931, in order to protest against the Colonial Exhibition, it organised an exhibition entitled 'the truth about the colonies', which denounced the system of colonial exploitation.

That said, unionism emerged late in French West Africa. For much of the colonial period, Africans did not have any right to unionise. The 1884 law legalising trade unionism in France reserved the right to French citizens, and the law was not applied in the colonies. Nevertheless, after World War I, a social movement did emerge in Africa. It was sometimes led by veterans who organised demonstrations or strikes after they came back from the front lines.[5] The prohibition of trade unionism was circumvented by creating mutual societies, assisted by the unions of metropolitan (i.e. mainland) France, which supported industrial action in the 1920s and 1930s. The railway unions, in particular, played an important role in structuring the labour movement in Africa.

In 1937, the *Front populaire* legalised unions in French West Africa, recognized the right to strike and provided collective agreements. However, these rights were reserved for 'Europeans and assimilated peoples'. To be entitled to unionise, it was necessary to be able to speak, read and write fluently in French and to hold a primary school graduation certificate. These conditions only applied to a very small elite of the so-called 'civilized natives'. These obstacles to unionism, set up by the French administration, may explain the role played by local intelligentsia, teachers and civil servants in the development of African trade unions.

Some African trade unions of civil servants and postal workers did appear in cities, under tight control of the French administration. African unions were branches of French trade unions. In the early unions, Europeans and Africans were separated. Further union demands subsequently emerged. In 1938, striking workers of the Dakar-Niger railway system demanded equal status and equal wages for all workers, whether French or African. This strike had some repercussions in France.

In 1940, the further development of trade unionism was arrested by the Vichy government, but the labour movement continued to exist in illegal ways. French Communist activists contributed directly to the establishment of unions. The CGT sent advisers, like Pierre Morley or Marcel Planes, to criss-cross West Africa between 1943 and 1948. During this period, 'communist study groups', linked to the colonial section of the French Communist Party, carried out propaganda and training work in French Africa. These groups were established especially in cities; they provided analytical frameworks, methods of organisation and action which pioneers

5 Coquery-Vidrovitch (2004), 'Le syndicalisme en Afrique Noire'.

of the African movement used to organise their parties or trade unions.[6] For example, Gaston Donnat was a communist teacher in Algeria.[7] In the 1940s, he applied for work in Cameroon, where he became director of the Regional School of Yaoundé. There, in June 1944, he secretly organised a Marxist study circle, which brought together (at his home, on Tuesday evenings) some twenty 'enlightened' Africans, who were teachers, employees and government officials. Among them was Ruben Um Nyobé, who later became a major figure in the nationalist movement in Cameroon. The aim was to train future leaders, to transmit knowledge as well as organisational, political and social skills. Thus in 1946 Gaston Donnat went with Ruben Um Nyobé, secretary of a regional union, to see the manager of a plantation and to demand the free exercise of trade union rights; he remarked on his 'great satisfaction at seeing an African trade union leader able not only to stand up to a French boss, but also to have the last word'. The similarity of working-class interests in metropolitan France and in the colonies was highlighted. Gaston Donnat, who at the time was first secretary of the USC (trade union confederation of Cameroon), declared that 'those who benefit from the wealth extracted from Africa are a handful of owners of capital who also exploit French workers'.

African trade unions flourished after the Second World War, with the abolition of the *Code de l'indigénat* (regulating the status of native subjects) and of forced labour, in 1946. At that time, there were 176 unions in French-speaking Africa, linked directly to the French confederations. This structure reflects the 'French way' of thinking about union cooperation, by fostering assimilation to the dominant model. Financial assistance, advisors and local leaders came straight from Paris.[8] Albert Bouezanquet, a leader of the CGT (who later joined the CGT-FO), spoke of union cooperation as an extension of the colonial undertaking: 'It is clear that unions exist in

6 Suret-Canale (1994), *Les groupes d'études marxistes.*

7 Donnat (1986), *Afin que nul n'oublie.*

8 However, some unions remained independent, most notably the powerful railway union.

those countries because they are recognized by metropolitan France. The expansion of French civilization should be continued by trade unions.'

In the beginning, union struggles involved demands for equal economic and social rights for all workers of the French Union. Frederick Cooper shows how workers' organisations seized the aim of 'assimilation', promoted by the colonial authorities, to demand equal treatment with the slogan 'Equal pay for equal work'.[9]

The post-war period was marked by a series of major industrial disputes, including the long African railway strike of 1947–48, which still plays an important role in the collective memory and which is the subject of a novel by Ousmane Sembene.[10] 20,000 workers from all of French West Africa ceased work. The reaction of the CGT was ambiguous; financial support for the strike was sent by metropolitan railway workers, but *Le Peuple*, the CGT newspaper, did not mention the strike. In West Africa, there were tensions between European and African unions. French and African workers had different statuses, and they often disagreed about their demands and claims. Overall, however, the CGT succeeded in unionising. In 1948 it had 42,500 members in West Africa, and it was by far the largest organisation, followed by the autonomous railway union. The CGT sought to link workers of colonies to the global communist movement, embodied by the Word Trade Union Federation (WTUF). The general secretary of the CGT in Sudan, Abdoulaye Diallo, became vice-president of the WTUF in 1953.

Union struggles from 1947 to 1953 were dominated by one major aim: the implementation of the Labour Code. The struggle for equal rights succeeded in December 1952, with the vote on the adoption of the Overseas Labour Code, which remains the basis of labour laws in most countries that were former French colonies. It included resolutions for equal employment and equal wages, minimum wages, the 40-hour week, the 8-hour day, family allowances, paid holidays, pension rights, protection of women and children, and the establishment of a Labour Inspectorate. The CGT

9 Cooper (1996), *Decolonisation and African Society*.
10 Sembene (1984), *Les bouts de bois de Dieu* (orig. 1960).

mobilised the rhetoric of assimilation to legitimize these rights. Thus a union newspaper in Sudan stated that '[t]here is no difference between a French person born on the banks of the Seine or the Loire and a French person born on the shores of the Senegal and the Niger'.[11]

The Code, which was a sort of culmination of struggles for equality, also paved the way for other claims. It was the beginning of the effort against the colonial administration, since it played a central role in the application of labour law and the extension of rights. Moreover the Code revised the alliances between French and Africans unions. Mobilisation for the application of law provided the foundation for a unitary African union movement. During the strike of 1953, which was triggered by the issue of wages, union leaders for the first time put forward the possibility of questioning links with France. Sékou Touré, who was an active member of the CGT, wrote: 'We say to the administration, quietly but firmly, that if it does not revise its position, we will go further in asking for things that are not only economic and social matters. African trade unionists will require revision of the ties that bind African territories to the French Union'.[12]

Further discussions were opened within the CGT on the issue of political autonomy, which had spanned the whole period of decolonisation. The union movement had developed in relationship to the political movement of emancipation, including the Rassemblement Démocratique Africain (RDA), established by Houphouët-Boigny in Bamako in October 1946. When in 1950 Houphouët-Boigny broke with the French Communist Party, he asked the RDA to break with the CGT. Union claims for independence appeared. Could the colonial system be fought by dependent unions? Sékou Touré accused the CGT of putting its aims and the rhetoric of proletarian internationalism before the recognition of African realities. In 1955, the unions of Senegal and Mauritania, followed by several other unions in French West Africa, quit the CGT and created the CGTA: the General Confederation of African workers whose leader was Sékou Touré.

11 Cooper (1996), *Decolonisation and African Society*.

12 Fall (1989), *L'Etat et la question syndicale au Sénégal*.

The CGTA broke with international organisations and gave priority to political struggles for independence over economic and social struggles. At first, the CGT denounced the claim of self-association, and presented it as a manoeuvre of colonialists to counteract wage demands. Leaflets of the CGT were ironic about the 'Administrative CGT, which was chatting about the African personality as it slavishly carries out the programme that comes straight from the federal building in Dakar' (the administration headquarters).[13] Indeed, tensions within the labour movement between the assimilationist and separatist trends were often fuelled by the colonial administration that welcomed the 'war of tracts'.

Eventually, the CGT supported the idea of independence. In 1957, the CGT, the CGTA and the powerful railway union created a new trade union at Cotonou, the Union Générale des Travailleurs d'Afrique Noire (UGTAN), which supported the unity of peoples of Africa and covered over 80 per cent of trade union members of French West Africa. At that time, the union movement was well established in French West Africa, especially in the public sector. African unionists, trained in French unions, were in a position to hold political office. Martens has identified 22 unionists of the CGT in new African governments in the late 1950s.[14]

The training of African leaders by the CGT

A second generation of African trade union leaders appeared during the independence struggles. More qualified than its elders, it occupied key positions in new states. Links with French trade unions and parties have also remained strong after independence. The Federation des Etudiants d'Afrique noire en France (FEANF) provided political training for many African students in France until the 1970s. Enrolment in the FEANF almost

13 Cooper (1996), *Decolonisation*.

14 Martens (1990), 'La coopération syndicale en Afrique'.

resembled entering an 'elite school' in West Africa. It taught rhetoric and political work, and contributed to consolidating African networks.[15]

Union relationships were rebuilt during the Cold War. Marxists grouped together in the World Federation of Trade Unions (WFTU), Social Democrats and American trade unionists created the International Confederation of Free Trade Unions (ICFTU), while Christians established the World Confederation of Labour (WCL). The political rivalries between international organisations led to intense activities in Africa. The Afro-American Centre of Labour of the AFL-CIO provided financial and political support. East Germany and West Germany competed through their powerful union foundations.

The presence of the CGT in Africa was part of the WFTU action, which had opened training schools in Africa. The CGT was responsible for the school in Conakry, which opened in 1960. Between 1960 and 1965 forty courses were organised, involving 466 activists, mostly from French-speaking countries.[16] Other union universities were opened in Mali and Congo. The CGT sent instructors. Many activists and future African leaders were then welcomed in the training centre of the CGT, at Courcelles near Paris. These training courses were developed throughout the 1960s. In 1975 the CGT opened the CERCI (Centre d'études et de recherches pour la cooperation internationale), which then became the Institute Louis Saillant, responsible for trade union training in French-speaking countries and developing countries, and supported by the WFTU until the late 1980s.

The survey shows the dynamics of these relationships, but also their misunderstandings and contradictions. International union organisations did not care about the specificities of the world of African labour nor of African societies. The trainers who were sent to Africa did not have any knowledge of the continent. Jean-Claude Poitou was designated by the CGT to run the board of education of the WFTU in Bamako (between

15 Diane (1990), *La FEANF et les grandes heures du mouvement syndical étudiant noir*.

16 Bressol (1996), *La place et les actions de la CGT dans le monde*.

1964 and 1966) because he was responsible for union education in France. He arrived in Mali with the programmes of the training courses of the CGT. Today, he is ironical about the gap between standard courses in Marxism, provided by visitors from Prague, and the social realities of Mali:

> It was incredible. The teachers came from Prague or Paris to talk about crisis of accumulation in a country where there was no capital. They explained the difference between sovkhoses and kolkhozes, but there were no factories in Mali [...] It was the same with me. I arrived with the training course curricula of the CGT. And then I quickly realized that it did not work. For colonial capitalism in Africa is not the same as ours. Colonial exploitation is very different from what happens at Citroen and Renault. It was necessary to review our view and practices.

He remembers that African trainees had a lot of difficulties talking about trade unionism in Bambara or in a language used in Mali. They invariably switched to French, for most union concepts could not be translated.[17] The modes of organisation and forms of action were just imitations of French practices, without reference to local traditions.

> For example, during a meeting, we had a role play: we had to hold a union meeting. I explained that the first thing to do was to appoint a session chair. They refused, and explained that the oldest would always lead the meeting. I protested, they didn't agree [...] Another example: later I realised that plays or theatrical sketches have an important role in African traditions. That is what they are doing today to fight against AIDS. We used to work through leaflets or newspapers and we had just transferred our habits. I do not mean that everything we did did not help, but there were obstacles that we could not see in the past.

In the 1960s there was an intensive international social life in Bamako, with Czechs, Russians, Chinese and other representatives of communist countries. This activist world was marked by competition. There were ideological conflicts related to the Cold War, and there were also rivalries between

17 These approaches can be contrasted by the work of Ruben Um Nyobe (1989) who, as shown by J. Mbembe, made a translation of the speech of the *Union des Populations du Cameroun* in the bush of southern Cameroon, using original forms of expression (songs, books of dreams, etc.) which was rooted in local culture.

members of the same international organisations. Within this context, French activists of the CGT used to stress their seniority and long term presence in Africa, in order to defend the model of French trade unionism, and this often succeeded. For example, there were conflicts over the reform of the labour code. A unionist from East Germany was instructed by the WFTU to assist the government of Modibo Keita to reform the labour code in Mali, drawing on the Soviet model. He arrived in Bamako without any knowledge of the African labour world, after three weeks of intensive training in French. Then he tried to adapt the labour code of East Germany. It was a failure, and the trade unionists of the CGT managed to maintain the code inherited from the colonial code.

The training courses used to be intended for future leaders or union officials. Subsequently, African educators were supposed to disseminate union principles throughout their country. This work had a significant impact. It explained the durability of the French model with respect to union strategies or union organisation. Training courses also allowed for social mobility and the political promotion for several African activists. In 1959, during the 32nd Congress of the CGT, a representative of the CGAT (the Congolese branch of the CGT) thus thanked 'the CGT and the WFTU which have kindly given us the brotherly aid and experience of the oldest union, our sister organisation, the CGT. The union school in Congo will help to develop the trade union movement; it will also give more than 100 young professionals from Chad, Central Africa, Gabon and Congo access to key positions.' The most motivated students hoped to obtain a long stay abroad, in other training centres of the WFTU, in East Germany, Budapest, Prague or Moscow. Union schools thus trained an international elite, taking its members away from African soil.

> East Germany had opened its school in the suburbs of Berlin: the Russians had Lulumba University, the Bulgarians too. They invited the elite for a year or two. In my opinion, this was not a good thing. I saw these friends when they left, I saw them when they came back: they were uprooted (J.C. Poitou).

Born out of the claim for equal rights, Franco-African labour relations were developed on the assumption that the same structures and the same policies were appropriate for French and African workers. Trade unionists used to proclaim equality, but the colonial context implied the subordination of African trade unions to their CGT 'parent'. After independence, labour relations retained traces of this initial contradiction. Questioning the ideological foundations of international cooperation has subsequently revealed the ambiguities of these unequal relations.

The Awakening of Union Relations

Since the 1990s, the ideological foundations of trade union internationalism have been strongly shaken. Trade union cooperation in Africa has been much reduced. The WFTU did not survive the collapse of the USSR and other communist governments. Most European trade unions have left it, and it is now reduced to working out of a house in the suburbs of Prague. The training institutes of the CGT that were mostly financed by the WFTU have closed, one after another.

The international priorities of the CGT have changed too. In 1995 it left the WTUF in order to be accepted by the European Trade Union Confederation (ETUC), which represents European unions at the European level. In 1999 the CGT became a member of ETUC and shifted its labour relations toward Europe. This shift brought protests within the organisation.[18] For example, in 1995 at the 45th Congress of the CGT, a trade unionist deplored the 'abandonment of our affirmation of international solidarity by the disaffiliation of the WFTU. By limiting our relations to European trade unionism we risk abandoning our concerns for workers of the Third World, who are the victims of shameful looting by European countries and North America, under the auspices of the IMF [...] Are we being called upon to become a reformist confederation, accompanying the construction of a Maastricht-based Europe?'

18 Wagner (2005), *Vers une Europe syndicale.*

Cooperation and the reproduction of relationships of domination

Questioning union relationships with Africa is not only a financial or political priority. The legitimacy of the cooperation no longer occurs without raising concerns. French trade unionists think that relations with African trade unions have to change. The ideological model has been relegated to the past. Unionists question the usefulness of 'diplomatic' meetings in trade union congresses or conferences. The CGT no longer wants to pay for international travel which is 'only for representative purposes'.

> Before, we used to invite people to the Congress of the CGT. Many of our international activities consisted in going to the Congresses of each other. I invite you to my congress; you invite me to your conference. This is what I call international representation. It is quite useless [...] Bad habits took hold. Such travel abroad also became a kind of 'rent'. We shouldn't pretend otherwise.

The relevance of union training courses, which are the mainstay of international cooperation, is also in question. 'We do not want to do union colonialism', said one trade unionist. Training courses used to be developed by training centres in Paris, and led by trainers without any foreign experience. They were criticized because they imposed a French model unilaterally, which is no longer considered the best one. 'Previously, we received unionists for two months. They attended CGT schools or Communist Party schools; it was the reproduction of a model, which had nothing to do with the reality of the countries.'

This rejection of 'union colonialism' does not come without a touch of condescension. A unionist explains that Africans are too 'passive' during training courses. Another one accuses them of admiring the French model too much. Interviewees deplore the tendency of some trade unionists to attend too many training courses ('When you discover that one had attended six different seminars on globalization, it makes you wonder '), or not to make good use of them ('We want follow-up. We do not want to train trade unionists if it does not change anything afterwards'). French trade unionists thus take on the contradictory position of being donors that demand accounts for how their gifts are used. Meanwhile, trade unionists do not want to interfere in African organisations, because it would lead unions to reproduce the relations of domination between rich and poor countries.

Nevertheless, international trade union cooperation cannot ignore these issues of domination. As Kester and Sidibé argue, African unions depend heavily on Western donors.[19] Many congresses can be convened only if accompanied by seminars, funded by donors. And yet, withdrawal of European trade union support is taking place at a time when African trade unionism has been markedly weakened at the national level. The 'structural adjustment plans' advocated by international financial institutions have resulted in waves of privatisation and layoffs, and trade unions have not been consulted in the implementation of these economic programmes. Moreover, privatisation and the expansion of the 'informal sector' undermine trade unionism that has traditionally been mainly established in the civil service and public sector.[20]

The search for legitimate partners

The renewal of African trade unions has undermined networks that were built up historically over time. International relations always rely on interpersonal contacts. Indeed, only complicity between individuals and confidence between them can overcome the barriers of cultural and national diversities between trade unions. International trade unionism has thus been based on the cohesion of a small group of actors, united by long term friendships. It takes time to understand the functioning of institutions, and African issues, as well as to create an address book in different countries. The capital of personal relationships and the quality of relationships between persons are essential elements in the efficiency of international cooperation. Seminars, forums and the Annual General Meetings of the International Labour Organisation in Geneva (which is a key moment of international sociability) are sometimes criticised for their apparent

19 Kester and Sidibé (eds) (1997), *Syndicats africains.*

20 Thomas (1995), *Globalization and Third World Trade Unions.*

uselessness. But they actually have an essential role in consolidating transnational, trade union networks.

Within these networks, French trade unionists used to meet African colleagues who would sometimes hold very high social positions in own their societies. Trade unions have trained several African presidents or political leaders. Many African union leaders come from teacher unions; they have often received higher education and they are in general well integrated in institutions of power. French trade unionists, for their part, come rather from the lower or middle classes, and some of them are fascinated by the high culture and lifestyle of African unionists.

> It is marvellous to see the status of unions in Africa. A general secretary is an important person. He regularly meets the President. It is not the same in France, Bernard Thibault (the General Secretary of the CGT) is not considered as an equal of the President of the Republic!

Thus Franco-African relations take on paradoxical aspects. Trade unionists are very close. They have attended the same training courses, they meet at the same forums and conferences and they are often friends. Yet at the same time complicity between individuals is somewhat misleading. It hides important disparities in their social positions in their respective societies.

Today French unions have to redefine relations with African partners, because trade unionism has changed in Africa. While single-party governments were based on a single union, since the 1990s multi-party governments have witnessed the birth of a very large number of unions, which are not always well known or clearly identified by the French trade unionists. Former partners are neither the only nor the most legitimate trade unions. Is the UTS, the Senegalese union which used to be the old partner of the CGT still representative of the labour movement in Senegal? Is it a good thing to continue to sustain organisations that owe their strength to the long-term relationships with French or European unions, more than to a nationally constructed legitimacy?

Thus the capital of interpersonal relations is depreciating because of changes in union staff. The personalisation of relationships may even hinder the effectiveness of cooperation. A trade unionist told me that, in Mali, he has mistakenly kept working with the former secretary of a federation, while the latter had not been re-elected and had created a new union. 'So it's complicated, because we would like to pursue cooperation, but with the other union. But we also have to take into account persons. This former secretary is my friend. I have welcomed him to my home; he has received me in Mali. I have to try not to deal with these two questions.'

Towards New Forms of Cooperation

Willingness to end the 'sacred nature' of international union relations, to replace diplomatic relations by concrete collaboration on the ground is the *leitmotif* of the present, main discourses on trade union internationalism. In a context of budgetary restraint, actions to foster international solidarity should not just be diplomatic. They have to be useful to the trade union movement.

Solidarity with unionists who are threatened in their countries remains important. Support from European trade unions can help unions in many countries without democratic freedom. It has often allowed them to survive in authoritarian regimes. For instance, the president of the Trade Union of Chad had to flee the country after the events of February 2008, and he was hosted for several months by activists of the CGT. A representative of the CGT intends to visit the Union's congress to show solidarity, which may be a resource for the Union in Chad to draw on. Last year in the Democratic Republic of Congo, the CGT protested against the arrest of union activists, organising a fax campaign to the Governor, and trade unionists were released.

The specificities of the world of African labour

Such solidarity is also more often than before organised as part of employment relationships. Privatisations have weakened African trade unions; they have also led to the development of cooperation within firms, which is more in line with the union ethos. French trade unions send experts, accountants, union representatives, to enable African trade unions to challenge the economic relevance of privatisations or to advise them in negotiations with employers. African employees are today in situations that can more easily be viewed as similar to French ones, especially when solidarity emerges in response to confrontational negotiations with well known multinational companies (Elf in Congo Brazzaville, EDF-GDF in Cameroon, Areva in Niger, etc.). For instance, the CGT recently organised demonstrations at the headquarters of French Bolloré to protest against the violation of trade union rights in Côte d'Ivoire and Burkina Faso, and it requested the reinstatement of workers at the port of Abidjan: 'It has worked because Bolloré dislikes that its practices appear to contradict its Corporate social responsibility.' The CGT has also mounted a project to support vocational training in three countries (Senegal, Mali, and Benin). Furthermore, it is conducting training on issues of health and safety in mines with Areva (the French company specialized in nuclear power) in Niger.

These guidelines pave the way for a new recognition of the specificity of African trade unionism and the world of African labour. Faced with a decline in their membership and a questioning of traditional links with governments, African unions are looking for other forms of legitimacy, which are also in line with international expectations. For a long time, they used to organise only in the formal sector. They were especially well established in the public sector or in state enterprises. Now, they are seeking to involve other workers, including workers in the countryside, and in the informal sector.[21] This requires a break with Western views of trade unionism. In his survey of a ship company in Dakar, Babacar Diouf shows that the daily work of a staff representative is far removed from the

21 Kester and Sidibé (eds) (1997), *Syndicats africains*.

western model.[22] A union delegate is more like a business agent who takes care of personal problems (often far removed from workers' professional problems). Such activities take place within a fabric of religious or friendly associations, village brotherhoods, and women's circles, all of which give workers identities that exist outside the framework of the work.

Links with NGOs

The brainstorming about informal labour has led to a redefinition of the concept of labour that goes with a new perception of unions. Unionism now claims the inclusion of new concerns, including health issues. On the subject of the fight against AIDS, the CGT thus associated itself with the association Aides to develop a project in Guinea, Senegal, Niger and Burkina Faso, in conjunction with local trade unions and with associations from civil society. This project, which has received funding from the French Department of Labour, provides training for actors, collective bargaining agreements, as well as actions to prevent and fight against discrimination among workers.

Changes in the views of legitimate international trade unionism have also leaded the CGT to work with new actors. Relationships are more frequent with NGOs, which have also more funding than unions. The trade unionist now in charge of relations with Africa within the CGT has been recruited because of his prior knowledge of the field of international solidarity in France. His aim is to build alliances with civil society organisations. The CGT participates in structures organising foreign aid. It works with humanitarian organisations. It is engaged in a project with the French Committee for international solidarity in Congo Brazzaville, with associations fighting against hunger, with Greenpeace and even with Catholic associations. The purpose is now to 'move closer to the labour movement and civil society'. Unions support anti-globalization demonstrations; the CGT has supported trade union participation in social forums

22 Diouf (1995), 'Syndicalisme, vie associative et identités ouvrières'.

in Bamako and Nairobi, and has encouraged African trade unions to be closer to associations of civil society.

The union's activity is at times very much like that of an NGO. The CGT federation of 'Mines and Energy' has developed humanitarian projects in Africa with African trade unions. The building of a water pump and the construction of schools or 'houses for all' are accompanied by 'solidarity trips' to enable young French workers to visit Africa. These actions have provoked resistance within the CGT: 'Our goal is to build the labour movement, not wells!' But these trips are also justified because they may 'open up' the international relations that have long concerned only the international department of the CGT, and to develop the international sensitivity in more workers. 'Clearly, French workers do not join a union to help Africa! We have to provide explanations. Explain that if we do not struggle against exploitation in Africa, rights of workers will be threatened in the entire world and also here. But solidarity is not spontaneous.'

Other initiatives aim to broaden the scope of international relations, by involving new actors. Trade unions try to mobilise immigrants; they sometimes work with migrant organisations to foster development projects. These African workers in France could be cultural intermediaries between the two labour worlds, which could generate other forms of relationships between French and African trade unionists.

Conclusion

Compared to the internationalisation of managers and leaders, the labour movement seems weak. Among business leaders, who have attended the same business schools, who are united by common interests and by the same business culture, who speak the same language, the creation of international networks follows harmoniously the globalization of production. Conversely, in unions, international relations have to overcome many barriers. Confederations have been built within different national histories: they are involved in different industrial relations systems. Moreover, workers are separated, more than elites, by language barriers and cultural distance.[23] Thus, because of the social selectivity of international activities, relations binding unions are often monopolised by a small number of trade unionists, who have become 'experts' of international issues.

Trade union relations with Africa, especially, highlight the difficulties in achieving the 'international solidarity among peoples' that founded union internationalism in the 19th century. In the colonial and post-colonial periods, the CGT had a crucial role in building African trade unionism. It has kept a privileged position in Africa as the representative of the international communist union. Trade union relationships have long been based on the illusion that it was possible to transpose the French pattern (or the international communist pattern) on Africa. The proximity of the individuals engaged in union relations, trained in the same union schools and often united by friendly relations, used to mask the great differences in social and economic contexts, and between the trade unions in their respective countries.

At the present time, the framework of such trade union cooperation is severely shaken. The CGT has partly disengaged from the African continent, with a shift towards Europe. Activities in Africa reflect doubt and questioning about what the proper form of association should be: actions by the CGT are sometimes very like aid agencies or anti-globalization organisations. This shift reflects a crisis in the old pattern of trade union cooperation. It may also pave the way to revival. The exchange of information and expertise within a multinational company, the twinning of works councils, as well as trade union participation in projects implemented by African immigrants constitute a set of devices – dispersed and disparate, little coordinated – but which nevertheless may rebuild a new internationalism, involving other actors closer to the ground, and thereby contributing to internationalise frameworks of thought and modes of union action.

23 Wagner (2007), *Les classes sociales dans la mondialisation.*

References

Bonvalot D. (1990) 'La politique internationale et l'activité internationale de la CGT', in G. Devin (ed.), *Syndicalisme. Dimensions internationales*, La Garenne-Colombes: Erasme.

Bressol, E. (ed.) (2006) *La place et les actions de la CGT dans le monde (1945–2000)*, Montreuil: Institut CGT d'Histoire sociale.

Collovald, A. (ed.) (2002) *L'humanitaire ou le management des dévouements*, Rennes: Presses universitaires de Rennes.

Cooper, F. (1997) 'UGTAN, the Loi-cadre, and the Break-up of AOF', in C. Becker, S. Mbaye, I. Thioub (eds), *AOF: réalités et héritages. Sociétés ouest- africaines et ordre colonial, 1895–1960*, tome 2, Dakar: Direction des Archives du Sénégal.

Cooper, F. (1996) *Decolonisation and African Society: The Labor Question in French and British Africa 1935–1960*, Cambridge: Cambridge University Press.

Coquery-Vidrovitch, C. (1994) 'Le syndicalisme en Afrique Noire des origines à nos jours: naissance tardive et difficultés face aux régimes autoritaires', in J. Sagnès (ed.), *Histoire du syndicalisme dans le monde*, Paris: Privat.

Diane, C. (1990) *La FEANF et les grandes heures du mouvement syndical étudiant noir*, Dakar: Editions Chaka.

Diouf, B. (1995) 'Syndicalisme, vie associative et identités ouvrières. L'exemple de Dakar Marine', in R. Cabanès, J. Copans, et M. Sélim (eds), *Salariés et entreprises dans les pays du Sud. Contribution à une anthropologie politique*, Paris: Karthala.

Donnat, G. (1986) *Afin que nul n'oublie. L'itinéraire d'un anti-colonialiste*, Paris: l'Harmattan.

Duhamel, R. (1981) *Aux 4 coins du monde*, Paris, Editions sociales.

Fall, M. (1989) *L'Etat et la question syndicale au Sénégal*, Paris: l'Harmattan.

Fonteneau, G. et al (2004) *Histoire du Syndicalisme en Afrique*, Paris: Karthala.

Kester, G. and Sidibé, OO. (eds) (1997) *Syndicats africains. A vous, maintenant! Pour une démocratie durable*, Paris: l'Harmattan.

Kriegel, A. (1998) *Les internationales ouvrières*, Paris: PUF.

Lebeau, Y., Boubacar N., Piriou A., and de Saint-Martin, M. (eds) (2003) *Etat et acteurs émergents en Afrique. Démocratie, incivilité et transnationalisation*, Paris-Ibadan: Karthala.

Martens, G. (1990) 'La coopération syndicale en Afrique. Mythe ou réalité?', in G. Devin (ed.), *Syndicalisme. Dimensions internationales*, La Garenne-Colombes: Editions européennes Erasme.

Marx, K. and Engels, F. (1848) *Manifesto of the Communist Party*, New York: Cosimo, 2005.

Sawicki, F. and Siméant, J. (2009) 'Décloisonner la sociologie de l'engagement militant. Note critique sur quelques tendances récentes des travaux français', *Sociologie du travail* 51(1): 97–125.

Sembene, O. (1984) *Les bouts de bois de Dieu* (orig. 1960), Abidjan: Les nouvelles éditions africaines.

Suret-Canale, J. (1994) *Les groupes d'études marxistes (GEC) en Afrique noire*, Paris, l'Harmattan.

Suret-Canale, J. (1997) 'Les syndicats confédérés (CGT) en AOF, 1943–1957. Quelques problèmes d'interprétation', in C. Becker, S. Mbaye, I. Thioub (eds), *AOF: réalités et héritages. Sociétés ouest- africaines et ordre colonial, 1895–1960*, tome 2, Dakar: Direction des Archives du Sénégal.

Thomas, H. (ed.) (1995) *Globalization and Third World Trade Unions: the challenge of rapid economic change*, London: Zed Books.

Um Nyobe, R. (1989) *Ecrits sous maquis*. Notes et introduction de J.A. Mbembe, Paris: L'Harmattan.

Wagner, A.-C. (2005) *Vers une Europe syndicale. Une enquête sur la confédération européenne des syndicats*, Paris: Le Croquant.

Wagner, A.-C. (2007) *Les classes sociales dans la mondialisation*, Paris: La Découverte.

Wagner, A.-C. (2008) 'L'internationalisation du syndicalisme: obstacles et dynamisme', in M.R. Mouriaux and J. Magniadas (eds), *Le syndicalisme au défi du 21ème siècle*, Paris: Syllepse.

JAMES A. JONES

The 1947–1948 Railway Strike in French West Africa

African trade unions developed in a starkly different environment than did their counterparts in Europe and North America. Instead of organising within a society structured into classes by economic privilege, African labour movements developed in colonial societies polarised by race. A white minority monopolised power and experimented with a number of initiatives intended to manipulate the black majority into performing work deemed useful for the empire at the lowest possible cost.[1] In French West Africa (Afrique occidentale française; henceforth FWA), their success was measured by the extent to which African workers demonstrated 'la regularité et la compétence ou, du moins, la facilité d'education'.[2] Africans were never given the chance to manage or create enterprises on their own, however, for fear that encouraging African initiative might also stir up resistance. Instead, to keep them from uniting, Europeans fomented divisions and as a result, African workers were cut off from each other and caught between conflicting obligations to their own societies and the Europeans who controlled their work place.

Fear of a unified African working class kept colonial authorities from legalising unions for many years. Although French citizens received the right to form unions in 1884, Africans had to wait until 1937, and even then, the right was granted only to those deemed to be assimilated.[3] The French goal was to limit labour resistance, not to reward loyal subjects, and consequently the leaders of the new unions presided over organisations that were created to serve the needs of management. Obliged to operate from

1 Jones (2002), *Industrial Labor*, 75–78.
2 'Notice Géographique 1890' in ANM 1 D 33.
3 Bernhard-Duquenet (1985), *Le Sénégal*, 37, 123–124, 141–145.

such a weak position, African union leaders spent much of their energy searching for allies among other unions, a few sympathetic colonial officials, international labour groups and the broader African population. Their task was made difficult because most of the lines of communications were controlled by the colonial administration, and the number of unionised Africans remained small. In FWA, the problem was ultimately solved by the railway workers, who possessed the largest union in the federation and controlled the main means of communication. During the strike that followed World War II, they showed that Africans could win a confrontation with Europeans without the need to seek support from other Europeans.

The 'great railway strike' of 1947–1948 lasted more than five months and involved roughly 17,000 workers on four lines in six colonies. It became FWA's longest industrial strike and achieved the same scale as the strike which closed France's Renault factories in 1947. Occurring just as France was organizing the Fourth Republic, and at the same time that the Cold War was reshaping world politics, the strike became part of a series of larger battles. Its effects were felt throughout francophone Africa, thanks in part to the centralisation favoured by the French, but also due to the ties that linked railway workers to the African population.

Before the 1920s, there was little coordination between France's African railways. Despite ambitious plans to connect the Mediterranean coast to Senegal and Lake Chad with railways,[4] the lines that made up the Chemins de Fer de l'AOF were each constructed independently over a period of more than seventy years. Work began first on the Dakar-Niger, which was built between 1881 and 1923 from the coast of Senegal to the port of Koulikoro on the Niger River just east of Bamako. A second line, the Conakry-Niger, extended eastward between 1900 and 1913 from the coast of French Guinea to the town of Kankan on the Milo River, a tributary of the Upper Niger River. The third line, the Abidjan-Niger, was constructed northward from the Guinea Coast between 1903 and 1934, and extended to Ouagadougou by 1954. The last line, the Benin-Niger, was built between

4 Kanya-Forstner (1959), *The Conquest*, 61–62.

1900 and 1936 from Cotonou to Parakou in central Dahomey.[5] Despite their names, only the first two actually reached the Niger River basin where, despite the creation of a 'service de navigation', they never functioned as a true network.[6] It was not until 1936 that the financial management of the four lines was centralised. In July 1946 they were combined under a single administration.[7]

Uniting the unions proved more difficult. Centralised management offered no help because it changed neither routes nor operating schedules, and the enormous distances that separated the lines – it was more than 2,000 kilometres from Dakar to Cotonou – prevented workers from interacting with their peers in other colonies.[8] Union leaders managed to form a centralised federation, the FSCA, in late 1945, but the organisation with the greatest potential to unite the African unions, the French Confédération Générale des Travailleurs (CGT), was completely unsuccessful. When representatives of the African unions and the CGT met in Dakar in October 1946, Africans remained unconvinced that the CGT's white members would support efforts to equalise African and European salaries. Leaders of the Dakar-Niger, Conakry-Niger, and Abidjan-Niger unions opted to remain autonomous, while the Benin-Niger union joined the rival Confédération Française des Travailleurs Chrétiens instead. Ironically, the main consequence of this meeting was to weaken the CGT in Africa

5 Dupré La Tour (2006), *Histoire*, 21–24. Other lines in francophone Africa were located in Togo, Cameroon, Gabon, Congo-Brazzaville, Madagascar, as well as Morocco, Algeria, Tunisia, Mauritania and Djibouti. See also Day (1964), *Railroads*, passim.

6 Rapids divide the Niger River into three navigable stretches, and plans to bypass them with locks and canals never materialized. There was river transportation between the termini of the Dakar-Niger and Conakry-Niger railways, but it was too costly and dependent on seasonal water levels to offer meaningful choices to shippers. For an overview of the subject, see Champaud (1961), 'La navigation fluviale'.

7 Inspection Générale du Travail de l'AOF (henceforth IGT), Annual Report 1947, 60–61, cited in Cooper (1996), 'Our Strike', 88. The history of the bureaucratic unification of the four railways and the two ports appears in Lakroum (1987), 'Chemin de Fer et Réseaux d'Affairs', 296–301.

8 Delanoue and Dewitte, 'La CGT', 107.

when some of its European members quit to form an all-white union, the Syndicat des Agents du Cadre Général.[9]

Even without a CGT affiliation, the African union leaders had no difficulty presenting the concept of a strike to their membership. Despite prohibitions against forming labour organisations,[10] workers on the Dakar-Niger went on strike as early as 1888.[11] In 1919 African and European workers shut down the Dakar-St. Louis branch of the Dakar-Niger, and in 1925 Africans staged a series of strikes that led to some improvement in working conditions.[12] In 1938 a wildcat strike closed the line once again, and turned lethal after troops fired into a crowd of strikers in the railway town of Thiès in Senegal.[13] That incident was still fresh in the minds of railway workers after the war ended in 1945.

Setting the Stage

The 1947–1948 strike took place during the period of worldwide labour unrest that followed World War II. Across FWA, European and African workers carried out strikes that culminated in a general strike that paralysed Senegal in January 1946.[14] Oddly enough, the union that represented the railway workers in Senegal, the Syndicat des Travailleurs Indigènes du

9 Suret-Canale (1978), 'Strike', 133–134; Morlet (1948), 'Une étape', 38.

10 In 1884 French workers received the right to unionise, but the law was not promulgated in Africa for fear that workers would be misled by demagogues. Bernhard-Duquenet (1985), *Le Sénégal*, 37. On the 1884 legalisation of French unions, see Stearns (1971), *Revolutionary Syndicalism*, 12.

11 Jones (2002), *Industrial Labor*, 15. For a reference to the 1888 strike, see Bouche, *Les Villages de Liberté*, 146.

12 Jones (2002), *Industrial Labor*, 50–51.

13 Thiam (1976), 'La tuerie', 300–338.

14 Much of the background to the 1947 general strike appears in Cooper (1991), 'La Grève Générale', 33–35. Additional details appear in Jones (2002), *Industrial Labor*, 53–54.

Dakar-Niger (STIN), did not join the twenty-seven unions that participated in the general strike. Scholars have attributed this to the influence of François Gning, the union's secretary-general, whose ties to local political leaders made him reluctant to challenge the administration.[15]

Gning was certainly well connected, having led the railway workers for seventeen years. Though born in Libreville, he grew up in Senegal, the land of his father, and after starting work at the railway, he became a decorated soldier in the French army during World War I. He returned from the war to a job in the railway's accounting office, and when the administration authorised the formation of a mutual aid association for railway workers, they elected Gning secretary general in 1929. During the next ten years, Gning mediated between the administration and the workers, and at key moments supported the administration's efforts to block reform. He also became active in the French Socialist party, which dominated local elections in Senegal. Gning's biggest test came in 1937 after France's Popular Front government passed laws that authorised the transformation of the association into a union, but only for full time workers who represented less than one-fifth of the Dakar-Niger's labour force. The majority were day workers (called auxiliares), most of whom worked side-by-side with the full time workers for much less pay and without formal contracts. When the day workers protested their exclusion from the new union, Gning backed the French administration. The immediate result was the disastrous wildcat strike of 1938, and it left many railway workers suspicious about Gning's loyalties. The decision to stay out of the 1946 general strike became the final provocation, and at the STIN annual conference in Thiès later that spring, Gning's opponents forced him to resign. On 25 May 1946 the delegates elected Ibrahima Sarr to take his place.[16]

Sarr was also a railway worker, but from a different generation. As a graduate of one of the colony's technical schools, he obtained a position working as a clerk at the railway headquarters in Thiès. During World War

15 Cooper (1996), 'Our Strike', 84. Bernhard-Duquenet (1985) made a similar charge about Gning's loyalties during the 1938 strike. See *Le Senegal*, 195.

16 Bernhard-Duquenet (1985), *Le Sénégal*, 39, 185–195; Cooper, 'Our strike,' 84–92.

II, he joined other Africans employed by the French in 'discussion groups' which viewed men like Gning as collaborators, and Sarr even went so far as to help edit an anti-government newspaper. His activities led the administration to transfer him away from Thiès, and by the time he was elected to head the union, he was working at Kayes in the Soudan.[17] According to most informants, Sarr was an effective speaker and administrator whose leadership was essential to the strike's success.[18]

After Sarr's election, events began to move rapidly. In July while Sarr was back in the Soudan, the administration announced a plan to combine the four rail lines, the wharfs in Côte d'Ivoire and Dahomey, and several 'supplementary and incorporated services'[19] into a corporation called the Chemins de Fer d'Afrique.[20] The new company would be 'semi-private' and that meant its employees would no longer enjoy the security of a government job. Fearing that this was the first step toward layoffs, the FSCA executive committee decided to take the initiative by presenting a list of grievances in August. They included issues like access to company housing, vacation time, safety conditions and the requirements for promotion, but the most important were the demand for a 'cadre unique' – a single pay scale for all workers regardless of race – and an end to the practice of hiring day workers to avoid creating permanent full time positions.[21] Tactically, the support of the day workers was critical since they outnumbered the full time workers and if they chose not to join a strike, they could enable

17 Cooper (1996), 'Our Strike', 85–86. On Sarr's assignment to Kayes, see Guèye interview.

18 Diombana, Guèye, and Sembene interviews, among others. See Jones (2002), *Industrial Labor*, 77.

19 Suret-Canale (1978), 'Strike', 131.

20 The Arrèté de 17 July 1946 (effective 1 January 1947), made the railway into a semi-private corporation. See 'Note sur la proposition de loi'.

21 'Cahiers de revendications' in ANS 17G 601 (152), cited in Ndour, 'Luttes laborieuses', 48. The FSCA executive committee included Ibrahima Sarr (Senegal), Edo Koffi (Dahomey), Adama Diop (Guinea), and Gaston Fiankan (Cote d'Ivoire). Sarr, as leader of the largest union, became the FSCA spokesperson. Traoré (1975), 'La Grève', 49.

the administration to continue railway operations.[22] Morally, the full time employees felt bound to support the day workers since they worked together and shared the same hazards.[23]

The next act in the prelude to the strike was a legal battle. The décret sur les syndicats professionels, which legalised unions in FWA in April 1937, included a detailed process for resolving labour disputes. Before a strike could begin, both sides were required to participate in an arbitration process that included representatives of the government as mediators. This was intended to reduce the likelihood of a strike, but in this case the situation was complicated by the fact that the government was also the owner of the railways and its revenue depended upon tariffs that were paid by the railway's biggest customers. As such, the government's neutrality was merely theoretical. The administration took two months to form an arbitration commission, and then waited another month before beginning hearings that dragged on into the following year. Many railway workers viewed the entire process as a farce, and as time passed, the pressure on Sarr and the FSCA to launch a strike became immense.[24]

While all of this was going on, most of the people of FWA got their first experience with mass democracy.[25] Between October 1945 and November 1946, they participated in five major elections – the election of the constituent assembly to draft a constitution for the Fourth Republic, the referendum that rejected the first constitution, the election of a second constituent assembly, the referendum that approved their work, and the election of delegates to the new national assembly.[26] Besides offering opportunities to mobilise large numbers of people, the elections that created the Fourth

22 Ndour (1991), 'Luttes laborieuses', 45.

23 Cooper (1996), 'Our Strike', 87.

24 Jones (2002), *Industrial Labor*, 55–56.

25 Citizens of the 'quatre communes' in Senegal – Dakar, Rufisque, Gorée and Saint Louis – elected their own representative to the National Assembly beginning in 1848. Diouf (1997), 'Assimilation', 838.

26 The people of FWA also got to witness the selection of members of the *Haut Conseil de l'Union Française*, but since this was done by territorial councils dominated by Europeans, the public did not participate directly. de Benoist (1982), *L'Afrique Occidentale Française*, 42–76.

Republic raised hopes among railway workers that their new representatives could settle their grievances without the need for a strike. That hope proved unrealistic, however, because as the new political landscape took shape, it became clear that the African delegates, who numbered only thirteen out of more than six hundred in the national assembly, could exert little pressure on their own. To improve their position, they met in Bamako in October 1946 and formed an autonomous African political party, the Rassemblement Démocratique Africain (RDA), but several prominent African politicians like Léopold Senghor of Senegal stayed away for fear of alienating potential metropolitan allies. As a result, following a convoluted mix of lobbying and subterfuge, Félix Houphout-Boigny of Côte d'Ivoire was chosen to lead the RDA. Fily Dabo Sissoko, the deputy from the Soudan, reluctantly endorsed the new group, but disappointed many by withholding his full support.[27]

As 1946 came to an end, the tension among union members increased. The arbitration commission began its deliberations on 5 December, but made no progress,[28] and at the beginning of the new year, the law that privatised the four railways went into effect.[29] Then in late January, the representative of the European railway workers at the arbitration commission withdrew his support for the *cadre unique*. In response, Sarr and Gaston Fiankan of the Conakry-Niger union walked out of the hearings on 9 February and decided to launch a strike.[30] They chose 17 April, the day that the new President of the Republic, Vincent Auriol, was due to arrive for a tour.[31] The strike lasted three days, and while it did not prevent Auriol from visiting Dakar, St. Louis, Conakry, Niamey, and Bamako,[32] it embarrassed the government and broke the negotiations logjam. The government's representatives agreed to accept the principle of the cadre unique and the

27 Kipré (1989), *Le congrès de Bamako*, 51–94.

28 'Note relative à la Grève'.

29 'Note sur la proposition de loi'.

30 Renseignements (10 February 1947), 1, in Archives de l'Afrique occidentale française (henceforth AOF) K 377 (26), cited in Cooper (1996), 'Our Strike', 89; Suret-Canale (1978), 'Strike', 135.

31 Morlet (1948), 'Une étape', 39; Cooper, 'La Grève Générale,' 37.

32 Traoré (1975), 'La Grève', 44.

use of worker qualifications, rather than the location of their work assignment, as a basis for setting salaries. The union's representatives accepted the need to reduce the size of the work force, while both sides agreed that the High Commissioner of FWA (HC-GGAOF) should decide how to promote day workers to full time status.[33] Thinking that progress had been made, the workers returned to their posts on 20 April.

They were mistaken. Instead of implementing the agreement, the administration stalled. On 15 June the arbitration commission resumed its deliberations,[34] but Sarr and the other union leaders boycotted the meeting in order to spend time meeting with workers in their respective territories.[35] In August the arbitration commission concluded its work, but issued recommendations that stopped short of the agreement that ended the April strike. The union leaders rejected the new proposal on 29 August[36] and issued a revised set of demands on 1 September, but continued to devote most of their time to preparing for a strike.[37] A week later, they notified the administration that the strike would resume on 10 October.[38] By the time that the arbitration commission rejected most of the September demands on 20 October, it no longer mattered.[39]

The Strike

While some workers wanted immediate action, Sarr and Fiankan used the rest of September and early October to organise their members.[40] They instructed local leaders to form strike committees at major rail centres and

33 'Note relative à la Grève'.
34 'Note relative à la Grève'.
35 Traoré (1975), 'La Grève', 49.
36 Suret-Canale (1978), 'Strike', 135–136; Ndour (1991), 'Luttes laborieuses', 49.
37 Police report (9 September 1947), in Archives de l'AOF, K457 (179).
38 Suret-Canale (1978), 'Strike', 136.
39 'Note relative à la Grève'.
40 Cooper (1996), 'Our Strike,' 92.

to hold daily information meetings for their workers. During the same period the workers' cooperative on the Dakar-Niger stockpiled food and supplies. Local farmers used the extra time to complete their harvest, which served two purposes: maximising local food reserves and increasing the pressure on export firms that needed to transport cocoa, coffee, peanuts, and especially bananas to the coast before they spoiled.[41]

French officials also made preparations. For example, in the Soudan the administration deployed troops to protect railway property and issued orders that limited public gatherings. Meanwhile, the police dispatched informers to report on the activities of strike committees.[42] Scholars have questioned the sincerity of these efforts, however, because police reports consistently claimed that the strikers were poorly prepared and predicted that a strike would last no more than a few days.[43] The director of the Dakar-Niger, Henri Cunéo, seemed especially unconcerned, and instead of making plans to operate trains with managers and volunteers, he merely sent a letter to the union leaders on 6 October, reminding them of the consequences of an illegal strike. After last minute negotiations failed, Cunéo sent a telegram to all stations on the 10th that ordered workers not to leave their posts,[44] but on 11 October he informed Paris that the strike would be over in no more than a few weeks.[45]

Cunéo was wrong. The strike began at midnight on the night of 10–11 October 1947 and lasted more than five months. It received almost total support from both day and full time railway workers, and on the first day

41 Suret-Canale (1978), 'Strike', 137, 148–149.

42 For examples of the administration's preparations in the Soudan, see police report (11 October 1947), in Archives. de l'AOF, K457 (179); and *Bulletin Quotidien de la Chambre du Commerce de Soudan* (7, 8, 11, 16, 24 and 27 October 1947).

43 Direction de la Suréte Générale to IGT AOF, 'Renseignements a/s Grève eventuelle des cheminots Africains (État d'esprit)' (7 October 1947), in Archives de l'AOF, K457 (179).

44 Morlet (1948), 'Une étape', 39; Suret-Canale (1978), 'Strike', 135–136.

45 Directeur Fédéral de la Régie to Directeur de l'Office Central des Chemins de Fer de la France Outre-Mer, IGT 13/2 (10 October 1947), cited in Cooper (1996), 'Our Strike', 103.

of the strike, only thirty-eight workers (out of more than 16,000) reported to their jobs. By 2 February, that number had risen to 836, mostly on the Abidjan-Niger, but the rate of desertion remained low on the other lines.[46] The strikers also demonstrated their discipline in other ways, so there were no significant incidents of violence or sabotage, and consequently, few arrests.[47] Instead there were examples of valour and self-sacrifice, like that of Mahmadou Cissé, the stationmaster from Tabako in the Soudan, who died rather than allow strike-breakers to transport him to the hospital at Bamako for medical treatment.[48] After both sides agreed to resume work on 19 March 1948, the workers returned to their jobs without taking reprisals against those who had gone back earlier.[49]

The strike became the longest work stoppage in African history. By all accounts, the workers were able to hold out because they received support from the rest of the population. Family members and neighbours provided food, merchants contributed money and trucks with which to move supplies, anti-French newspapers took up collections, the CGT donated money, and all but the most prominent religious leaders urged support for the strikers.[50] But the real strength of the movement, according to one participant, was 'our solidarity and our faith'.[51] Unlike the CGT, whose notion of solidarity was based on the struggle against imperialism,[52] the African strikers understood solidarity in terms of 'the idea of family in its most noble, most dedicated form' in which no one wanted to be the first to betray the others.[53] Scholars have, without reservation, accepted

46 IGT AOF, 'Situation des effectifs de la Régie' (Renseignements fournis par la Régie le 6–1–48), in Archives de l'AOF, K457 (179), cited in Ndour (1991), 'Luttes laborieuses', 50.
47 Jones (2002), *Industrial Labor*, 59.
48 Diombana, interview; Traoré (1975), 'La Grève', 65.
49 Cooper (1996), 'Our Strike', 112.
50 Ibid., 93–97.
51 Guèye interview.
52 Morlet (1948), 'Une étape', 41.
53 Jones (2008), 'Ousmane Sembene', 147–148.

the role of the ideal of solidarity in the success of the strike, and devoted significant energy to exploring its sources.[54]

That sense of solidarity did not extend to the African politicians who were preoccupied with the struggle to wield influence in the Fourth Republic. For them, the strike offered an opportunity to attract support from the railway workers, but it also presented a challenge since support for the strike was tantamount to opposition to France's governing coalition. That endangered their efforts to form alliances with metropolitan delegates who might support African initiatives. The problem was particularly acute for deputies like Lamine Guèye and Fily Dabo Sissoko, whose Socialist party remained dominant in Senegal and closely associated with the railway administration.[55] After the French Communists left the ruling coalition on April 1947, it became somewhat easier for their African allies, Houphouët-Boigny in the National Assembly and Gabriel D'Arboussier (of Moyen-Congo) in the Assembly of the French Union, to declare their support for the strike.[56]

Houphouët-Boigny's support had its limits, however.[57] He was a successful cocoa planter and he derived much of his support from other planters in Côte d'Ivoire. That made him especially susceptible to pressure to restore rail service in order to transport crops to the coast. As early as November 1946, police informers reported that he criticised the union leadership in private conversations,[58] and in January 1947 the only serious breakdown in union discipline took place in his home territory.[59] Years

54 Cooper subtitled the relevant section of one of his articles 'Solidarity and Survival', while Jean Suret-Canale concluded a section of his article entitled 'Solidarity' with 'in general the strikers were sustained by the entire African population'. Cooper (1996), 'Our Strike', 93; Suret-Canale (1978), 'Strike', 146–147.

55 Cooper (1998), *Decolonization*, 73–75.

56 Ndour (1991), 'Luttes laborieuses', 52. On Houphouë-Boigny's and d'Arboussier's positions in the government, see de Benoist (1982), *L'Afrique Occidentale Française*, 77, 82.

57 Suret-Canale (1978), 'Strike', 147.

58 Renseignements (Côte d'Ivoire, 5 November and 18 November 1947), in Archives de l'AOF K379 (26), cited in Cooper (1996), 'Our Strike', 98.

59 N'Dour (1991), 'Luttes laborieuses', 50.

later strikers still remembered what they believed to have been Houphouët-Boigny's duplicity.

They had even harsher criticism for Fily Dabo Sissoko.[60] As the son of a chief who won election to the second constituent assembly, and then won a seat in the National Assembly, his ancestry and electoral success gave him the most prestige of any deputy from FWA. But his loyalty to the French kept him from offering whole-hearted support to the RDA, and after Houphouët-Boigny outmanoeuvred him for the RDA leadership, the two men became rivals. While Houphouët-Boigny professed support for the strikers,[61] Sissoko declared his opposition to the strike as early as December 1947,[62] and as it dragged on, he tried to position himself as a power-broker. At the end of January, he convinced the administration to agree to some minor concessions so that he could use them to pry a back-to-work order out of the FSCA leadership. Sarr appeared interested, but the FSCA executive committee remained firm, and Sissoko tried to salvage his effort by appealing directly to the workers. He sent a telegram to all stations that claimed a settlement had been reached and instructed everyone to return to their posts. The union sent their own telegram and in the end, only a handful of workers followed Sissoko. Sissoko lost all credibility with the union[63] and the Soudanese railway workers never forgot his betrayal.[64]

By mid January 1948, the strike had entered its third month. Even though the administration managed to restore limited rail service using soldiers, new hires and union defectors,[65] the two sides remained deadlocked. The union could see some favourable signs, such as the resolution approved on 8 January by the Assembly of the French Union that called

60 Diombana (1989), '1938–1948', 6.

61 de Benoist (1982), *L'Afrique Occidentale Française*, 62, 67–68.

62 Fily Dabo Sissoko to Minister of Colonies, telegram IGT 3 December 1947, cited in Cooper (1996), 'Our Strike', 101.

63 Cooper (1996), 'Our Strike', 101–102.

64 Diombana interview; Jones, 'Ousman Sembene', interview, 146. Worker dissatisfaction with Sissoko is also mentioned in Traoré (1975), 'La Grève', 73.

65 'Note relative à la Grève'.

for an end to the strike, and the donation of a half million francs by the CGT to the union. But Houphouët-Boigny and d'Arboussier failed to get the Assembly to approve a stronger resolution in support of the union's demands,[66] and at about the same time a large number of strikers returned to work on the Abidjan-Niger. The union appeared to suffer another setback a month later when the administration authorised the formation of a rival union, headed by none other than François Gning.[67]

Through the early months of 1948 the export economy remained paralysed and the pressure continued to mount back in France. The breakthrough finally came after a new Foreign Minister, Marius Moutet, recalled HC-GGAOF Réné Barthes at the end of January. Barthes' replacement, Paul Béchard, arrived at Dakar on 22 February and quickly called a meeting that included the Dakar-Niger director Henri Cunéo; African deputies Léopold Senghor, Lamine Guèye, Fily Dabo Sissoko, Gaston d'Arboussier and Hamani Diori (of Niger); and the union's lawyer, Léon Boissiers-Palun.[68] They worked out an agreement to end the strike and then waited two weeks while Béchard presented it to administrators in Bamako, Conakry and at posts in the Upper Niger Valley.[69] After a final meeting to sign the agreement, Béchard announced the end of the strike on 16 March. Sarr did the same on the 17th, and work resumed on the 19th.[70]

The agreement was only a partial victory for the union, since it was based on the results of the arbitration decision from the previous October. It left unresolved such thorny questions as how to simultaneously reinstate the strikers, upgrade the day workers to full time status, and reward the new

66 'Les Élus du RDA à l'Assemblée de l'Union appuyés par les Élus communistes mettent le Gouvernement en face de ces responsabilités dans la Grêve des Cheminots Africains', and Blacas, 'Solidarité Active de la C.G.T.', both in *Le Réveil* (8 January 1948).

67 Police report (8 February 1948), in Archives de l'AOF, K457 (179), cited in Cooper (1996), 106.

68 Diombana (1989), '1938–1948', 7; Cooper (1998), *Decolonization*, 247.

69 Announcements of Béchard's trip appeared in issues of *Sud Quotidien* from 20 February through 17 March 1948.

70 Suret-Canale (1978), 'Strike', 149.

workers hired during the strike with permanent jobs on a railway system that the administration claimed was overstaffed. On the other hand, the agreement prohibited retribution by the administration against the strikers, recognised the union's right to represent them, and most importantly, codified the right to equal pay for equal work.[71] What was even more important in the long run, the union had demonstrated its ability to conduct a long strike, and the outcome appeared to African observers as an act of capitulation by the administration. From 1948 until independence in 1960, the terms of the battle to determine labour conditions were altered. The old tactics of patronage and punishment gave way to legal battles fought by lawyers and politicians.

Remembering the Strike

An event of such magnitude, involving thousands of workers and hundreds of thousands of eyewitnesses, was not likely to be forgotten. Yet as time passed the memory of the strike became simplified as details experienced by participants were left out of the stories passed on to the next generation. Written accounts did little to prevent the loss, because they were surprisingly scarce. The strike was the subject of numerous newspaper reports while it was underway, and a French union activist named Pierre Morlet published an account right after it ended in 1948,[72] but there were no more written accounts after that until independence in 1960. There is ample evidence however, that even without written accounts, the memory of the strike influenced other unions during the passage of the *Code du Travail* in 1952 and the *Loi Cadre* in 1956, the formation of the Union Général des

71 'Note relative à la Grève'.

72 Morlet (1948), 'Une étape'. Morlet was the secretary of the Union des syndicats confédérés of the Soudan. After the governor expelled him in July 1947, he returned to the AOF as a CGT delegate at the beginning of 1948.

Travailleurs Africains in 1957, and the transition to independence between 1958 and 1960.[73] In each case, leaders drew lessons from the strike about the importance of remaining autonomous from European institutions and the value of the ideal of solidarity as a means to attract popular support. As the main character expressed it in Ousman Sembene's novel about the strike, 'It depends on you, workers of Dakar, whether our wives and our children will ever see a better life. There is a great rock poised across our path, but together we can move it.'[74]

Although it stimulated a new round of writing about the strike, independence proved disastrous for the railway unions, especially in Senegal and Soudan. The unions had always been more interested in improving labour conditions than in breaking away from France, so they were left behind as reform movements turned anti-colonial in the 1950s. By the time independence arrived in June 1960, the desires of the union had become secondary to the need for nation-building. Even though the new Mali Federation, formed from the territories of Senegal and the Soudan, contained all of the region served by the Dakar-Niger railway, when disputes about the structure of the new government threatened the federation's survival, its leaders did not hesitate to divide it in two, even though that meant sacrificing the railway itself.[75]

To make matters worse for railway workers, the head of the Soudanese government, Modibo Keita, called on all Soudanese to return home from Senegal. Since many were employed at the main railway workshops in Thiès or at other stations in Senegal, the order had particularly dire implications for members of the union. Many had to abandon their homes and families, and after they returned, they discovered that Keita's promises of jobs in the Soudan (renamed the Republic of Mali on 22 September) were meaningless because most of the railway's equipment remained behind in Senegal. By the end of August, the breakup of the Mali Federation fractured the

73 Jones (2002), *Industrial Labor*, 66–67.

74 Sembene (1986), *God's Bits of Wood*, 218.

75 On the creation of the Mali Federation, see Mortimer (1969), *France and the Africans*, 343–371. For the Senegalese and Malian views on its dissolution, see République du Sénégal (1960), *Livre Blanc* and Ndiaye (1980), *L'Échec* respectively.

union along territorial lines, and then the Soudanese contingent divided again over whether or not to return home.[76]

Keita launched a campaign to win the railway workers' support that invoked, among other things, the 1947–1948 strike. His RDA party's newspaper, *L'Essor*, carried a front page story and photo showing Keita travelling by train, rather than by airplane, to Dakar for the 'Conference Inter-états du Mali' which ended the federation on 20 August. Throughout September and October, *L'Essor* published a series of upbeat stories about the new 'Fédération National des Cheminots du Mali' while disparaging the 'soit-disant Syndicat des Cheminots en Residence au Senegal'. It also ran numerous articles about the mistreatment of the Soudanese who remained behind in Senegal, described negotiations for foreign aid to finance new railway construction in Mali, and published letters of support for the new government from groups with names like 'Cheminots du Soudan'.[77]

The coverage culminated on 29 October with an entire issue devoted to the exodus of several thousand railway workers and their dependents from Senegal. Besides photographs of the 'refugees' and stories of their mistreatment, the same issue carried a poem called 'Hommage aux cheminots du Mali' that included two stanzas that referred directly to the 1947 strike.[78]

> Tu demontais en '47 la preuve
> de la maturité au cours d'une épreuve
> qui restera encore longtemps dans l'histoire
> et s'inscrira en lettres d'or dans les memoires.
>
> Tu sortais victorieux de ce conflit unique
> dans l'histoire de la grande Afrique.
> Sur toi, les frères opprimés prenent exemple
> ont alors engagé la lutte pour libérer leur peuple.

76 Diombana interview.

77 Various issues of *L'Essor* from 13 August through 28 October 1960, in the Archives Nationales du Mali.

78 Sissoko, 'Hommage aux cheminots' in *L'Essor* (29 October 1960).

Maturity, the struggle against oppression, and the liberation of 'their people' – these were all useful distractions for unemployed workers in an impoverished state like Mali. Other verses in the poem referred to the workers' patriotism, discipline, willingness to accept sacrifice and in particular, their readiness to abandon their houses and families in Senegal in order to serve their country.[79]

Some of the same values appeared in *God's Bits of Wood*, the 1960 novel by Ousman Sembene that became the best-known account of the strike. Although Sembene was in France during the strike, he grew up in Dakar near the railway union's headquarters and absorbed many of the ideas that influenced the 1947–1948 strike. Unlike Nodibo Keita, Sembene used the story of the strike to promote working class solidarity rather than national unity, and later explained that he disapproved of how independence divided FWA into national states. He especially condemned the way that the new leaders focused on creating their own power bases, so he used his narrative of the strike to emphasise the solidarity of the workers, their links to the larger population, and the difference between leaders who served themselves and those who served the community.[80]

While Africans reconsidered the strike in the context of independence, scholars in other parts of the world began to examine it in relation to the Cold War. A year after Sembene's book was published, a German political scientist named Franz Ansprenger described the strike as an effort by French communists, working through the CGT, to introduce the Cold War into colonial Africa.[81] His thesis provoked more than two decades of spirited debate about whether the CGT 'controlled' the African railway unions.[82]

79 Ibid.

80 Jones (2000), 'Fact and Fiction', 118–121. On Sembene's relationship to the railway union, see Jones (2008), 'Ousmane Sembene', 148–149. For a discussion of antagonisms between trade unions and independent African governments, see Freund (1988), *African Worker*, 94–96.

81 Ansprenger (1961), *Politik im Schwarzen Afrika*, 85.

82 Mortimer (1969), *France and the Africans*, 118; Pfefferman (1967), 'Trade Unions', 213–230. For a critique of Ansprenger's thesis, see Allen (1975), 'Union-Party Relationships', 99–125.

The conclusion accepted by most scholars was that the CGT had offered assistance in the hope of gaining some influence, but the African railway union had been truly autonomous before, during and after the strike.[83]

The debate started by Ansprenger raised new questions about the applicability of European models to the 1947–1948 strike. Troubled by the dearth of primary sources in the Cold War analyses, a pair of Europeans who had lived through the strike used their personal archives and interviews with African acquaintances to produce more detailed accounts. Jean Suret-Canale, a French communist who had worked with Pierre Morlet, wrote about the strike's contribution to the unity of workers, not only within Africa but also between Europeans and Africans.[84] Joseph Roger de Benoist, a missionary who was critical of the communists, stressed the damage done to the colonial system, but admitted that the strike established a 'working class consciousness' in West Africa.[85]

The search for African sources turned into an effort to preserve the memory of the strike. Individual Africans began the process in the 1970s,[86] but the task had become urgent by the 1990s as elderly strike participants began to die of old age. The best known effort was led by Babacar Fall of the Université Cheikh Anta Diop in Dakar who, assisted by Frederick Cooper, directed graduate students on an oral history project that examined 'the events that have marked the social, political, and labour history of Senegal between 1946 and 1960'.[87] At about the same time, the author of this chapter interviewed strike participants in Mali for a doctoral dissertation.[88] Both efforts yielded similar conclusions about the railway workers' perceptions of the strike and the uses to which its memory had been put in subsequent years. All emphasised that Africans had come together in an effort to make the colonial government live up to its promises, not to ignite an insurrection.

83 Dewitte (1981), 'La CGT', 15; Delanoue and Dewitte (1983), 'La CGT', 107.

84 Suret-Canale (1978), 'Strike', 129–154.

85 de Benoist, 'La grande bataille', 21–28.

86 Traoré (1975), 'La Grève'; Diombana (1989), '1938–1948'.

87 Fall (2003), 'Orality and Life Histories', 60.

88 Jones (1995), 'The Impact'.

By the mid 1990s, a new group of people looked to the strike for inspiration. Faced with structural adjustment programs that required the public sector to shrink, the governments of Senegal, Mali, Côte d'Ivoire and Bénin sold their rail systems to private firms, while Guinea closed down its railway completely.[89] As the new owners made politically unpopular decisions to curtail service and lay off workers, the people living along the rail lines organised to protest. The anti-privatisation movement was particularly well-organised along the former Dakar-Niger line, and in addition to modern methods like web sites and appeals to international human rights groups, its leaders invoked the memory of the strike as a means to rally local support. For example, when railway workers from Mali and Senegal met to discuss strategy in March 2003, they chose Thiès, the centre of worker agitation during earlier strikes, as the site for their meeting. At its conclusion, they issued a 'Déclaration de Thiès' that recalled the 1947–1948 strike and claimed that history was repeating itself in 2003.[90] Meanwhile, opponents of privatisation organised themselves as the Collectif citoyen pour la restitution et le développement intégré du rail malien (Cocidirail), and during the following summer, the group's president invoked the 'événements historiques de la mémorable grève de 1947' in a position paper that also emphasised the 'solidarité exemplaire' of the 1947 strikers and their 'coup décisif' against colonial authority.[91] Most recently in February 2008, leaders of the union representing workers on the 'Petit train de banlieue' on Dakar protested the demolition of the main train station in the centre of town with a reminder that railway workers had fought to liberate Africa and opposed 'l'exploitation de l'homme par l'homme'.[92]

89 Dupré la Tour (2006), 'Histoire des chemins de fer', 30–32. In the same book, see also Traore, 'L'impact de la privatisation', and Ouedraogo, 'Rôle du chemin de fer'.

90 'Privatisation du chemin de fer Dakar-Koulikoro', *l'Essor* (24 March 2003).

91 Traoré (2007), 'Tous ensemble'. Traoré was the secretary-general of the *Syndicat des Travailleurs du Rail* (Sytrail), until he was fired in September 2004. See Daou (2004), 'Privatisation du chemin de fer'.

92 Sarr (2009), 'Sénégal: Démolition de la gare ferroviaire'.

Conclusion

Pierre Prier, writing in *Le Figaro*, claimed that in Mali and Senegal, 'le train Dakar-Bamako reste avant tout le centre d'une geste mythologique'. The strike became 'the first act of decolonisation' whose memory still motivates workers at the main workshops in Thiès.[93] As time has passed, that memory has become simplified to three basic ideas: the solidarity of the African population in opposition to threats, the autonomy of African institutions from foreign organisations, and the righteousness of opposition to governments that fail to keep their promises. The first two ideas have faced few political challenges since both serve the needs of leaders who invoke solidarity to rally support from the population and autonomy to discredit their opponents as foreign agents. The third idea has proven more controversial because unions and other dissidents have used it to accuse their leaders of collaborating with the forces of globalisation. Meanwhile, other goals of the strike, such as the desire to obtain equality with the West, have been lost.

References

Newspapers

Le Réveil, 1947–1948
Sud Quotidien, 1947–8
L'Essor, 1960
L'Essor on-line at http://www.essor.gov.ml), 2003
Bulletin Quotidien de la Chambre du Commerce de Soudan, October 1947

93 Prier (2004), 'Train de légende'.

Official Reports

'Main d'oeuvre' in *Notice Géographique* (1890), in Archives Nationales du Mali, Series 1D 33, fonds anciens.

'Note relative à la Grève des Cheminots Africains' (n.d. [April 1948]), in Archives Nationales du Mali, Série K 70, fonds recents.

'Note sur la proposition de loi presentés par M. Mamadou Konaté tendant a la création d'un cadre unique des chemins de fer de l'AOF' (n.d. [1950]), in Archives du Gouvernment Général de l'Afrique Occidentale Française, Series K43 (1).

Books and Articles

Allen, C.H. (1975) 'Union-Party Relationships in Francophone West Africa: A Critique of "Téléguidage" Interpretations', in R. Sandbrook and R. Cohen (eds), *The Development of an African Working Class*, Toronto: University of Toronto Press.

Ansprenger, F. (1961) *Politik im Schwarzen Afrika: Die modernen politischen Bewegungen im Afrika französischer Prägung*, Köln: Opladen.

de Benoist, J.R. (1981) 'La grande bataille des cheminots (1947–1948)' in *Afrique histoire* 4: 21–28.

de Benoist, J.R. (1982) *L'Afrique Occidentale Française de 1944 à 1960*, Dakar: Nouvelles Editions Africaines.

Bernhard-Duquenet, N. (1985) *Le Sénégal et le Front Populaire*, Paris: L'Harmattan.

Blacas, J. (8 January 1948) 'Solidarité Active de la C.G.T.', *Le Réveil.*

Bouche, D. (1968) *Les Villages de Liberté en Afrique Noire Française, 1887–1910*, Paris: Mouton.

Champaud, J. (1961) 'La navigation fluviale dans le moyen Niger', in *Cahiers d'Outre-Mer* 14(55): 255–292.

Cooper, F. (1990) 'The Senegalese General Strike and the Labor Question in Post-War French Africa', *Canadian Journal of African Studies* 24(2): 165–215.

Cooper, F. (1991) 'La Grève Générale de 1946 et la grève des cheminots de 1947–1948', *Historiens-Géographes du Sénégal* 6: 32–42.

Cooper, F. (1996) '"Our strike": Equality, anticolonial politics and the 1947–48 railway strike in French West Africa', *The Journal of African History* 37(1): 81–118.

Cooper, F. (1998) *Decolonization and African Society: the labor question in French and British Africa*, Cambridge: Cambridge University Press.

Daou, M. (6 September 2007) 'Privatisation du chemin de fer. ATT mis en accusation par Cocidirail', *Les Echos*, Bamako. Downloaded from http://www.maliweb.net/category.php?NID=21818 on 29 May 2008.

Day, J.R. (1964) *Railways of Northern Africa*, London: Arthur Baker.

Delanoue, P. and Dewitte, P. (1983) 'La CGT et les syndicats de l'Afrique noire de colonisation française, de la Deuxième Guerre mondiale aux indépendances', *Le Mouvement Social* 122: 103–121.

Dewitte, P. (1981) 'La CGT et les syndicats d'Afrique occidentale française (1947–1957)' in *Le Mouvement Social* 117: 3–32.

Diombana, C.S. (1989) '1938–1948: Dix Années de l'histoire syndicale des cheminots de Dakar-Niger', Bamako, unpublished monograph.

Diombana, C.S. (1992) interview by J.A. Jones, Bamako, transcript at http://courses.wcupa.edu/jones/his311/archives/intindex.htm.

Diouf, M. (1997) 'Assimilation coloniale et identités religieuses de la civilité des originaires des Quatre Communes (Sénégal)' in C. Becker, S. Mbaye and I. Thioub (eds), AOF: Réalités et Héritages; sociétés oust-africain et ordre colonial, volume 2, Paris & Dakar: Archives du Sénégal.

Dupré la Tour, F. (2006) 'Histoire des chemins de fer d'Afrique Noire francophone. De la construction aux privatisations', in J.-L. Chaléard, C. Chanson-Jabeur et Chantal Béranger (eds), *Le chemin de fer en Afrique*, Paris: Karthala.

Fall, B. (2003) 'Orality and Life Histories: Rethinking the Social and political History of Senegal', *Africa Today* 50(2).

Freund, B. (1988) *The African Worker*, Cambridge: Cambridge University Press.

Guèye, A.B. (1992) interview by J.A. Jones, Thiès, transcript at http://courses.wcupa.edu/jones/his311/archives/intindex.htm.

Jones, J.A. (1995) 'The Impact of the Dakar-Niger Railway on the Middle Niger Valley', Newark, DE: University of Delaware, PhD dissertation.

Jones, J.A. (2000) 'Fact and Fiction in *God's Bits of Wood*', *Research in African Literatures* 31(2): 117–131.

Jones, J.A. (2002) *Industrial Labor in the Colonial World: The African Workers of the Chemin de Fer Dakar-Niger*, Portsmouth, NH: Heinemann.

Jones, J.A. (2008) 'Ousmane Sembene' in A. Busch and M. Annas (eds), *Ousmane Sembene Interviews*, Jackson: University Press of Mississippi.

Kanya-Forstner, A.S. (1959) *The Conquest of the Western Sudan*, Cambridge: Cambridge University Press.

Kipré, P. (1989) *Le congrès de Bamako*, Paris: Chaka.

Lakroum, M. (1987) 'Chemin de Fer et Réseaux d'Affairs en Afrique Occidental: le Dakar-Niger 1883–1960', University of Paris VII, doctorat d'état.

Morlet, P. (1948) 'Une étape de la lutte anticolonialiste; la grêve des cheminots africains d'A.O.F.', *Servir la France* 37: 36–42.

Mortimer, E. (1969) *France and the Africans: 1944–1960*, New York: Walker and Co.

Ndour, B. (1991) 'Luttes laborieuses en "situation colonial": cheminots du Dakar-Niger, 1919–1951', *Historiens-Géographes du Sénégal* 6: 43–53.

Ndiaye, G. (1980) *L'Échec de la Fédération du Mali*, Dakar: Nouvelles Editions Africaines.

Ouedraogo, D. (2006) 'Rôle du chemin de fer dans l'économie du Burkina Faso: les révélations de la crise ivoirienne' in J.-L. Chaléard, C. Chanson-Jabeur and C. Béranger (eds), *Le chemin de fer en Afrique*, Paris: Karthala.

Pfefferman, G. (1967) 'Trade Unions and Politics in French West Africa during the Fourth Republic', *African Affairs* 66: 213–230.

Prier, P. (9–11 August 2004) 'Train de légende: le Dakar-Bamako' in *Le Figaro*, Paris.

République du Sénégal (1960) *Livre Blanc sur le Coup d'État manqué du 19 au 20 août 1960*, Dakar: Ministère de l'Information de la Presse et de la Radiodiffusion.

Sarr, M. (27 February 2009) 'Sénégal: Démolition de la gare ferroviaire - Les travailleurs du petit train de banlieue en ordre de bataille'. Downloaded from http://fr.allafrica.com/stories/200902270748.html on 23 August 2009.

Sembene, O. (1984) *Les bouts de bois de Dieu* (orig. 1960), *God's Bits of Wood*, London: Heinemann Educational Books.

Sembene, O. (1992), interview by J.A. Jones, transcript at http://courses.wcupa.edu/jones/his311/archives/intindex.htm.

Sissoko, M. (29 October 1960), 'Hommage aux cheminots du Mali', *L'Essor* 3505, Bamako.

Stearns, P.N. (1971) *Revolutionary Syndicalism and French Labor: A Cause without Rebels*, New Brunswick. NJ: Rutgers University Press.

Suret-Canale, J. (1978) 'The French West African Railway Workers' Strike, 1947–1948', in P. Gutkind, R. Cohen and J. Copans (eds), *African Labor History*, Beverly Hills, Sage Publications.

Thiam, I.D. (1976) 'La tuerie de Thiès de Septembre 1938, essai d'interprétation', *Bulletin de l'Institute Fondamentale de l'Afrique Noire* 38(2): 300–338.

Traore, A. (2006) 'L'impact de la privatisation de la RCFM sur l'économie malienne' in J.-L. Chaléard, C. Chanson-Jabeur and C. Béranger (eds), *Le chemin de fer en Afrique*, Paris: Karthala.

Traoré, C.H. (1975) 'La Grève des Cheminots Africains 10 Octobre 1947–19 Mars 1948', Bamako: École Normale Supérieur.

Traoré, T. (2 July 2004) 'Tous ensemble pour construire un monde juste et solidaire. Le chemin de fer Dakar-Bamako-Koulikoro: Une construction coloniale privatisée 100 ans après', downloaded from http://penserpouragir.org/espace-de-reflexion/forum-des-peuples-kita-2004,16/article/le-chemin-de-fer-dakar-bamako,102.html on 25 May 2009.

ELIZABETH SCHMIDT

Trade Unions and Nationalism in French Guinea, 1945–1958

Trade unionism in French Guinea emerged from a culture of protest that began during World War II. Burdened by the war effort, rural dwellers fled from military recruiters and resisted the labour, tax, and crop requisitions imposed by government-appointed chiefs. When forced labour was abolished in 1946, conscripts deserted their work sites in droves.[1] Campaigning for benefits commensurate with those of their European counterparts, returning war veterans provided the slogan, 'Equal sacrifices = equal rights', that would inspire the nascent trade union movement.[2] As anti-colonial sentiment escalated, France convened the historic Brazzaville Conference in January 1944 and promised a series of political, economic, and social reforms to be implemented at the war's end. Employing the language of assimilation to justify continued domination, France was confident that the Brazzaville concessions would ensure the survival of its empire and its claim to great power status.[3] While 'enlightened' imperialism did breathe new life into the old empire, it also gave African activists room to manoeuvre. Increasingly, they seized on French claims that the rights of citizenship were

1 Research for this chapter was conducted at the Archives Nationales du Sénégal (ANS) in Dakar, the Archives de Guinée (AG) in Conakry, the Centre de Recherche et de Documentation Africaine (CRDA) in Paris, and the Centre des Archives d'Outre-Mer, Archives Nationales (de France) (CAOM) in Aix-en-Provence. Unless otherwise indicated, I conducted all interviews in Conakry, Guinea, with the assistance of Siba N. Grovogui. Material from this chapter was previously published in Schmidt (2005), *Mobilizing the Masses*, and Schmidt (2007), *Cold War and Decolonization*.

2 Echenberg (1991), *Colonial Conscripts*, 104.

3 Suret-Canale (1971), *French Colonialism in Tropical Africa*, 484–485.

universal and demanded parity with Frenchmen in all domains.[4] It was in this context that the majority of Guinean trade unions moved beyond purely workplace concerns to promote the broader political struggle for African autonomy and independence.

If anti-colonial protests began during the war, so, too, did the incipient labour movement. In 1937, the French Popular Front government had recognized the right of Africans to organise trade unions. However, the Vichy regime had put an end to virtually all trade union activity in French West Africa. In 1943, shortly after the federation transferred its allegiance to the Free French, metropolitan unions began to initiate contacts with African workers, and in August 1944 a government decree reiterated the right of African workers to organise.[5] Many of the first African unions were affiliates of French trade unions, which in turn were associated with French political parties. Territorial branches were grouped together in federal organisations that represented workers in French West and Equatorial Africa. As multiethnic, trans-territorial African associations, trade unions played a crucial role in the development of national and international identities that united diverse peoples in common cause.

Most of the French West African trade unions established during the first postwar decade were affiliated with the French Confédération Générale du Travail (CGT), which in turn was associated with the Parti Communiste Français (PCF). The CGT branch in Guinea (officially the Union des Syndicats Confédérés de Guinée) was led by Sékou Touré. By 1950, the Guinean CGT had 2,000 members and included eighteen unions representing workers in both the public and private sectors.[6] The CGT

4 Cooper (1996a), *Decolonization*. See also Chafer (2002), *End of Empire*.

5 Morgenthau (1964), *Political Parties*, 28; Kéïta (1978), *P.D.G.*, 1:175–176; Cooper (1996b), 'Our Strike', 88–89; Cooper (1996a), *Decolonization*, 227–228.

6 ANS, 1K44, Inspection Territoriale du Travail de la Guinée Française, 'Décision de la Commission Mixte Locale du 1er Juillet 1950 fixant les Salaires des Travailleurs du Batiment et de l'Industrie de la Guinée Française'; 17G271, Gouverneur, Conakry, à Haut Commissaire, Dakar, 'A/S Activité Syndicale', 25 Feb. 1952, #85/APA; 17G529, Guinée Française, 'Liste des Organisations Professionnelles', 1952; Kéïta (1978), *P.D.G.*, 1:256–257; Mortimer (1969), *France and the Africans*, 200.

unions were closely allied to the Guinean branch of the Rassemblement Démocratique Africain (RDA), an inter-territorial coalition of political parties with affiliates in most of the fourteen territories of French West Africa, French Equatorial Africa, and the United Nations trusts of Togo and Cameroon. From 1947 to 1950, the RDA was also associated with the PCF, with which it formed a parliamentary alliance.[7]

Although the CGT was by far the largest, it was not the only trade union federation in Guinea. Its primary rival was the much smaller Confédération Française des Travailleurs Chrétiens (CFTC), which had only four member unions and was supported financially by the Catholic missions.[8] Established in France in 1919, the CFTC was conceived as a Christian alternative to the Marxist-oriented workers' struggle. After World War II, it worked closely with the Christian democratic Mouvement Républicain Populaire (MRP), a party founded by anticommunist Catholic resistance leaders who promoted settler and commercial interests and in French West Africa.[9] Even more pro-settler and anticommunist was the CGT-Force Ouvrière (CGT-FO), which split from the CGT in 1948 and was associated with the Section Française de l'Internationale Ouvrière (SFIO, the French Socialist Party). In Guinea, the CGT-FO, which recruited primarily among civil servants and office workers, was composed almost exclusively of European workers.[10] Finally, there were autonomous African unions that chose to remain independent of all French

7 Schmidt (2007), *Cold War and Decolonization*, 29–34, 46–50.

8 Kéïta (1978), *P.D.G.*, 1:257.

9 Morgenthau (1964), *Political Parties*, 44–45; Mortimer (1969), *France and the Africans*, 71; Pfeffermann (1967), 'Trade Unions and Politics', 215; Jean Suret-Canale (1977), 'Strike Movements', 53.

10 Meynaud and Bey (1967), *Trade Unionism in Africa*, 29–30, 78–79; Pfeffermann (1967), 'Trade Unions and Politics', 222; Kéïta (1978), *P.D.G.*, 1:257. The hostility between the SFIO and the PCF dated to 1920, when the SFIO's left wing seceded to form the PCF. While the communists generally disparaged the socialists as opportunists who were willing to ally with the political right, the socialists considered the communists to be dupes of Moscow and dangerous fomenters of revolution. The secessionist party initially was called the Section Française de l'Internationale Communiste. It became the PCF in October 1921. Chafer (2002),

trade union federations and political parties. The most important of these were the Fédération des Syndicats des Cheminots Africains de l'A.O.F. (FSCA), an alliance of French West African railway workers' unions, and the Syndicat du Personnel Enseignant Africain de Guinée, the Guinean African teachers' union.[11]

Emergence of the Guinean Labour Movement

The first African trade union in Guinea was the CGT-affiliated Syndicat Professionel des Agents and Sous-Agents Indigènes du Service des Transmissions de la Guinée Française. Established by postal, telegraph, and telephone (PTT) workers in March 1945, the Guinean union was part of a federation-wide body with branches across French West Africa. Led by the union's secretary-general, Sékou Touré, Guinean PTT workers joined a federation-wide strike on 20 December 1945. Like African military veterans who compared their lot to Frenchmen and demanded equal treatment for their wartime sacrifices, Guinean PTT workers campaigned under the banner 'equal pay for equal work'. While the strike lasted for only a few days in most of French West Africa, in Guinea it lasted until 4 January 1946, paralyzing government services in the major urban centers of Conakry, Kindia, Mamou, and Kankan.[12]

End of Empire, 92; Tiersky (1972), *French Communism*, 14–15; Ross (1982), *Workers and Communists*, 4.

11 ANS, 2G53/187, Guinée Française, Governor, 'Revues Trimestrielles des Événements, 3ème Trimestre 1953', 12 Sept. 1953, #862/APA; interviews with Adama Diop (first secretary-general of the Guinean FSCA), Conakry, 14 and 18 March 1991; Suret-Canale (1978), 'Railway Workers' Strike', 132–133; Cooper (1996a), *Decolonization*, 242; Cooper (1996b), 'Our Strike', 88–89; Jones (2002), *Industrial Labor*, 55.

12 AG, 2Z27, 'Syndicat Professionnel des Agents et Sous-Agents Indigènes du Service des Transmissions de la Guinée Française', Conakry, 18 March 1945; interview with Léon Maka, Conakry, 20 Feb. 1991; interviews with Joseph Montlouis (first assistant

In Guinea, as elsewhere in colonial Africa, trade unions did not focus exclusively on wages and working conditions. From the outset, they entertained political questions and became increasingly politicized with time. A central theme of the PTT workers' strike was equality between African and metropolitan workers. In addition to federation-wide demands for an established minimum wage for various categories of workers, higher and more equitable wages and benefits throughout the job hierarchy, integration of auxiliary workers into the regular civil service ranks, and general promotion of African workers, Guinean leaders included overtly political demands, including the abolition of forced labour and suppression of the *indigénat*, the harsh system of arbitrary justice applied to colonial subjects. Laws abrogating both of these systems were passed the following year.[13] The PTT workers' strike the stage for more expansive and radical trade union action in Guinea. In March 1946, Sékou Touré organised the Union des Syndicats Confédérés de Guinée, which joined together all Guinean affiliates of the CGT. In contrast to its predecessors, which tended to group workers by rank, the CGT unions united all workers of a single industry or service without regard to professional hierarchy. Focusing on common ground, rather than competing interests, CGT unions were well suited to broad based, coordinated collective action.[14]

If PTT workers were among the first to mobilize successfully, railway workers were not far behind. Like their colleagues in the postal and telecom-

---

secretary-general of the Guinean PTT workers' union), Conakry, 3 and 6 March 1991; Kéïta (1978). *P.D.G.*, 1:176–177; Cooper (1996a), *Decolonization*, 228–229.

13 Personal Archives of Joseph Montlouis: 'Revendications d'Ordre Général Accordé à l'Employé un Traitement qui lui Permettre de Vivre Décemment', n.d.; interview with Léon Maka, 20 Feb. 1991; Kéïta (1978), *P.D.G.*, 1:177–178; Cooper (1996a), *Decolonization*, 228–229. The Houphouët-Boigny Law (April 1946) ended most forms of forced labour, while the Lamine Guèye Law (May 1946) abolished the category of subject and granted citizenship to all residents of the French empire. Seizing on French claims of universalism, African workers increasingly compared their wages, benefits, and working conditions to those of their metropolitan counterparts and demanded equal pay and benefits for equal work. Cooper (1996a), *Decolonization*, 229, 286, 292.

14 Kéïta (1978), *P.D.G.*, 1:180; Suret-Canale (1971), *French Colonialism*, 388.

munications industry, African railway workers agitated for wages, benefits, and working conditions on par with those of their European counterparts. Easy communication along railway lines and at associated ports permitted these workers to organise quickly and effectively. The FSCA united all African railway workers, including engineers, office workers, mechanics, and manual labourers, grouping permanent employees and auxiliary workers in a single organisation.[15]

On 8 September 1947 the FSCA put forth a list of demands, including the establishment of a single staff system that would integrate all African and European workers into one professional hierarchy in which workers of equal rank would receive the same wages and benefits, without regard to race or national origin. The union warned that if its demands were not satisfied, a federation-wide railway workers' strike would begin at midnight on 10 October 1947.[16] The railway administration ignored the deadline, and the strike began. Three weeks later, only thirty-eight of some 17,277 French West African railway workers remained on the job.[17] From 10 October 1947 until 18 March 1948, when the strike finally

15 Interview with Adama Diop, Conakry, 14 March 1991; Adama Diop, 'Le Syndicat des Cheminots Africains de la Région Conakry-Niger Proteste contre l'Arrestation de Dianè Yayé, Touré Faciné et Mamby Diawara', Part I, *Réveil*, 15 April 1948, p. 4; Suret-Canale (1978), 'Railway Workers' Strike', 131; Cooper (1996b), 'Our Strike', 87–88.

16 ANS, 26K365, 'Motion Votée à l'Unanimité par le Comité Fédéral des Syndicats des Cheminots Africains de l'A.O.F.', Thiès, 1 Sept. 1947; 26K365, Direction de la Sûreté Générale, Dakar, 'Compte-Rendu Réunion Tenue aux Ateliers du D.N. A/S Revendications des Employés du D.N.', 11 Sept. 1947, #4066; 26K365, Inspecteur Général du Travail à Haut Commissaire, 10 Oct. 1947; 179K457, Inspection Générale du Travail de l'A.O.F., 'Différend Collectif du Travail entre la Régie des Chemins de Fer de l'A.O.F. et son Personnel Africain', 24 Jan. 1948, #16/C/IGT/AOF; interviews with Adama Diop, Conakry, 14 and 18 March 1991; Suret-Canale (1978), 'Railway Workers' Strike', 132, 136; Cooper (1996b), 'Our Strike', 82, 85–87, 89–90, 92, 115 n. 128; Cooper (1996a), *Decolonization*, 242–243; Kéïta (1978), *P.D.G.*, 1:251–252.

17 ANS, 26K365, Gendarmerie Nationale, Détachement de l'A.O.F.-Togo, Section de Conakry, Colonie de la Guinée, 'Rapport du Lieutenant Berge, Commandant la Section', Conakry, 11 Oct. 1947, #152/4; 26K379, Haut Commissaire, Dakar, à Ministre, F.O.M., Paris, 11 Oct. 1947, #701 AP; 179K457, 'Quelques Jours d'Économie

ended, economic activity in French West Africa was seriously disrupted. Perishable crops rotted; inadequate roads were clogged with trucks; import and export goods accumulated at the ports and wharves.[18] In Guinea, the work stoppage was virtually total. African workers in the shipyards, public works, and port joined railway workers in walking off the job.[19]

Colonial officials had anticipated a quick end to the strike, believing that poorly paid auxiliary workers could not have substantial resources in reserve. However, they failed to consider the importance of kin and community to daily survival. African railway workers were linked by family and neighbourhood to traders and shopkeepers in the urban areas and to agricultural producers in the interior. Women formed the crucial links. As market traders, kitchen gardeners, and rural agriculturalists, they played a critical role in sustaining the strike. Mobilizing through trade and kinship networks, market women provided food, largely grown by female farmers, to workers and their families. They raised funds for the strikers and made their own cash contributions. In the absence of male wages, women's income-generating activities grew in importance. Finally, they played a crucial role in building morale and maintaining solidarity.[20]

Guinnéene', *La Guinée Française*, 20 Nov. 1947; 179K457, Direction Fédérale de la Régie des Chemins de Fer de l'A.O.F., 'Situations des Effectifs de la Régie des Chemins de Fer au 2 Janvier 1948'; 179K457, Inspection Générale du Travail, 'Différend Collectif du Travail ...', 24 Jan. 1948; AG, 5B49, Guinée Française, Gouverneur, Conakry, à Haut Commissaire, Dakar, 'Revue des Événements du 4ème Trimestre 1947', 17 Feb. 1948, #35/APA; Suret-Canale (1978), 'Railway Workers' Strike', 129, 137, 152 n. 5 & n. 6; Cooper (1996a), *Decolonization*, 241, 243; Cooper (1996b), 'Our Strike', 81, 93.

18 ANS, 179K457, Inspecteur du Travail de la Guinée Française, Conakry, à Inspecteur Général du Travail de l'A.O.F., Dakar, 26 Nov. 1947, #578/IT.Gu (includes 'Quelques Jours d'Économie Guinéenne', *La Guinée Française*, 15 Novembre 1947); Suret-Canale (1978), 'Railway Workers' Strike', 129–131, 143, 146, 148–149.

19 ANS, 179K457, Inspecteur du Travail de la Guinée Française, Conakry, à Inspecteur Général du Travail de l'A.O.F., Dakar, 19 Nov. 1947, #34/C/IT/Gu; 26K365, Gendarmerie Nationale, 'Rapport du Lieutenant Berge ...', Conakry, 11 Oct. 1947; AG, 5B49, 'Revue des Événements du 4ème Trimestre 1947.'

20 ANS, 179K457, Inspection Générale du Travail, 'Différend Collectif du Travail ...', 24 Jan. 1948; Suret-Canale (1978), 'Railway Workers' Strike', 147–148; Cooper

The strike seriously disrupted French West African railway operations for more than five months and cost the railway administration hundreds of millions of francs.[21] The outcome was a victory for the union, if only a partial one. African workers were granted a twenty per cent increase in wages and most allowances, and the principle of the single staff system was accepted – although numerous privileges for European workers remained. While thousands of auxiliaries were integrated into the single staff system, the majority retained their auxiliary status, and thousands more lost their jobs altogether.[22] In Guinea, the inspector of labour noted that the CGT, which gave moral and material support to the railway workers, 'represents the large majority of civil servants' unions'. He warned that civil servants' future demands concerning cost of living allowances would be linked to the railway workers' success on this point.[23]

Indeed, the successful French West African railway strike stimulated an explosion in trade union membership throughout the federation. As workers challenged France to keep the promises of 'enlightened' imperialism, the CGT and other unions provided the means to mobilize. The early 1950s witnessed a proliferation of successful strikes, most of them led by the CGT. The 1950 general strike in Guinea would revolve around the minimum wage, while family allowances would be central to the general strike of 1953.[24]

(1996a), *Decolonization*, 241, 244, 247; Cooper (1996b), 'Our Strike', 82, 93–97, 103, 108.

21 ANS, 179K457, Inspection Générale du Travail, 'Différend Collectif du Travail ...', 24 Jan. 1948. For the return to work on March 19, 1948, see Suret-Canale (1978), 'Railway Workers' Strike', 129, 149; Cooper (1996b), 'Our Strike', 111; Cooper (1996a), *Decolonization*, 247.

22 ANS, 179K457, Inspection Générale du Travail, 'Différend Collectif du Travail ...', 24 Jan. 1948; interview with Adama Diop, 18 March 1991; Suret-Canale (1978), 'Railway Workers' Strike', 149–150; Cooper (1996b), 'Our Strike', 109–114; Cooper (1996a), *Decolonization*, 247.

23 ANS, 179K457, Inspecteur du Travail à Inspecteur Général du Travail, 19 Nov. 1947.

24 Cooper (1996a), *Decolonization*, 287, 303.

Despite their philosophical differences, the CGT and CFTC formed a strong alliance in 1950 and, together with the autonomous railway workers' union, mounted Guinea's June 9–10 general strike.[25] Harkening to the rhetoric of assimilation, the unions noted the disparity in African and European workers' wages and the fact that French workers received accommodations, while African workers did not. To rectify the situation, the unions demanded a minimum wage of 134 francs per day for unskilled African workers, and a 67.5 per cent across-the-board increase for all other African workers.[26] When their demands were not met, a forty-eight hour general strike ensured. The governor of Guinea described the strike as 'partial' on June 9 and 'almost total' on 10 June.[27] The inspector general of labour for French West Africa noted that, 'The totality of unskilled workers of the public and private sectors, commercial, industrial, and construction workers, workers on the ports and those in bakeries and butcher shops, as well as domestic workers, participated in this movement.' Of an estimated 6,000 to 6,500 wage-workers in Conakry, 4,500 to 5,000 (75 per cent) went out on strike. About half of these were unskilled labourers directly affected by the minimum wage. The remainder understood that a victory concerning the minimum wage, which would result in corresponding increases in other categories, was in their interest as well. The strike's outcome was a clear victory for the unions. The minimum daily wage for unskilled workers was raised, reaching 134 francs within the year. The ripple effect resulted in territory-wide increases for skilled

25 ANS, 1K44, Inspecteur Général du Travail, Dakar, 'Note Schématique Concernant la Grève des 9 et 10 Juin 1950 à Conakry', 12 June 1950, #108/C IGT/AOF.

26 ANS, 1K44, Comité Intersyndical, C.F.T.C., C.G.T., Conakry, 'Travailleurs Guinéens: L'Union dans L'Action', 31 May 1950; 1K44, C.F.T.C., C.G.T., 'Camarades Travailleurs', Conakry, 10 June 1950; 1K44, Inspecteur Général du Travail, Dakar, 'Rapport: Fixation du Salaire Minimum en Guinée et Grève des 9 et 10 Juin 1950', 19 June 1950, #113/C IGT/AOF; 1K44, Inspecteur Général du Travail, Dakar, 'Rapport: Le Salaire Minimum en Guinée et les Conditions de Résorption des Séquelles de la Grève des 9 et 10 Juin 1950', 21 Aug. 1950, #145/C IGT/AOF; Rivière (1977), *Guinea: The Mobilization of a People*, 56.

27 ANS, 1K44, Télégramme Arrivée, Haut Commissaire, Dakar. Envoyé par Gouverneur, Guinée Française, Conakry, 11 June 1950, #44.

workers in construction, industry, commerce, banking, and insurance, as well as for bakers, chauffeurs, and domestic servants.[28]

The Overseas Labour Code and the General Strike of 1953

The battle over the minimum wage was part of a larger struggle for a comprehensive overseas labour code. Hoping to contain labour unrest by establishing standards for African workers, some colonial officials pressed for an overseas labour code – similar, but not identical, to the one that regulated labour in metropolitan France. African trade unions, in contrast, demanded a labour code that recognized no distinction between African and metropolitan workers. In October 1952 some seventy French West African trade union leaders representing the CGT, CFTC, FSCA, and other autonomous unions met in Dakar to devise a strategy. A one-day general strike on November 3 signalled their determination.[29]

The federation-wide general strike of 3 November 1952, prompted by the government's failure to enact a democratic overseas labour code, was a remarkable success in most French West African territories.[30] While noting

28 ANS, 1K44, Inspecteur Général du Travail, '... Salaire Minimum ... et Grève des 9 et 10 Juin 1950', 19 June 1950; 1K44, Inspection Territoriale du Travail, 'Décision ... du 1er Juillet 1950 ...'; 1K44, Les Unions des Syndicats Confédérés C.F.T.C. et C.G.T. de Guinée, à Haut Commissaire, Dakar, 4 July 1950; 1K44, Inspection Territoriale du Travail de la Guinée Française, 'Décision de la Commission Mixte Locale portant avenant de la Convention Collective du 12 Novembre 1947 intéressant les Chauffeurs d'Automobiles de la Guinée', ca. 3 Aug. 1950; 1K44, Inspecteur Général du Travail, '... Salaire Minimum ... et ... la Grève des 9 et 10 Juin 1950', 21 Aug. 1950; Kéïta (1978). *P.D.G.*, 1:263.

29 Cooper (1996a), *Decolonization*, 286, 292, 303–304; Kéïta (1978). *P.D.G.*, 1:257, 269; Jones (2002), *Industrial Labor*, 66, 115 n. 54.

30 AG, 1F20, JS/LL, #7234, 'Nouvelles de l'Union Française', *West Africa*, 22 Nov. 1952 (retyped article); Cooper (1996a), *Decolonization*, 303–304; Cooper (1996b), 'Our Strike', 117.

massive work-stoppages in Senegal, Ivory Coast, Upper Volta, Dahomey, and French Soudan, *West Africa* magazine observed that 'the strike seems to have been the most complete in French Guinea'.[31] Military police in Guinea affirmed that Mamou had been brought to a standstill, with virtually all of the public and private sector workers adhering to the strike call.[32] In the capital, a police commandant worried, 'We witnessed in Conakry the birth of an African proletariat that will necessarily become a struggling proletariat with a class consciousness.'[33]

Pushed by the general strike, the French National Assembly adopted an overseas labour code on 22 November, which took effect in French West Africa on 24 December 1952. The code applied to all wage workers in the public and private sectors, but excluded from its provisions informal sector workers and 'customary labour', a category that included sharecroppers, labour tenants, and the unpaid family labour of peasant women, junior men, and children, as well as rural subjects working for their chiefs.[34] In Guinea, the vast majority of the population fell into the informal sector or 'customary labour' categories. Women, in particular, were generally defined outside the category of 'worker'.[35] Workers covered by the labour code – those in the relatively small capitalist economic sector – were guaranteed a number of rights. Using the metropolitan labour code as its model, the overseas code granted workers the right to one day off per week. Forty hours became the legal length of the work week in all public and private establishments. Beyond that, employers were required to pay overtime. The principle of 'equal pay for equal work' was underscored; wages were to be determined by workers' qualifications and job categories, not by race

31 AG, 1F20, JS/LL, #7235, 'Nouvelles de Union Française.'

32 AG, 1E42, Guinée Française, Gendarmerie Nationale, Commandant la Brigade de Mamou, 'Rapport sur une Grève des Employés de Divers Services à Mamou', ca. 3 Nov. 1952, #7/4.

33 Quoted in Kéïta (1978). *P.D.G.*, 1:273.

34 Cooper (1989), 'Free Labor to Family Allowances', 754–755; Cooper (1996a), *Decolonization*, 294–296, 313–314, 319; Kéïta (1978). *P.D.G.*, 1:273–274; Morgenthau (1964), *Political Parties*, 228.

35 Cooper (2003), 'Industrial Man Goes to Africa', 129.

or civil status. While civil servants had obtained equal family allowances in 1950, private sector workers were now eligible for family allowances, equal or otherwise, to be implemented by local government decree. Public and private sector workers were guaranteed paid holidays and clean, safe workplaces. Their right to organise trade unions was reaffirmed; procedures for conciliation and arbitration were spelled out, as were the circumstances for legal strikes and lock outs.[36]

The lengthy debates over the labour code had focused on a handful of key issues. One was the duration of the standard work week. In the major cities of French West Africa, the normal work week was forty-eight hours. In other parts of the federation, it was often longer. However, in metropolitan France, the work week was forty hours. Hence, the RDA, the PCF, and others argued that forty hours should be the standard overseas. They demanded strict application of the 1946 Constitution, which accorded equal rights to inhabitants of metropolitan France and the overseas territories.[37] Unsettled was the question of pay. African representatives argued that if the length of the work week were reduced, the hourly rate would have to increase accordingly or workers would lose money in the process. The implementation of the forty-hour work week, and the amount that workers would be paid for it, would be central issues in the 1953 general strike.

A second debate revolved around the issue of family allowances, one of the most contested benefits in the overseas labour code. Since 1932, metropolitan workers had received guaranteed family allowances in the form of a supplementary bonus for each child. Colonial officials argued, however, that African and European societies were totally different in nature. The practice of marrying multiple wives and the demands of the elastic African family would rapidly consume benefits intended only for monogamous nuclear families. The costs of supporting a dramatically expanded system were enormous. Yet, the receipt of family allowances

36 The second Lamine Guèye Law (1950) mandated equal benefits for all civil servants, and equal wages for all civil servants of the same grade. Cooper (1996a), *Decolonization*, 281–282, 296–297, 303; Cooper (1989), 'Free Labor to Family Allowances', 754–755; Cooper (2003), 'Industrial Man Goes to Africa', 133–134.

37 Cooper (1996a), *Decolonization*, 178, 296, 298.

was more important to African workers than any other single issue. It was significant philosophically – African and European families were of equal value, and materially – child supplements were critical to the survival of the large families of minimum wage earners.[38]

Implementation of the labour code was left to the colonial governments, which were generally ill-disposed toward equalizing African and European benefits. It was the failure to implement the labour code that set the stage for the next phase of the struggle. Throughout 1953, the federation's principal urban centres were plagued by strikes. The most intensive labour actions occurred in Guinea, where trade unions were especially strong and the RDA had consolidated its position in the urban areas, largely due to its championship of the overseas labour code. The trade union – RDA alliance has been cemented in 1952, when Sékou Touré, secretary-general of the CGT's Union des Syndicats Confédérés de Guinée, assumed the leadership of the Guinean RDA.[39]

As 1953 wore on, and the French West African administration failed to implement the labour code, preparations were made for a federation-wide general strike of unlimited duration. The strike, which began on 21 September 1953, included skilled and semi-skilled workers in the public and private sectors, represented by the CGT, CFTC, and FSCA.[40] In Guinea, the capital city was the most severely affected. On the first day of the strike, there were no African workers on construction sites or in the mines, and only a few isolated railway workers were on the job. With the exception of the banks, virtually all commercial enterprises were closed. The governor estimated that 80 per cent of Conakry's private sector was on strike.[41]

38 For an extensive discussion of the debate over family allowances, see Cooper (1996a), *Decolonization*, 281–282, 284–285, 300–305; Cooper (1989), 'Free Labor to Family Allowances', 755–756; Cooper (2003), 'Industrial Man Goes to Africa', 133–134.

39 Morgenthau (1964), *Political Parties*, 228–229; Kéïta (1978). *P.D.G.*, 1:278–281; Kéïta (1998), *Ahmed Sékou Touré*, 118.

40 Morgenthau (1964), *Political Parties*, 229; Kéïta (1978). *P.D.G.*, 1:284; Cooper (1996a), *Decolonization*, 308.

41 ANS, 17G277, Télégramme Arrivée, Haut Commissaire, Dakar. Envoyé par Gouverneur, Guinée Française, Conakry, 21 Sept. 1953, #205; 17G277, Télégramme

As in previous strikes, the trade unions actively solicited community support. African civil servants waged a three day solidarity strike on 29–31 October, and military veterans were invited to join the strikers.[42] Messages of support poured in from trade unions in neighbouring territories, the unions' federal headquarters in Dakar, and from unions affiliated with the metropolitan CGT.[43] Sékou Touré and other trade unionists spoke daily in Conakry neighbourhoods, generating crowds of several thousand people.[44] Rural women contributed rice, manioc, and other foodstuffs. Urban women sold their own jewellery, clothing, and cooking utensils, took up collections, and fed striking workers and their families without charge. At low tide, brigades of women fished for their families' meals.[45]

Arrivée, Haut Commissaire, Dakar. Envoyé par Gouverneur, Guinée Française, Conakry, 22 Sept. 1953, #207; 17G277, Télégramme Arrivée, Haut Commissaire, Dakar. Envoyé par Gouverneur, Guinée Française, Conakry, 25 Sept. 1953, #215–216.

42 ANS, 17G277, Télégramme Arrivée, Haut Commissaire, 22 Oct. 1953; 17G277, Télégramme Arrivée, Haut Commissaire, Dakar. Envoyé par Gouverneur, Guinée Française, Conakry, 24 Oct. 1953, #280–282; 17G277, Guinée Française, Services de Police, 'Renseignements Objet: La Grève à Conakry', 27 Oct. 1953, #2245/1206, C/PS.2; 17G277, Télégramme Arrivée, Haut Commissaire, 28 Oct. 1953; 17G277, Télégramme Arrivée, Haut Commissaire, Dakar. Envoyé par Gouverneur, Guinée Française, Conakry, 28 Oct. 1953, #290–291; 17G277, Télégramme Arrivée, Haut Commissaire, 29 Oct. 1953; 17G277, Télégramme Arrivée, Haut Commissaire, Dakar. Envoyé par Gouverneur, Guinée Française, Conakry, 3 Nov. 1953, #300–303.

43 ANS, 17G277, Guinée Française, Services de Police, 'Renseignements Objet: La Grève à Conakry', 26 Octobre 1953, #2224/1192, C/PS.2.

44 ANS, 2G53/189, Guinée Française, Gendarmerie Nationale, Détachement de l'A.O.F.-Togo, Compagnie de la Guinée, 'Fiche sur la Situation du Territoire de la Guinée au Cours du 4ème Trimestre 1953', Conakry, 31 Dec. 1953, #182/4; Morgenthau (1964), *Political Parties*, 229.

45 CRDA, Claude Gérard, 'Incidents en Guinée Française, 1954–1955', *Afrique Informations*, no. 34, 15 March–1 April 1955, p. 11; interviews with Tiguidanké Diakhaby, 12 Jan. 1991; Namankoumba Kouyaté, 31 Jan. 1991; Léon Maka, 20 Feb. 1991; Joseph Montlouis, 3 March 1991; Fatou Diarra, 17 March 1991; Louis Marquis Camara, 27 March 1991; Fatou Kéïta, 7 April 1991; Néné Diallo, 11 April 1991; Morgenthau (1964), *Political Parties*, 229; Kéïta (1978). *P.D.G.*, 1:290.

On 28 November, the overseas minister increased the French West African minimum hourly wage by 20 per cent. The strike was over.[46] The strike's resolution weighed heavily in the workers' favour. Their central demand had been met; the 20 per cent minimum wage increase was an unequivocal victory. Moreover, strikers were guaranteed re-employment in their previous positions.[47] However, it was not until 1956 that France implemented a regime of family allowances in French West Africa that included African workers outside the civil service.[48] Politically, the strike enhanced Guinea's standing in the West African labour scene, as Guinean leaders were credited with the hourly wage increase. The number of trade union members in Guinea skyrocketed from 4,600 at the beginning of 1953, to 20,000 in 1954, and 44,000 in 1955.[49]

Trade Unions and African Autonomy

The workers' victory did not bring an end to demands, but instead stimulated new ones. Moreover, the 1953 general strike had enhanced the alliance between the RDA and the workers' movement and reinforced the linkages

46 ANS, 17G529, Télégramme Départ, Gouverneur Général, Dakar, à Ministre, F.O.M., Paris 20 Nov. 1953, #424–426; 17G277, Télégramme Départ, Haut Commissaire, Dakar, à Ministre, France Outre-Mer, Paris, 25 Nov. 1953, #428; 2G53/189, Gendarmerie Nationale', ... Situation ... de la Guinée ... 4ème Trimestre 1953'; Cooper (1996a), *Decolonization*, pp. 309–310, 566, n. 137; Morgenthau (1964), *Political Parties*, 229; Kéïta (1978). *P.D.G.*, 1:285.

47 ANS, 17G529, Télégramme Arrivée, Gouverneur Général, Dakar. Envoyé par Gouverneur, Guinée Française, Conakry, 16 Dec. 1953, #385–387.

48 Although African civil servants had won the right to family allowances after a 1946 strike, equality within the ranks had to wait for the Lamine Guèye Law of 1950. Cooper (1996a), *Decolonization*, 281–282, 296–297, 303, 317–318, 320; Cooper (1989), 'Free Labor to Family Allowances', 754–756; Cooper (2003), 'Industrial Man Goes to Africa', 133–135; Kéïta (1978). *P.D.G.*, 1:276–277; Morgenthau (1964), *Political Parties*, 228; Rivière, *Guinea*, 56.

49 Morgenthau (1964), *Political Parties*, 229.

between metropolitan and local trade unions and local unions of diverse tendencies.[50] Fearful of the long-term political consequences, the government of Guinea launched an all-out campaign to destroy the unity of the trade union movement. In fact, the government's determination to drive a wedge between the RDA and the CGT predated the general strike. Since 1947, the French government had used the RDA's communist affiliations to justify repression, convincing some political leaders that the RDA-PCF alliance should be abandoned. On 18 October 1950 RDA parliamentarians severed all ties to the PCF and began to forge an alliance with the ruling coalition.[51] In Guinea, Sékou Touré and other RDA activists opposed this move and refused to sever ties with the PCF-linked CGT. Police spies noted that Sékou Touré was using his trade union base as a launching pad for political leadership. They also reported that African labour leaders were frustrated by the refusal of their metropolitan counterparts to give primacy to African concerns and to allow them a voice in policy-making. Aware of Sékou Touré's political ambitions, the French government was convinced that he could be persuaded to lead an African secession from the CGT.[52]

The schism was expected to occur at the French West African CGT conference in Bamako on 22–27 October 1951. Sékou Touré was expected to mount a coup, establishing an African trade union federation independent of the French communist-linked CGT. However, the rupture did not occur.[53] Sékou Touré was taken to task for his inaction, not only by the government, but by the RDA's inter-territorial president, Ivory Coast Deputy Félix Houphouët-Boigny. Many of the delegates to the

50 ANS, 17G529, Télégramme Départ, Gouverneur Général, Dakar, à Ministre, F.O.M., Paris, 25 Nov. 1953, #429–432; 17G529, Télégramme Arrivée, Gouverneur Général, 6 Dec. 1953.

51 Costigliola (1992), *France and the United States*, 66–67; Cooper (1996a), *Decolonization*, 285, 409; Mortimer (1969), *France and the Africans*, 180.

52 Cooper (1996a), *Decolonization*, 410, 414; Chafer (2002), *End of Empire*, 123.

53 ANS, 17G573, 'Partis Politiques en Guinée, 1er Semestre 1951'; 17G573, Haut Commissaire à Ministre, FOM, 28 April 1952; Cooper (1996a), *Decolonization*, 409–410.

conference were both CGT and RDA members, and most had ignored the inter-territorial RDA president's orders that they break with the CGT. Houphouët-Boigny held Sékou Touré accountable.[54] While Houphouët-Boigny subsequently forced Ivorian RDA members to choose 'unequivocally between the C.G.T. and the R.D.A.', in other territories, it was not so simple.[55] Sékou Touré continued to walk a fine line, bowing to the RDA's new collaborationist agenda in his political work, but adhering to the CGT's more militant stance in his trade union activities.[56]

This anomaly persisted for several years. However, in July 1955, under increasing pressure from both the inte-rterritorial RDA and the colonial administration, Sékou Touré publicly introduced the prospect of a new labour federation under African control.[57] In November 1955, the CGT's Senegalese-Mauritanian branch broke from the metropolitan body. In January 1956, shortly after elections that had garnered the Guinean RDA two seats in the French National Assembly, Sékou Touré joined the Senegalese-Mauritanian unions in forming the autonomous Confédération Générale des Travailleurs Africains (CGTA). Within months, Sékou Touré would become the CGTA's federal president.[58] Under Sékou Touré's leadership, the CGTA would reject the notion of class struggle in Africa, proclaiming

54 Cooper (1996a), *Decolonization*, 410.

55 AG, 1E41, Côte d'Ivoire, Services de Police, Abidjan, 'Renseignements A/S Position du R.D.A. Après le Congrès Cégétiste de Bamako', 5 Nov. 1951, #5446/757/PS/BM/C. See also Cooper (1996a), *Decolonization*, 410; Chafer (2002), *End of Empire*, 123.

56 ANS, 17G573, Police, 'Rapport Hebdomadaire, Semaine du 29 Octobre au 4 Novembre 1951.' See also 17G573, Haut Commissaire à Ministre, FOM, 28 April 1952. Cooper (1996a), *Decolonization*, 410.

57 Morgenthau (1964), *Political Parties*, 241–242, 307; Cooper (1996a), *Decolonization*, 407–408, 418–419.

58 ANS, 21G215, Union des Syndicats Sénégal-Mauritanie, Confédération Générale des Travailleurs Africains (C.G.T.A.), Kaolack, 'Appel à tous les Travailleurs Africains', 12 Nov. 1955; 21G215, Sûreté, Sénégal, 'Renseignements sur la Scission au Sein de l'Union Territoriale des Syndicats C.G.T.K. Sénégal-Mauritanie', 15 Nov. 1955, #1916 C/Su; 2G55/152, 'Rapport Politique Annuel, 1955'; 2G56/138, 'Rapport Politique Mensuel, Février 1956'; Milcent (1958), *L'A.O.F. Entre en Scène*, 133–134; Meynaud and Bey (1967), *Trade Unionism in Africa*, 58; Rivière (1977), *Guinea*, 59; Cooper (1996a), *Decolonization*, 414.

the common interests and inherent unity of all Africans – thus subordinating the workers' struggle to that of national liberation.[59]

By 1956, it was clear that Sékou Touré's nationalist ambitions had eclipsed his trade union loyalties. He broke with the CGT, but only after the RDA's electoral sweep and his own election as deputy to the French parliament. As the undisputed leader of the Guinean RDA, whose position had been consolidated by his sensational electoral victory, Sékou Touré could now abandon the CGT without jeopardizing his national stature or influence.[60] In Guinea, the CGT unions rapidly fell into line behind their erstwhile leader. When a Guinean branch of the CGTA was formed in May 1956, twenty-two of Guinea's twenty-seven CGT unions joined, and Sékou Touré was elected secretary-general.[61]

59 Pfeffermann (1967), 'Trade Unions and Politics', 221, 223; Cooper (1996a), *Decolonization*, 416–417.

60 One month after the rupture, the coordinating committee of the French West African CGT acknowledged the new reality and expelled Sékou Touré from its ranks. ANS, 2G55/152, 'Rapport Politique Annuel, 1955'; 2G56/138, Guinée Française, Gouverneur, 'Rapport Politique Mensuel, Mars 1956', 19 April 1956, #185/APA; Mortimer (1969), *France and the Africans*, 247; Meynaud and Bey (1967), *Trade Unionism in Africa*, 58–59; Kéïta (1978). *P.D.G.*, 2:119.

61 ANS, 2G56/138, 'Rapport Politique Mensuel, Mars 1956'; 17G271, Guinée Française, Services de Police, 'Renseignements A/S Réunion Intersyndicale tenue le 28 Avril 1956 au Cinema 'Rialto' à Conakry, par Touré Sékou en vue de la Constitution de la C.G.T.-A.', 29 April 1956, #781/258, C/PS; 179K432, Sékou Touré, Secrétaire Général, et Mamady Kaba, 1er Secrétaire, Union des Syndicats Confédérés de Guinée, Conakry, à Inspecteur Général du Travail, Conakry, 9 May 1956; 179K432, Abdoulaye N'Diaye, Secrétaire Général, C.G.T., Conakry, à Inspecteur Territorial du Travail, Conakry, 10 May 1956, #1/US/CGT/G; 17G271, Guinée Française, Services de Police, 'Renseignements d'Activités Nationalistes, *Objet*: AOF – 'C.G.T.A.' Activités de Sékou Touré', 11 May 1956, #65/68, ex./10; 179K432, Guinée Française, Inspecteur Territorial du Travail, Conakry, à Inspecteur Général du Travail, Dakar, 19 May 1956, #67T; 2G56/138, 'Rapport Politique Mensuel, Mai 1956'; Johnson (1970b), 'The Parti Démocratique', 347; Kéïta (1998), *Ahmed Sékou Touré*, 88–89; Cooper (1996a), *Decolonization*, 414.

Having severed their ties to the French parent body and formed an independent African federation, CGTA unions were at the forefront of the new movement.[62] African trade unions and student, youth, and political organisations, convinced that French and African interests were not synonymous, agitated for autonomy from France.[63] In July 1956, the African CFTC unions ended their association with their French parent body and reorganised themselves as the Confédération Africaine des Travailleurs Croyants (CATC). Although the new federation welcomed both Muslim and Christian members, it continued to be subsidized by the Catholic Church.[64] With the majority of Guinean unions at least nominally independent of their French progenitors, trade union leaders prepared to make further advances toward African unity. Sékou Touré urged all Guinean unions to unite under the banner of the Guinean CGTA. He then advanced the inter-territorial CGTA's proposition that all trade unions in French Africa join together in one pan-African confederation.[65] In January 1957, this plan was largely realized. At a conference in Cotonou, Dahomey, the majority of rival African trade union bodies agreed to unite in a single inter-territorial confederation under exclusively African leadership. Joining the new Union Générale des Travailleurs d'Afrique Noire (UGTAN) were the

62 ANS, 21G215, Union des Syndicats Sénégal-Mauritanie (C.G.T.A.), Appel à tous les Travailleurs Africains', 12 Nov. 1955; 21G215, Sûreté, Sénégal, '... Scission ... Syndicats C.G.T.K. Sénégal-Mauritanie', 15 Nov. 1955; 2G55/152, 'Rapport Politique Annuel, 1955'; 2G56/138, 'Rapport Politique Mensuel, Février 1956'; 179K432, Sékou Touré et Mamady Kaba à Inspecteur Général du Travail, 9 May 1956; Meynaud and Bey (1967), *Trade Unionism in Africa*, 58; Kéïta (1978). *P.D.G.*, 2:119.

63 For the trade unions' move toward autonomy, see: Morgenthau (1964), *Political Parties*, 108–109, 241–242; Cooper (1996a), *Decolonization*, 407–408; Kéïta (1978). *P.D.G.*, 2:119–121; Meynaud and Bey (1967), *Trade Unionism in Africa*, 58–59.

64 Milcent (1958), *A.O.F. Entre en Scène*, 132–133; Meynaud and Bey (1967), *Trade Unionism in Africa*, 59–60; Kéïta (1978). *P.D.G.*, 2:120–121; Rivière, *Guinea*, 54 n. 2, 59.

65 ANS, 17G271, Police, '... Réunion Intersyndicale tenue le 28 Avril 1956 ... en vue de la Constitution de la C.G.T.-A.', 29 April 1956; 179K432, Sékou Touré et Mamady Kaba à Inspecteur Général du Travail, 9 May 1956; 2G56/138, 'Rapport Politique Mensuel, Mai 1956'; Meynaud and Bey (1967), *Trade Unionism in Africa*, 58.

CGT, the CGTA, and a number of autonomous unions, including those of teachers and railway workers. Protesting UGTAN's political orientation, the CGT-FO and the CATC refused to sign on, but more than two-thirds of all French West African trade unionists were now united in a single, autonomous federation.[66]

Self-Government, Independence, and the Suppression of the Labour Movement

In 1956, France once again embarked on a program of imperial reform in order to save the empire. In June, a new legal framework (loi-cadre) authorized the French government to implement reforms leading to limited self-government in the overseas territories. African-dominated governments with increased powers over local affairs were established in 1957. In Guinea, the local government, established in May 1957 with Sékou Touré at the helm, was dominated by the RDA.[67] Critics charged that the loi-cadre system, which promoted individual territories at the expense of the French West and Equatorial African federations, undermined the potential for inter-

66 ANS, 17G586, Guinée Française, Services de Police, 'Renseignements d'Activités Communistes et Apparentés, La Réunion de Conakry', 11 Oct. 1956, #1160/Y (or 67/68 ex./9); 17G613, Guinée Française, Services de Police, Conakry, 'Renseignements A/S Retour en Guinée des Délégués à la Conférence de Cotonou', 23 Jan. 1957, #188/86, C/PS.2; Morgenthau (1964), *Political Parties*, 111–112; Milcent (1958), *A.O.F. Entre en Scène*, 135–137; Kéïta (1978). *P.D.G.*, 2:122–124; Kéïta (1998), *Ahmed Sékou Touré*, 89–90; Rivière (1977), *Guinea*, 59; Meynaud and Bey (1967), *Trade Unionism in Africa*, 59–61; Cooper (1996a), *Decolonization*, 414–415.

67 ANS, 20G136, Télégramme Départ, Afcours, à tous Gouverneurs, 4 July 1956, #80237; 20G136, Télégramme Départ, Haut Commissaire, Dakar, à tous Gouverneurs, 20 July 1956, #80266; 20G136, Gouverneur, Guinée Française, Conakry, à Haut Commissaire, Dakar, '*Objet*: Suffrage Universel dans les T.O.M.', 3 Aug. 1956, #2072, CB/SL; Morgenthau (1964), *Political Parties*, 66–70, 246; Mortimer (1969), *France and the Africans*, 258–261.

territorial action by dividing French Africa into small, economically fragile units that remained dependent on metropolitan France. At its founding congress in January 1957, UGTAN condemned loi-cadre for Balkanizing French West Africa.[68]

If loi-cadre weakened the great federations, it also undermined the African labour movement. In eight of the nine territories comprising French West Africa and Togo, former labour leaders occupied new positions as ministers of labour or the civil service. Seven of these ministers were UGTAN members. Their new responsibilities led them to cater to government rather than workers interests. Like their colonial predecessors, their goals were to reduce costs and to maintain law and order. Toward these ends, they opposed public sector wage increases and warned workers not to strike against African-led governments. Loi-cadre laid the groundwork for labour repression and the eclipse of independent worker movements by the broader nationalist agenda.[69]

In Guinea, the autonomous teachers' and railway workers' unions criticized the compromises of loi-cadre and accused the RDA-led local government of attempting to quash the independent labour movement by bringing all trade unions under RDA control.[70] At its August 1957 congress,

68 Cooper (1996a), *Decolonization*, 424–431; Morgenthau (1964), *Political Parties*, 69; Mortimer (1969), *France and the Africans*, 248, 271.

69 Cooper (1996a), *Decolonization*, 415–419.

70 ANS, 17G613, Guinée Française, Services de Police, Conakry, 'Renseignements A/S Mécontentement Regnant Chez les Évolués Guinéens, Après la Parution des Décrets d'Application de la Loi-Cadre Modifiés par le Conseil de la République', 30 April 1957, #966/393, C/PS.2; 17G622, Guinée Française, Services de Police, 'Renseignements A/S Syndicat Autonome des Cheminots Africains du C.F.C.N.', 23 July 1957, #1623/633, C/PS.2; 17G622, Guinée Française, Services de Police, 'Renseignements A/S Activité du Syndicat Autonome des Cheminots Africains', 27 July1957, #1671/651, C/PS.2; 17G622, Guinée Française, Services de Police, 'Renseignements A/S Activités du Syndicat Autonome des Cheminots Africains du Conakry-Niger, Assemblée Générale tenue le Samedi 27 Juillet 1957 à Conakry, devant le Local de ce Syndicat', 30 July 1957, #1690/658, C/PS.2; 17G622, Guinée Française, Services de Police, 'Renseignements A/S Exclusion du R.D.A. de KOUYATÉ Diéli Bakar et Répercussions en Ville', 31 July 1957, #1701/662, C/PS.2; 17G622, Guinée

the Syndicat du Personnel Enseignant Africain de Guinée adopted a motion criticizing loi-cadre. It also decried the annual transfer of its members, a technique used silence critics that had begun under the old regime, but had continued under loi-cadre. To signal their discontent, the teachers voted to strike in October 1957.[71] Koumandian Kéïta, a personal and political rival of Sékou Touré, was reelected as the union's secretary-general – a move

---

Française, Services de Police, 'Renseignements A/S 6ème Congrès des Enseignants Africains qui s'est Ouvert à Mamou, le 6 Août Dernier', 10 Aug. 1957, #1800/692, C/PS.2; 17G622, Guinée Française, Services de Police, 'Renseignements A/S Conférence Publique tenue dans la Salle du Cinéma de Mamou, par les Enseignants, le Samedi 10 Août Dernier', 16 Aug. 1957, #1837/709, C/PS.2; 17G622, Guinée Française, Services de Police, 'Renseignements A/S Conférence Publique tenue le Samedi 17 Août Dernier, par la S/Section P.D.G.-R.D.A. de Kindia', 28 Aug. 1957, #1920/734, C/PS.2; 17G622, Guinée Française, Services de Police, 'Renseignements A/S Répercussions à Mamou, de l'Article Intitulé 'Communiqué du P.D.G.' Publié dans le Dernier Numéro du Journal *La Liberté*, Organe de ce Parti', 6 Sept. 1957, #2029/773, C/PS.2; 17G622, Guinée Française, Services de Police, 'Renseignements A/S Rebondissement du Conflit des Enseignants Africains', 8 Nov. 1957, #2485/919, C/PS.2; 17G622, Guinée Française, Services de Police, 'Renseignements A/S Conflit des Enseignants Guinéens', 12 Nov. 1957, #2500/929, C/PS.2; 17G622, Guinée Française, Services de Police, 'Copie du Communiqué du Comité Directeur du P.D.G.', Conakry, 12 Nov. 1957, C/PS.2; 17G622, Guinée Française, Services de Police, 'Renseignements A/S Exclusion du P.D.G./R.D.A. de Plusieurs Dirigeants de la S/Section de Mamou', 15 Nov. 1957, #25__/941, C/PS.2; 2G57/128, Guinée Française, Police et Sûreté, 'Synthèse Mensuelle de Renseignements, Novembre 1957', Conakry, 25 Nov. 1957, #2593/C/PS.2; Personal Archives of Bocar Biro Barry, 'Travaux du Congrès de Mamou (6–10 Août 1957): Motion sur la Loi-Cadre', *L'École Guinéenne*, 1957–1958, p. 1; Johnson (1970b), 'Parti Démocratique', 347–369; Cooper (1996a), *Decolonization*, 410–412, 422–424; Chafer (2002), *End of Empire*, 203–204.

71 ANS, 17G622, Police, '... 6ème Congrès des Enseignants Africains ...', 10 Aug. 1957; 17G622, Police, '... Conférence Publique ... par les Enseignants ...', 16 Aug. 1957; 17G622, Police, '... Conférence Publique ... S/Section P.D.G.-R.D.A. de Kindia', 28 Aug. 1957; 2G57/128, Police et Sûreté, 'Synthèse Mensuelle de Renseignements, Novembre 1957', 25 Nov. 1957; Personal Archives of Bocar Biro Barry, '... Congrès de Mamou ... Motion sur la Loi-Cadre'; Johnson (1970b), 'Parti Démocratique', 358, 364; Kéïta (1978). *P.D.G.*, 2:101, 103.

that was harshly criticized by the RDA board of directors.[72] Kéïta, who was also president of the RDA's primary rival, the Bloc Africain de Guinée, was contemptuous of Sékou Touré, whom he considered an ill-educated *arriviste*.[73] Although the vast majority of Guinea's African teachers RDA members, they saw no conflict between their party membership and their loyalty to their union leader.[74] Among the transferred dissidents was Ray Autra, a founding member of the Guinean RDA and press secretary of the teachers' union. Although the teachers had struck in October 1957, they voted to strike again on November 19 to protest Autra's transfer, and

72 See 'Communiqué du P.D.G.–Le Congrès des Enseignants à Mamou Lié à la Nouvelle Situation Politique', *La Liberté*, no. 127, 27 Aug. 1957, quoted in ANS, 17G622, Police, '… Répercussions à Mamou, de l'Article Intitulé 'Communiqué du P.D.G.' …', 6 Sept. 1957; 17G622, Police, '… Conflit des Enseignants Guinéens', 12 Nov. 1957; 17G622, Police, '… Exclusion du P.D.G./R.D.A. de Plusieurs Dirigeants de … Mamou', 15 Nov. 1957; Personal Archives of Bocar Biro Barry, 'Nouveau Bureau Directeur [Syndicat du Personnel Enseignant Africain de Guinée]', *L'École Guinéenne*, no. 1 (1957–1958).

73 ANS, 2G53/187, Guinée Française, Governor, 'Revues Trimestrielles des Événements, 3ème Trimestre 1953', 12 Sept. 1953, #862/APA; 17G586, Guinée Française, Services de Police, Conakry, 'Renseignements *Objet*: Activité de l'Union du Mandé', 17 Jan. 1955, #109/46, C/PS.2; 2G55/150, Guinée Française, Gouverneur, 'Rapport Politique Mensuel, Août 1955', 28 Sept. 1955, #487/APAS/CAB; 2G57/128, Police et Sûreté, 'Synthèse Mensuelle de Renseignements, Novembre 1957', 25 Nov. 1957; 17G622, Police, '… 6ème Congrès des Enseignants Africains …', 10 Aug. 1957; 17G622, Police, '… Conférence Publique … par les Enseignants …', 16 Aug. 1957; AG, 2D297, Guinée Française, Secrétaire Général du Comité de Coordination des Syndicats de l'Enseignement Primaire Public de l'AOF, Conakry, à Gouverneur, Conakry, 11 Oct. 1954, #1/CCE; interview with Bocar Biro Barry, 21 Jan. 1991; Johnson (1970b), 'Parti Démocratique', 358, 364; Kéïta (1978). *P.D.G.*, 2:99.

74 ANS, 17G586, Guinée Française, Services de Police, Kankan, 'Renseignements A/S P.D.G. et Congrès de Dabola', 24 Sept. 1956, #1965/682, C/PS.2; 17G622, Police, '… Répercussions à Mamou, de l'Article Intitulé 'Communiqué du P.D.G.' …', 6 Sept. 1957; 17G622, Police, '… Exclusion du P.D.G./R.D.A. de Plusieurs Dirigeants de … Mamou', 15 Nov. 1957; interview with Bocar Biro Barry, 21 Jan. 1991; Johnson (1970b), 'Parti Démocratique', 358. An estimated 90 per cent of Guinea's African teachers were RDA members. ANS, 17G586, Police, Kankan, '… P.D.G. et Congrès de Dabola', 24 Sept. 1956.

again on December 9–10 if the November strike did not result in Autra's reinstallation in Conakry.[75]

As the conflict between the RDA and the teachers simmered, the Syndicat des Cheminots Africains also became embroiled. A few months previously, Diéli Bakar Kouyaté, secretary-general of the railway workers' union, had been expelled from the RDA for insubordination. In November, Kouyaté urged railway workers to demonstrate solidarity with the teachers if the latter struck to protest Ray Autra's transfer. According to the police, Kouyaté was pleased to 'lead the struggle so that trade unionism would not be dominated by the dictatorship of any political party'.[76]

Under attack by trade unionists and other dissidents, Guinea's RDA government became increasingly intolerant of criticism. Its attempt to silence its critics culminated in a crackdown on the Mamou RDA subsection, where many dissident elements had found a home.[77] In November 1957, the Mamou RDA subsection, composed primarily of teachers, was expelled for insubordination and 'Left deviationism'. To the outrage of the

75 Subsequent arbitration by UGTAN resulted in the cancellation of the strike. ANS, 17G622, Police, '… Rebondissement du Conflit des Enseignants Africains', 8 Nov. 1957; 17G622, Guinée Française, Services de Police, 'Renseignements A/S Conférence d'Information Syndicale tenue le 7 Novembre Dernier, à Mamou, Salle du Cinéma 'REX', par les Enseignants Africains de cette Ville', 12 Nov. 1957, #2503/932, C/PS.2; 17G622, Guinée Française, Services de Police, 'Copie du Communiqué du Bureau Directeur, Syndicat des Enseignants', ca. 12 Nov. 1957, C/PS.2; 17G622, Télégramme Arrivée, Haut Commissaire, Dakar. Envoyé par Gouverneur, Guinée Française, Conakry, 15 Nov. 1957, #329; 2G57/128, Police et Sûreté, 'Synthèse Mensuelle de Renseignements, Novembre 1957', 25 Nov. 1957; Kéïta (1978). *P.D.G.*, 2:101, 103; Johnson (1970b), 'Parti Démocratique', 358–360.

76 ANS, 17G622, Police, '… Exclusion du R.D.A. de KOUYATÉ Diéli Bakar …', 31 July 1957; 17G622, Guinée Française, Services de Police, 'Renseignements A/S des Répercussions Causées par la Radiation du R.D.A. du Secrétaire Général du Syndicat Autonome des Cheminots du C.F.C.N. KOUYATÉ Diéli Bakar', 5 Aug. 1957, #1746/675, C/PS.2; 17G622, Guinée Française, Services de Police, 'Renseignements A/S Réunion du Comité Directeur du Syndicat des Cheminots Africains', 14 Nov. 1957, #__531/118, C/PCF; 2G57/128, Police et Sûreté, 'Synthèse Mensuelle de Renseignements, Novembre 1957', 25 Nov. 1957.

77 Johnson (1970b), 'Parti Démocratique', 349–350.

RDA's loi-cadre government, the Mamou subsection had publicly taken up the refrain of trade unionists, accusing RDA officials of styling themselves as a new colonial bourgeoisie and condemning the compromises of self-government. Moreover, the Mamou subsection had been outspoken in its support of RDA dissident, Ray Autra.[78] Outside of Mamou, other teachers were also purged from the party. Activists in Labé were expelled for demonstrating solidarity with the Mamou dissidents, while other perceived enemies were arbitrarily transferred.[79] Simultaneous with the internal crackdown, the Guinean RDA embraced some of its critics' positions. During the third party congress, held in January 1958, RDA leaders decried the limits of loi-cadre and demanded complete internal autonomy.[80] They also took steps to bring dissidents back into line. In the future, all Guinean trade unions would join the Union des Syndicats des Travailleurs de Guinée, the local UGTAN branch. The UGTAN branch, in turn, would become a specialized organ of the Guinean RDA. Through

78 ANS, 17G622, Police, '... Exclusion du P.D.G./R.D.A. de Plusieurs Dirigeants de ... Mamou', 15 Nov. 1957; 17G622, Guinée Française, Services de Police, 'Renseignements A/S Conférence Publique tenue à Mamou, le 14 Novembre 1957, par l'Ex-Sous-Section du P.D.G./R.D.A.', 19 Nov. 1957, #2565/954, C/PS.2; 2G57/128, Police et Sûreté, 'Synthèse Mensuelle de Renseignements, Novembre 1957', 25 Nov. 1957; 17G622, Guinée Française, Services de Police, 'Renseignements A/S Activité de l'Ex-S/Section R.D.A. de Mamou', 20 Dec. 1957, #2798/1018, C/PS; interview with Mamdou Bela Doumbouya, 26 Jan.1991; interview with Kadiatou Meunier, 5 March 1991; interview with Fanta Diarra and Ibrahima Fofana, 24 May 1991; Johnson (1970b), 'Parti Démocratique', 347–348, 352, 354–355, 358, 362, 365.

79 ANS, 17G622, Police, '... Rebondissement du Conflit des Enseignants Africains', 8 Nov. 1957; 17G622, Police, '... Conflit des Enseignants Guinéens', 12 Nov. 1957; 17G622, Police, '... Conférence d'Information Syndicale ... Mamou ... par les Enseignants Africains ...', 12 Nov. 1957; 17G622, Police, '... Communiqué du Comité Directeur du P.D.G.', Conakry, 12 Nov. 1957; 17G622, Police, '... Exclusion du P.D.G./R.D.A. de Plusieurs Dirigeants de ... Mamou', 15 Nov. 1957; 2G57/128, Police et Sûreté, 'Synthèse Mensuelle de Renseignements, Novembre 1957', 25 Nov. 1957; 17G622, Police, '... Activité de l'Ex-S/Section R.D.A. de Mamou', 20 Dec. 1957; Johnson (1970b), 'Parti Démocratique', 358–360, 362, 365.

80 Kéïta (1978). *P.D.G.*, 2:108–110, 131; Morgenthau (1964), *Political Parties*, 248.

this manoeuvre, the labour movement would officially be subordinated to the political party.[81]

UGTAN's subordination of class struggle to national liberation highlighted the division between trade union leaders, who had been integrated into the loi-cadre governments, and rank-and-file members, who had not. Since 1946, African trade unions had wielded the language of French universalism to win ever greater parity with metropolitan workers. As UGTAN leaders became ministers in the loi-cadre governments responsible for paying African civil servants and other public sector workers, many did an about face on the parity issue. They claimed that the new African-led governments could not afford the high wage and benefit packages the unions had previously negotiated. Workers were castigated for using French workers as the standard for own wage and benefit demands. They were admonished to compare their lot with that of their own countrymen and to cease their demands for even greater privilege. Sékou Touré and his labour minister cautioned Guinean workers that while striking against colonial employers was both justified and necessary, striking against an African government undermined African unity and would not be permitted.[82]

As the RDA struggled to assert its predominance over labour in Guinea, a political crisis was brewing in France. The critical situation in Algeria and a narrowly-averted coup d'état in France brought Charles de Gaulle back to power. Upon assuming office in June 1958, he ordered an overhaul of the constitution that he hoped would bind French territories to the Republic, even as they agitated for greater autonomy. The document he proposed would seal the fate of overseas territories as perpetual minors in the French empire, henceforth dubbed the French Community. Africans would no longer be represented in the French National Assembly. The federations of French West and French Equatorial Africa would be dissolved, and with them, the Grand Councils that had brought Africans together from all the territories. The constitution would be voted up or down in a

81 Rivière (1977), *Guinea*, 60; Kéïta (1998), *Ahmed Sékou Touré*, 92.

82 Pfeffermann (1967), 'Trade Unions and Politics', 227–229; Cooper (1996a), *Decolonization*, 416–424; Morgenthau (1964), *Political Parties*, 67.

popular referendum on 28 September 1958. Rejection of the constitution would result in immediate independence.[83] French West African political and trade union leaders met in Dakar on 27 August to discuss the proposed constitution. UGTAN's board of directors pronounced itself in favour of a 'no' vote. Its position was ratified by a cadre conference on September 11.[84] Three days later, Guinea's local government also declared itself in favour of the 'no'. On 28 September, Guinean voters overwhelmingly rejected the constitution and opted for immediate independence.[85]

The Guinean government's relations with the trade union movement deteriorated rapidly after independence. In November 1961, the teachers' union, led by Sékou Touré's long time nemesis, Koumandian Kéïta, demanded more pay to compensate for dramatically increased student enrolments after independence. The union also had a political agenda. Angered by the perks granted to politicians based on position rather than merit, teachers decried the bourgeois turn taken by the post independence government and used their trade union to promote the Parti Africain de l'Indépendance, a small Marxist party founded in 1957 by French West African university graduates. Accused of fomenting a leftist plot to overthrow government, Koumandian Kéïta and Ray Autra were each sentenced to ten years' imprisonment, while Djibril Tamsil Niane, Ibrahima Bah, and Ibrahima Seck were given five year prison terms. Demonstrations in

83 Morgenthau (1964), *Political Parties*, 71–72, 75, 77, 113–114, 311; Mortimer (1969), *France and the Africans*, 238–239, 307–312; Kéïta (1978). *P.D.G.*, 2:132–133.

84 CAOM, Carton 2181, dos. 6, Gouverneur à Haut Commissaire, 27 Aug. 1958, #1960/CAB; Carton 2181, dos. 6, 'S.T. Presse Communiqué', *Agence France-Press*, Conakry, 29 Aug. 1958; Chaffard (1967), *Les Carnets Secrets*, 2: 202; Mortimer (1969), *France and the Africans*, 295, 318, 320–321; Morgenthau (1964), *Political Parties*, 253.

85 CAOM, Carton 2181, dos. 6, Gouverneur, Guinée Française, Conakry, à Ministre, FOM, Paris, 'Discours Prononcé par le Président Sékou Touré, le 14 Septembre 1958', 15 Sept. 1958, #0191/CAB; Carton 2181, dos. 6, 'Motion du Parti Démocratique de la Guinée en date du 14 Septembre 1958', 15 Sept. 1958, #0191/CAB. See also 'Unanimement le 28 Septembre la Guinée Votera Non', *La Liberté*, 23 Sept. 1958, pp. 1–2; 'La Résolution', *La Liberté*, 23 Sept. 1958, p. 2; 'Les Résultats du Scrutin', *La Liberté*, 4 Oct. 1958, p. 5; Kéïta (1978). *P.D.G.*, 2:147–148; Morgenthau (1964), *Political Parties*, 219, 399.

support of the teachers were brutally crushed. Schools were closed and students were dispersed to their homes across the country.[86]

Conclusion

The postwar period in Guinea was one of tremendous political and labour ferment. Workers' demands were explicitly linked to the role Africans had played during the war and to the wartime promises of reformed imperialism. Their demands for equal pay and benefits bore a striking resemblance to those of military veterans, who rallied under the banner, 'Equal sacrifices = equal rights'. Skilfully employing the French language of assimilation, as well as forceful strike action, African workers obtained many of the benefits previously reserved for their metropolitan counterparts. CGT unions, linked both to their French parent body and the PCF, were at the forefront of the Guinean labour movement. The MRP-linked CFTC unions played a lesser but important role, while autonomous unions independent of French trade union and political bodies were also significant actors. In the mid-1950s, influenced by the broader political movement for African unity and autonomy, most Guinean unions severed their ties to French organisations and established autonomous federations under exclusively African leadership.

Simultaneous with the emergence of organised labour, political parties began to agitate for a greater role in African governance. In Guinea, the RDA used the labour movement, with its broad ethnic and class alliance, as a launching pad for its political program. While supportive of protests

86 Morgenthau (1964), *Political Parties*, 154–155, 160; Mortimer (1969), *France and the Africans*, 287–290; Rivière (1977), *Guinea*, 126–128; B. Ameillon (1964), *La Guinée: Bilan d'une Indépendance*, 179–181; Johnson (1970a), 'Sekou Touré and the Guinean Revolution', 357–358; Straker (2009), *Youth, Nationalism, and the Guinean Revolution*, 48–55, 63.

against the colonial government, RDA leaders altered their stance after the establishment of an African-led government in May 1957. Although their powers were circumscribed, African leaders were now in charge of local affairs. Increasingly intolerant of dissent, they felt threatened by labour's persistent demands. Within the party, trade unionists were sanctioned for disobedience and obstructionism. The interests of labour, long the mainstay of the RDA program, were now subordinated to those of the wider nationalist movement. Although the Guinean labour movement led the campaign for complete independence in 1958, the particular interests of workers were cast aside in the process, and the anti-labour actions of the loi-cadre government foreshadowed further repression to come.

References

Ameillon, B. (1964) *La Guinée: Bilan d'une Indépendance*, Cahiers Libres, nos. 58–59, Paris: François Maspero.

Chafer, T. (2002) *The End of Empire in French West Africa: France's Successful Decolonization?*, New York: Berg.

Chaffard, G. (1967) *Les Carnets Secrets de la Décolonisation*, Paris: Calmann-Lévy.

Cooper, F. (1989) 'From Free Labor to Family Allowances: Labor and African Society in Colonial Discourse', *American Ethnologist* 16(4).

Cooper, F. (1996a) *Decolonization and African Society: The Labor Question in French and British Africa*, New York: Cambridge University Press.

Cooper, F. (1996b) '"Our Strike": Equality, Anti-colonial Politics and the 1947–48 Railway Strike in French West Africa', *Journal of African History* 37(1).

Cooper, F. (2003) 'Industrial Man Goes to Africa', in L.A. Lindsay and S.F. Miescher (eds), *Men and Masculinities in Modern Africa*, Portsmouth, NH: Heinemann.

Costigliola, F. (1992) *France and the United States: The Cold Alliance since World War II*, New York: Twayne.

Echenberg, M. (1991) *Colonial Conscripts: The Tirailleurs Sénégalais in French West Africa, 1857–1960*, Portsmouth, N.H.: Heinemann.

Johnson, R.W. (1970a) 'Sekou Touré and the Guinean Revolution', *African Affairs*, 69(277).

Johnson, R.W. (1970b) 'The Parti Démocratique de Guinée and the Mamou "Deviation"', in C. Allen and R.W. Johnson (eds), *African Perspectives: Papers in the History, Politics and Economics of Africa Presented to Thomas Hodgkin*, Cambridge: Cambridge University Press.

Jones, J.A. (2002) *Industrial Labor in the Colonial World: Workers of the Chemin de Fer Dakar-Niger, 1881–1963*, Portsmouth, NH: Heinemann.

Kéïta, S.K. (1978) *Le P.D.G.: Artisan de l'Indépendance Nationale en Guinée (1947–1958)*, Conakry: I.N.R.D.G., Bibliothèque Nationale.

Kéïta, S.K. (1998) *Ahmed Sékou Touré: L'Homme et son Combat Anti-Colonial (1922–1958)*, Conakry: Éditions S.K.K..

Meynaud, J. and Bey, A.S. (1967) *Trade Unionism in Africa: A Study of its Growth and Orientation*, trans. Angela Brench, London: Methuen.

Milcent, E. (1958) *L'A.O.F. Entre en Scène*, Paris: Bibliothèque de l'Homme d'Action.

Morgenthau, R.S. (1964) *Political Parties in French-Speaking West Africa*, Oxford: Clarendon Press.

Mortimer, E. (1969) *France and the Africans, 1944–1960: A Political History*, New York: Walker.

Pfeffermann, G. (1967) 'Trade Unions and Politics in French West Africa during the Fourth Republic', *African Affairs* 66(264).

Rivière, C. (1977) *Guinea: The Mobilization of a People*, trans. V. Thompson and R. Adloff, Ithaca: Cornell University Press.

Ross, G. (1982) *Workers and Communists in France: From Popular Front to Eurocommunism*, Berkeley: University of California Press.

Schmidt, E. (2005) *Mobilizing the Masses: Gender, Ethnicity, and Class in the Nationalist Movement in Guinea, 1939–1958*, Portsmouth, N.H.: Heinemann.

Schmidt, E. (2007) *Cold War and Decolonization in Guinea, 1946–1958*, Athens: Ohio University Press.

Straker, J. (2009) *Youth, Nationalism, and the Guinean Revolution*, Bloomington: Indiana University Press.

Suret-Canale, J. (1971) *French Colonialism in Tropical Africa: 1900–1945*, trans. Till Gottheiner, New York: Pica Press.

Suret-Canale, J. (1977), 'Strike Movements as Part of the Anti-colonial Struggle in French West Africa', *Tarikh* 5(3).

Suret-Canale, J. (1978) 'The French West African Railway Workers' Strike, 1947–1948', in P. Gutkind et al (eds), *African Labor History*, Beverly Hills: Sage.

Tiersky, R. (1972) *French Communism, 1920–1972*, New York: Columbia University Press.

DAVID PERFECT

Trade Unions in The Gambia, 1929–2010

This chapter charts the history of the Gambian labour movement since the foundation in 1929 of the country's first trade union, the Bathurst Trade Union (BTU). It argues that although Gambian unions have on occasion played a critical role in their country's history and have produced two major leaders in E.F. Small and M.E. Jallow, more frequently they have been weak and ineffective.[1]

Background Context

Prior to 1960 the focus of Gambian politics was the Legislative Council.[2] Established in 1843, its unofficial (and official) members were appointed, rather than being directly elected, until 1947. In 1960, it was replaced by a unicameral House of Representatives with 34 members, 19 of whom were elected directly by universal suffrage. The first election to the new body was narrowly won by the People's Progressive Party (PPP) led by D.K. (later

1 There has been no full-length published study of the Gambian trade union movement to date. The main sources remain Hughes and Perfect (1989), 'Trade Unionism' and Perfect (1987), 'Organised Labour'. Since then, new information has become available on the colonial and post-independence periods, including records at the National Archives, Kew, London, in the Colonial Office (CO) and Ministry of Labour (LAB) series, and at the Trades Union Congress archive, Modern Record Centre, University of Warwick (MSS 292/966 series).

2 Hughes and Perfect (2006), *Political History*, provide the fullest analysis of Gambian political history.

Sir Dawda) Jawara, which achieved an overall majority for the first time in 1962. Thereafter, the PPP won six successive general elections between 1966 and 1992. The Gambia became a republic in 1970, following a national referendum, with Jawara automatically becoming President. Direct presidential elections were first contested alongside the parliamentary elections in 1982, with Jawara easily winning the three held up to 1992.

In July 1994, the Jawara government was overthrown in a military coup led by Yahya Jammeh. The House of Representatives was abolished and political activities banned. Civilian rule was restored in 1996 under a new constitution, which included the establishment of a National Assembly. Jammeh won the first presidential election in 1996 (and subsequent elections in 2001 and 2006), while his party, the Alliance for Patriotic Reorientation and Construction (APRC), comfortably won the Assembly elections of 1997, 2002 and 2007, winning 42 out of 48 seats in 2007. Jammeh is expected to win the next presidential election that is due to take place in September 2011.

Even in the 2000s, The Gambia remains a predominantly agricultural country. In 2003, 51 per cent of the employed population worked in agriculture, animals or fisheries; 15 per cent in trade; 12 per cent in community and social services; and only 5 per cent in manufacturing.[3] Before World War II, very few Gambians were in paid employment and almost all of these worked in the capital, Bathurst (renamed Banjul in 1973); even during the 'trade season', when the groundnut crop was loaded onto ocean-going vessels, probably no more than 3,000 manual workers were employed in total. Wage employment increased only marginally after the war; even in the mid 1950s, less than 5,000 manual workers were employed in Bathurst. Between 1959 and 1961, employment increased sharply, with over 11,000 manual workers employed in the latter year, but then declined, with employment levels not exceeding this figure again until 1973. Overall employment increased steadily in the 1970s and by 1983, more than 30,000 men and women were in paid employment, with three out of four being employed in the public sector. But public sector employment fell sharply

3 Heintz et al (2008), *Development Strategy*, 52 (Table A8).

in the mid 1980s and may not have returned to the old levels since then; thus in June 2007, there were only 13,599 civil servants in post with the civil service.[4]

The Mandinka have always been the largest ethnic group nationally, while the Wolof remained the largest group in the capital in 2003 and most prominent trade union leaders have either been Mandinka or Wolof. The small Aku community, consisting of the descendants of Liberated Africans, also provided a number of trade union leaders in the colonial period.[5]

Trade Unions under Colonial Rule

Labour organisation and action before 1929

The origins of Gambia trade unions lie in the societies (associations) formed by craft workers in Bathurst in the nineteenth and early twentieth centuries, their main purpose being to meet the burial expenses of their members. Many such societies catered for specific ethnic groups or for a variety of social activities, but some covered specific trades. A 'Shipwrights' Society', covering masons and carpenters as well as shipwrights (and both Christians and Muslims), was established around 1850 and may have organised the first recorded strike in Bathurst in 1856. This was probably an attempt to secure the abolition of the 'truck' system by which merchants paid their employees partly in goods that they valued well above the normal retail price in Bathurst. After 1865, societies were required to register under the Friendly Societies Ordinance and a magistrate could regularly investigate

4 See Hughes and Perfect (1989), 'Trade Unionism', 549–550; Heintz et al (2008), *Development Strategy*, 33.

5 See Hughes and Perfect (2008), *Historical Dictionary*, 3, 140–141, 243, 261.

their subscription books. Strikes were not outlawed, but they remained a rarity, the only other known strike before the 1920s occurring in 1882.[6]

Between 1914 and 1920, the cost of living in Bathurst doubled as imports were restricted during World War I.[7] At a time of labour shortages, this led to strikes by sailors in September 1920 and by artisans employed in the Public Works Department (PWD) or by commercial firms in March and April 1921. Both were resolved in the strikers' favour after government intervention; in April 1921, Governor C.H. Armitage drew up a scale of wages for skilled workers, which resulted in a one shilling (5p) increase in the daily rates of pay of carpenters, shipwrights, masons and headmen. This scale was accepted by the firms and by a 'Deputation of Workmen, representing the Labour (Government and Mercantile) of the Colony', which consisted of the leaders of the Carpenters' and Shipwrights' Society (CSS). A new organisation, the CSS is likely to have combined the Mohammedan Carpenters' Society (which had been registered in 1890) and the Gambia Shipwrights' Society (registered in 1903) and possibly other societies of carpenters. It was probably led by a carpenter, Biram (Ibrahim) Jobe.[8]

Establishment of the Bathurst Trade Union and the 1929 strike

In May 1929, the CSS was revived to resist wholesale pay cuts carried out by private sector employers. Meeting as the Chamber of Commerce, the employers had resolved on 25 April 1929, in response to a poor trade season, to cut the wages of the artisans and sailors they employed by approximately 20 per cent from 1 June. The CSS leaders, who were poorly educated Muslim

6 See Hughes and Perfect (2006), *Political History*, 61–65; Grey-Johnson (2002), *Small*, 41. The truck system was eventually abolished in 1858.

7 See Hughes and Perfect (2006), *Political History*, 36.

8 Perfect (1987), 'Organised Labour', 28–32. Jobe was described by Small as 'the pioneer of the whole [trade union] movement' in 1941, so probably headed the CSS in 1921; see Perfect (1987), 'Organised Labour', 45 (note 26).

Wolof artisans lacking literacy in English, now sought the assistance of the educated Aku Christian, E.F. Small, to negotiate on their behalf.[9]

The illegitimate son of an Aku tailor, Edward Francis Small had initially trained to become a Wesleyan Methodist minister, but had been dismissed for insubordination by the Methodist Church in 1918. Radicalised by his treatment, he had become politically active and in 1920 had set up the Gambia Section (branch) of an inter-territorial organisation, the National Congress of British West Africa (NCBWA). Leaving Bathurst in 1933, he moved first to Senegal and then to London, during which time he established a newspaper, *The Gambia Outlook and Senegambian Reporter*. Returning to Bathurst in 1927, he re-launched his newspaper, but unable to revive the moribund Gambia Section of the NCBWA, sought to establish a new political base through organising urban workers (and farmers).[10] Thus in May 1929, Small converted the CSS into the Bathurst Trade Union (BTU), with the CSS as the union's first 'trade branch'. Small became its Chairman, with other executive posts being filled by prominent Wolof artisans (or retired artisans), such as the carpenters, Biram Jobe, Bai Ceesay and Marie Kebbeh, and the shipwrights, Momadu Jahumpa and Joseph Lemu N'Jie. Over the next few months, the BTU gradually took shape. It formally adopted a constitution, which had been supplied by the Labour Research Department (LRD), a London organisation linked with the British Labour Party; appointed an educated Wolof, Thomas Collingwood Fye, as its General Secretary; and gradually incorporated new groups of workers, including masons, drivers, fitters, painters, blacksmiths and sailors. No attempt, however, was made to recruit unskilled labourers or salaried civil servants.[11]

9 Perfect (1987), 'Organised Labour', 31–33.

10 On Small's political career in the 1920s, see Hughes and Perfect (2006), *Political History*, 85–96. According to Grey-Johnson (2002), *Small*, 44–45, an unsuccessful attempt had been made in 1928 to form a union.

11 All the BTU leaders were Muslims, except Small and N'Jie (who was a Roman Catholic); Jahumpa and Kebbeh in fact headed two of the three main Muslim societies in Bathurst. See Perfect (1987), 'Organised Labour', 29, 37–42, 53. Jahumpa is profiled in Hughes and Perfect (2008), *Historical Dictionary*, 102–103.

1929 general strike

Fye outlined the union's wage demands on 8 October and warned that if these were not met, then notices of withdrawal of labour would be issued a week later. But far from entering negotiations, two of the commercial employers, Palmine Ltd and the United Africa Company issued lock-out notices to all their employees. Moreover, Palmine's Danish manager, George Christensen, specifically warned his employees to resign from the union or face dismissal. Consequently, on 26 October, Fye informed the Chamber of Commerce that henceforth union members would be forbidden to work for less than the rates outlined on 8 October or to work under non-union foremen. He also warned the Colonial Secretary that from 30 October, union member would be forbidden to accept 'piecework contracts' in the PWD.

The 1929 strike continued for three weeks amongst private sector workers, although for only a week in the PWD. Gradually the union gained the upper hand. The employers withdrew the April wage cuts on 29 October; belatedly recognised the union on 7 November; and, finally, after feelings had been inflamed by a police bayonet charge against a group of unarmed strikers on 14 November, conceded substantial wage increases for all categories of skilled craft workers at a 'Round Table Conference' of employers and union leaders held on 15–16 November.[12]

The strike was thus one of the most successful in colonial Africa before World War II and many skilled and semi-skilled workers joined the BTU during, or immediately after, it. Small later claimed that union membership doubled to 1,000 between the strike and April 1930; if true, this meant that most of Bathurst's skilled and semi-skilled employees were now unionised.[13] Unusually, the strike also received considerable international attention. This was due to the LRD coordinating a highly effective campaign in England on the union's behalf, involving left-wing Labour MPs asking questions in

12 The fullest account of the strike is in Perfect (1987), 'Organised Labour', 50–63.

13 A total of 1,100 artisans (and 1,300) unskilled workers were recorded in Bathurst in the April 1931 Census. See Perfect (1987), 'Organised Labour', 7, 62.

the House of Commons to embarrass the Ramsay MacDonald government and a number of district trade and local councils writing protest letters attacking Palmine Ltd for its anti-union stance. The union also received strong support from the British Section of the League Against Imperialism through its Secretary, Reginald Bridgeman, but the British Trades Union Congress (TUC) refused to intervene or offer any support.[14]

Decline of the BTU, 1931–35

The 1929 strike settlement was a significant achievement for the BTU, but this success was never to be repeated. The union's rapid decline in the early 1930s stemmed initially from internal factional conflict, first between Small and the General Secretary, T.C. Fye, and then between Small and some members of the union's Executive led by the shipwright, J.L. N'Jie, and two carpenters, John L. Owens and Marie Kebbeh. Each side accused the other of misappropriating funds, while some Wolof artisans, including N'Jie, Owens and Kebbeh, resented the control exerted by Small (and other Aku), although other Wolof, including Jobe and Jahumpa, remained loyal to him. In addition, Small was also absent from Bathurst (mainly in Europe) for long periods in 1930 and 1931, which weakened his grip over the union.[15]

During 1932 and 1933, the breach widened as Small's political opponents became involved in the dispute. By the summer of 1932, Bathurst was divided into two political camps. A conservative faction headed by Sir Samuel Forster, the leading African member of the Legislative Council, had formed the Gambia Representative Committee (GRC), while a more radical group, the Rate Payers' Association, was led by Small. Sensing an opportunity to destroy Small's base in the labour movement, the GRC

14 Perfect (1987), 'Organised Labour', 55; Hughes and Perfect (2006), *Political History*, 97–98.

15 Perfect (1987), 'Organised Labour', 79–82; Hughes and Perfect (2006), *Political History*, 98–99. Small was in Europe primarily to develop a co-operative marketing scheme for groundnut farmers.

encouraged the N'Jie faction in March 1933 to register itself as the BTU under the Trade Union Ordinance, which had been passed by the Legislative Council in December 1932. The legislation, introduced as a response to the famous Passfield Memorandum of September 1930, made the registration of trade unions compulsory and prevented any two unions from operating under the same name. Thus the BTU became the first legally registered union in colonial Africa and meant that Small and his supporters could no longer operate legally without changing the name of their union. Small reacted furiously, complaining to the TUC about 'a dozen scabs [who] have conspired to deprive us of our proper title and rights we have acquired'; he argued, with some justification, that one outcome was that wages were falling as employers no longer felt bound by the November 1929 agreement. But neither the TUC nor the Secretary of State for the Colonies, Sir Philip Cunliffe-Lister, would intervene on Small's behalf and the LRD was in no position to help.[16]

E.F. Small and the Gambia Labour Union: 1935–58

After two years of trying without success to regain control of the BTU, Small finally cut his losses and established a rival trade union, the Gambia Labour Union (GLU) that was officially registered in May 1935. He became Chairman of the new body, a position he held until his death in 1958, while other GLU officials were Aku Christians and loyal Wolof Muslims, such as Jahumpa, Jobe and Ceesay. Like the BTU, the GLU catered primarily for artisans and did not seek to represent unskilled labourers. Initially it had few members with a stated income from dues in 1935 of only £9 (although this was £4 more than the BTU's income). Nor did the GLU make much progress in the next decade; its income from membership dues probably never exceeded £20 per annum between 1936 and 1945. The BTU was no stronger and, not surprisingly, government officials, external commentators

16 Hughes and Perfect (2006), *Political History*, 96–103; Perfect (1987), 'Organised Labour', 82–87. See also MSS 292/966/1, Small to TUC, 22 April 1933.

and even Small himself commented on the weakness of the trade union movement in this period.[17]

In 1944, the British TUC announced its intention of organising an inaugural World Trade Union Conference in London. At a meeting in Bathurst in April 1944, Small was selected as the Gambian representative, with Ibrahima M. Garba-Jahumpa, a young Wolof Muslim who had been General Secretary of the GLU since 1942, chosen to accompany him. But soon after the conference, which eventually took place in February 1945, the two men quarrelled bitterly. The root cause of the dispute was that the politically ambitious Garba-Jahumpa was determined to make his mark in both politics (including the wider Pan-African movement) and trade unionism, and he was frustrated by Small's reluctance to give him free rein. By October, the breach between the two men was irreconcilable, with Small complaining to the TUC about Garba-Jahumpa and other 'pro-fascist elements who are out to break our Trade Union Movement'. Eventually, in January 1947, with the apparent assistance of the European Labour Officer, David Barrett, Garba-Jahumpa established a rival trade union to the GLU, the Gambia Amalgamated Trade Union (GATU). Most trade unionists appeared to have joined the GATU, as the GLU's membership shrank.[18]

Both Small and Garba-Jahumpa contested the first direct election to the Legislative Council in November 1947 for the single seat available. While Small described himself as a journalist, rather than as a trade unionist, in his nomination papers, Garba-Jahumpa did stand as a union leader. The latter clearly hoped that sufficient GATU members would vote for

17 Perfect (1987), 'Organised Labour', 88–95. Table 4.4 (p. 93), gives information on the GLU's income from membership dues between 1935 and 1945 (data are missing for 1938 and 1942); this ranged from £4 in 1941 to £17 in 1940. The BTU's income ranged from £0 in 1936 to £15 in 1944.

18 See Perfect (1987), 'Organised Labour', 95–113; Hughes and Perfect (2006), *Political History*, 110–114. See also MSS 292/966/3, Small to Kemmis, 20 October 1945, 5 April 1947. In the second letter, Small complained about Barrett's 'undue interference'. Barrett claimed in 1947 that the GATU possessed between 250 and 1,000 members and the GLU less than 50.

him to ensure his victory, but he finished a well-beaten third behind Small and Sheikh Omar Fye, a former member of the council.[19] In July 1948, Garba-Jahumpa dissolved the GATU and ceased to be active in labour affairs. Former GATU members rejoined the GLU, which now enjoyed something of a revival, with income from subscriptions reaching £125 in 1949, the highest total since 1929–30, and the union claiming 420 paid up members in 1950. But after 1950, union income declined as the organisation lapsed into inactivity, with its income largely being spent on sending delegates to international conferences, the GLU having affiliated to the International Confederation of Free Trade Unions (ICFTU) on its foundation in 1949. By the time of Small's death in January 1958, the GLU, like the BTU, was virtually moribund. It would soon be superseded by a new union, the Gambia Workers' Union (GWU).[20]

The establishment of the Gambia Workers' Union, 1956–60

The GWU was founded in December 1956 as a general workers' union by Momodou E. Jallow, who became its General Secretary and was to remain the key figure in the Gambian labour movement for the next three decades. A Fula originally from Georgetown in the Protectorate, who had been educated in Bathurst, Jallow had won a scholarship in 1954 to attend the Co-operative College in Ibadan, Nigeria. On returning to Bathurst, he had been employed as a Co-operative Inspector, but in August 1955, he was convicted of stealing £30 from a co-operative society and dismissed. He then established the Gambia Construction Employees' Society, which he subsequently converted into the GWU.

19 On the 1947 election and the role of organised labour in it, see Hughes and Perfect (2006), *Political History*, 113–116; Perfect (1987), 'Organised Labour', 113–115.

20 See Perfect (1987), 'Organised Labour', 116–122. Allen (1970), 'Trade Unionism', 409 (note 3), calculated that the GLU spent no less than £550 on affiliation fees, conference expenses and allied items between 1951 and 1955 – or some £24 more than its total income. The BTU was deregistered in 1960, while the GLU's income did not exceed £20 between 1955 and 1959.

During 1957, the new union organised several strikes, with some success, but progress was not sustained. However, in November 1958, Jallow (together with A.W. Loum, the GLU's Deputy Secretary) secured a place on a four-month course on trade unionism at the ICFTU's Kampala Labour College. Before returning to Bathurst in March 1959, the two men visited Ghana and Guinea (both of which were now independent of colonial rule), where they obtained substantial funding. They also took the crucial decision to concentrate thereafter on recruiting unskilled labourers then being employed in increasing numbers in the Bathurst area rather than artisans like earlier unions. They also briefly established a new union, the Industrial and Commercial Workers' Union, but quickly reverted to the GWU name. At the end of May 1959, the ICFTU managed to persuade the GWU and GLU to affiliate, but the merger was short-lived and collapsed in July 1959 with both sides complaining bitterly about its failure.[21]

1960 general strike

Following the merger's collapse, the GWU sought to build its membership through supporting industrial action by unskilled labourers against low pay. This period of industrial unrest, the most significant since 1929, culminated on 2 February 1960 with a one day general strike in Bathurst, which received significant backing from both unionised and non-unionised daily paid workers. Caught off guard by the first major strike for 30 years and anxious to avoid trouble in the run up to the first national election to the House of Representatives in May, the government agreed to make substantial concessions. The Panda-Lewis Commission was appointed to make recommendations about wage rates and its suggestion of a 25 per cent increase in the legal minimum wage was accepted by the government; the

21 On the early years of the GWU, see Perfect (1987), 'Organised Labour', 129–135. MSS 292/966/3 also contains extensive information on the dispute between the GLU and GWU. Jallow is profiled in Hughes and Perfect (2008), *Historical Dictionary*, 104–105.

Commission also established four Joint Industrial Councils (JICs) as the formal method for negotiating wages, terms and conditions of daily paid workers in the public and private sectors. Bathurst's workers responded by joining the GWU in increasing numbers; by mid 1960, the union could claim 1,158 paying members. It did not, however, seek to recruit salaried civil servants. In contrast, the GLU, that had denounced the strikers as 'hooligans', lost further ground.[22]

1961 general strike

Over the next few months, the GWU maintained its momentum through effective use of the JICs, which resulted in important concessions on terms and conditions, backed up by the threat of industrial action. It then demanded a 90 per cent increase in the minimum wage at a meeting of the Commerce JIC (CJIC) on 10 January 1961. The timing was particularly effective for it was known in Bathurst that the Bain Commission was about to recommend substantial salary increases for civil servants. The CJIC was due to debate the issue on 24 January, but on 20 January, groundnut carriers involved in a separate dispute refused to load an ocean-going vessel at Kuntaur, an up river port. They were encouraged to do so by GWU officials and labour unrest soon spread to Georgetown, the administrative capital of the Protectorate. When the government responded on 23 January by denouncing these developments, Jallow sought permission to hold a demonstration in Bathurst on the following day. When this was refused by the Commissioner of Police, the GWU organised a public meeting at which it was agreed that a two day general strike would begin on 24 January. Most daily paid workers in the public and private sectors in Bathurst (and many elsewhere) supported the strike. When the employers refused to negotiate

22 See Perfect (1987), 'Organised Labour', 135–141. Further information, especially on the response of the colonial authorities, is in CO 554/2497–2498. Civil servants were briefly organised in the Gambia Civil Service Union in early 1961, but this soon collapsed. See Perfect (1987), 'Organised Labour', 148 and CO 554/2498.

until the strikers returned to work, the GWU convened a public meeting on 25 January. Afterwards, a large crowd of strikers (and others) surged into the Marine Yard in Bathurst despite the authorities having refused the union permission to hold a demonstration. On this occasion (unlike in 1960), the crowd was dispersed by tear gas and police action, and Jallow (along with around 30 others) was later arrested for incitement to riot.

The government's response did not crush the strike as anticipated; instead, public opinion was inflamed and Jallow was hailed as a nationalist hero and the victim of colonial oppression, a view reinforced when Jallow was subsequently convicted of taking part in a riot and fined £75. Fearing that strikers might resort to violence, the private sector employers quickly opened informal negotiations with the GWU with the tacit approval of the government. A further 13 per cent increase in the minimum wage was agreed and later confirmed at a CJIC meeting on 30 January. The five day strike, in which more than 3,000 workers had participated, thus came to an end. The outcome was a triumph for the GWU and later the government and employers conceded the check-off system (which they had previously refused to do), allowing union dues to be deducted at source. Consequently, union income from entrance fees and subscriptions increased four-fold in 1961 to £1,652.[23]

The GWU's popularity was now at its peak, while the GLU, which had again denounced the strike, was eclipsed. Jallow's personal reputation was also very high and he was invited to attend two constitutional conferences in Bathurst and London in 1961 (albeit as an Independent, rather than as a trade union leader).[24] He was also actively courted by the ICFTU, although the GWU did not formally affiliate to that body until March 1963, thereby paving the way for Jallow to become secretary of its African Regional Organisation (AFRO) in April 1964. Affiliation to the ICFTU also meant that the union was now eligible formally to receive financial assistance ('subvention'), having previously received funds from

23 See Perfect (1987), 'Organised Labour', 142–150. Further information is in CO 554/2498–2500 and MSS 292B/966/5.

24 On the 1961 conferences, see Hughes and Perfect (2006), *Political History*, 149; Perfect (1987), 'Organised Labour', 166–168.

the US trade union centre, the AFL-CIO. However, neither Jallow's foray into international trade unionism nor subvention ultimately benefitted the union. Jallow's term of office with AFRO was not a success and in July 1965, he was dismissed for misappropriation of funds. Meanwhile, since subvention was provided in cash, rather than being tied to particular projects, most of the money was misappropriated or otherwise misused by GWU officials who also paid less attention than hitherto to resolving members' grievances as their own salaries were now guaranteed.[25]

Trade Unions after Independence

Although the GWU had failed to make much progress since 1961, its paying membership remained surprisingly high at independence in February 1965. But by 1967, this had fallen by more than two-thirds. There were two main reasons for this. First, having remained neutral in both the 1960 and 1962 general elections, the GWU unwisely became more involved in party politics that led to a loss of members to rival unions.[26] Secondly, in an attempt to regain the initiative, the GWU called a general strike in February 1967 that was a complete failure and further damaged the organisation.

1965 referendum

A few months after independence, in May 1965, the Prime Minister, Sir Dawda Jawara, announced that the PPP government intended to replace

25 See Perfect (1987), 'Organised Labour', 172–173; 187–190; Allen (1970), 'Trade Unionism', 419–421. Jallow's career at AFRO is discussed in LAB 13/1550 and 13/2236.

26 On the two elections, see Hughes and Perfect (2006), *Political History*, 137–157. Perfect (1987), 'Organised Labour', 159–171 examines the GWU's (and GLU's) stance.

the monarchy with a republic. The 1964 constitution required an amendment to an 'entrenched clause' (as this was) to be endorsed by two-thirds of the elected members of Parliament and confirmed by a two-thirds majority of those voting in a subsequent national referendum. The Republic Bill was duly passed in Parliament in June despite the criticisms of the opposition party, the United Party (UP), with the GWU also coming out against the bill despite being in favour of a republic in principle. The union argued that fundamental human rights would be damaged if The Gambia became a republic under an executive president and warned that it would be followed by a crackdown on unions and strikes (as had happened in Ghana). Clearly Jallow also calculated that defeating the bill would help to re-establish his domestic reputation which had been badly tarnished by his dismissal from AFRO.

The government failed by just 758 votes (or just 0.8 per cent of those voting) to achieve the required two-thirds majority. The GWU could claim some of the credit, but far from strengthening its position, the outcome of its opposition to the Republic Bill was that a number of PPP supporters resigned in protest from the union. Some of these joined the National Farmers and General Workers' Union (NFGWU), another general workers' union. Founded in early 1963 by a former General Secretary of the GLU, Henry Forster (although not registered until about April 1965), the NFGWU gained momentum when Baba M. Touray, a Kampala-trained former GLU official, joined the organisation. A Mandinka who had been an unsuccessful PPP candidate in the 1962 election, Touray was influential amongst dockworkers (many of whom were also Mandinka) and in October 1965, around half of them resigned from the GWU to join the NFGWU.[27]

27 Hughes and Perfect (2006), *Political History*, 160–163 on the referendum; Perfect (1987), 'Organised Labour', 184–194 discusses this and the NFGWU. See also MSS 292B/966/5, which contains Forster and Touray's correspondence with the TUC. In October 1965, the NFGWU claimed to have 200–300 members in total; see Slater Report, October 1965.

1966 election and establishment of GNU

Having alienated pro-PPP members through opposing the 1965 referendum, Jallow then angered pro-UP rank and file when he stood against the UP leader, P.S. N'Jie, in his Bathurst North constituency in the May 1966 general election. He won only 115 votes (3.5 per cent of those cast) with pro-UP union members clearly preferring N'Jie. Jallow's poor showing reflected his failure to devote 'adequate attention' to union affairs or organise 'a rigorous or honest election campaign'; and 'his personal behaviour (drinking, womanising and quarrelling)', all of which antagonised the electorate.[28] In the following month, Tairu A.K. John, a Kampala-trained former GWU official, who had left the GWU in 1963 over its failure to pay a fine he had incurred on union business, established yet another general workers' union, the Gambia National Union (GNU). The GNU was strongly pro-UP; John had been an unsuccessful UP candidate in the 1966 election, the union's President, Momodou C. Cham, had been the UP MP for Tumana since 1962, and the union's official address was the party's headquarters. The GNU quickly built up support through organising a series of short-lived, but relatively effective, strikes in private sector organisations in 1966.[29]

1967 and 1970 general strikes

By early 1967, therefore, the labour movement was increasingly fragmented, with four general workers' unions – the GWU, GLU, NFGWU and GNU – covering a wage labour force of a few thousand workers. Not surprisingly, many workers reacted to labour disunity by ceasing to be members of any union. In an attempt to regain the initiative, the GWU (supported by the

28 Hughes and Perfect (2006), *Political History*, 163–169 analyse the election. See also Perfect (1987), 'Organised Labour', 194–198 and LAB 13/2167, Slater to Seaward, 22 July 1966, on Jallow's motives and performance.

29 Perfect (1987), 'Organised Labour', 198–200; Allen (1970), 'Trade Unionism', 423; Slater Report, January 1967.

GNU) called the first general strike since independence in January 1967 in support of a general wage increase. The PPP government countered that the union's claim was unjustified and would be economically damaging; the strike was also opposed by the pro-government NFGWU and GLU, with the latter warning workers that they might lose their jobs if they participated in it. Most workers either accepted the government's arguments or heeded the GLU's warning and the strike collapsed on the second day. The GWU was later forced to accept humiliating compromise proposals put forward by the government.

Following the strike's failure, some rank and file members in government departments ceased to pay check-off to the GWU and some of its officials resigned. The impact on the GNU was even greater, for not long afterwards, Tairu John gave up trade unionism after gaining a job with the firm, Wimpeys, with the GNU eventually being wound up in 1970.[30] Meanwhile, Jallow responded to this setback by attempting to foster unity between the unions in October 1967 through the establishment of a single 'national' union under his leadership, but his arguments were rejected by the other unions and came to nothing.[31] Over the next few years, the GWU made little progress and when, under pressure from rank and file members, Jallow called another general strike in February 1970, it collapsed on the second day without any concessions being achieved.[32]

Revival of labour unrest: 1975–76

In the first decade after independence, the Gambian economy performed reasonably well, but in the mid 1970s, inflation began to rise rapidly.

30 Perfect (1987), 'Organised Labour', 200–203; Allen (1970), 'Trade Unionism', 424. See also Slater Report, May 1968. John later re-emerged as President of the GWC; see Jaiteh (2001), 'Union Boss'.

31 Perfect (1987), 'Organised Labour', 269–270; see also Slater Report, October 1967, May 1968.

32 Perfect (1987), 'Organised Labour', 213–222 examines the reasons for the strike and describes the course of events.

Responding to this, the Jawara government established the Waller (Salary) Commission in April 1974 and conceded interim wage increases in July and December 1974 and an 18 per cent increase in the minimum wage at the end of June 1975. On 8 July 1975, President Jawara informed a delegation of union leaders that the minimum wage would be increased again and that the final rate would be announced within a fortnight. But when no announcement was made, the GWU leadership lost patience and called another general strike on 28 July. The strike lasted five days and, unlike those of 1967 and 1970, was extremely successful; most daily paid workers in both the public and private sectors in Banjul (and many outside it) went on strike. It ended only after the government had conceded a further 7.7 per cent increase in the minimum wage. Several factors account for the strike's success. First, the government was caught unawares; unlike in 1967 and 1970, no prior negotiations had taken place in the JICs and a strike was not thought to be imminent. Second, the government could not persuade pro-PPP strikers to stay at (or return to) work. Third, and most importantly, the strike coincided with a major political crisis, the dismissal from the Cabinet on 29 July of the former Vice-President and prominent PPP leader, Sheriff Dibba.

In the short term, the strike provided a much needed boost for the GWU and union membership rose significantly. But the government now considered the union leadership irresponsible and willing to call general strikes (and disrupt the economy) without prior warning. Some PPP leaders may also have feared that Jallow would unite with Dibba, who had established a new opposition party, the National Convention Party (NCP), in September 1975, to challenge the PPP's predominance at the next general election due in 1977. In fact, however, the GWU leadership was generally unsympathetic to the NCP and distrusted Dibba for his past reputation as an anti-labour politician.[33]

33 Perfect (1987), 'Organised Labour', 225–232 examines the strike and the GWU's view of the NCP and Dibba. On Dibba's sacking from the Cabinet and the NCP, see Hughes and Perfect (2006), *Political History*, 187–190.

The government's antagonism towards the GWU increased as labour unrest reached a new peak during 1976 and, very significantly, affected white-collar employees of the public corporations, including workers in essential services. In October 1976, the government responded by securing parliamentary approval for an amendment to the Trade Union Act. Previously, unlike in virtually all other African states, no restrictions had been placed on the right to strike; now 21 days' notice would be required before a strike could lawfully be called in essential services and 14 days' notice was needed in non-essential services. The amendment placed the GWU leadership in a dilemma; a refusal to support strikers in future would undoubtedly cost it popular support, but the penalties for infringement of the act (a *dalasi* 1,000 (£200) fine and two years' imprisonment) were severe and could result in the union's destruction.

A few weeks later matters came to a head. Earlier in 1976, technicians at the Gambia Utilities Corporation (GUC), which was responsible for the provision of electricity and water, had organised two relatively successful strikes on their own account. But when, in mid November, they staged another protest over the repeated failure of the GUC's management to resolve their grievances, nine middle management men, who had been acting as their representatives, were sacked. Most shop floor workers immediately walked out, without giving any notice as was now required by law. GWU leaders disagreed over the proper response. Some members of its Executive Committee, probably including Jallow, were reluctant to act, but two leading officials, Araba Bah and Matarr Ceesay, were determined to support the sacked GUC men. Their view was upheld at a union meeting on 18 November. However, the strike, which began the following day, was badly organised, was opposed by some sections of the union, notably the dockworkers, and, unlike in 1975, the government remained in complete control of the situation. Both Bah and Ceesay were quickly arrested (although the government wisely did not arrest the still popular Jallow) and when the union's Administrative Secretary, Tim Sosseh, ordered workers who had gathered outside the union's offices to disperse, the strike rapidly collapsed. Bah and Ceesay were later put on trial; the former was acquitted, the latter convicted and fined.[34]

Deregistration of the GWU, 1977

The government now resolved to rid itself of the GWU once and for all and in January 1977, its certificate of registration was withdrawn. Consequently, it was barred from the JICs, it could no longer receive check-off payments and its funds were frozen. It now became an offence for anyone to have any dealings with it. Registration had been legally compulsory since the 1930s, while presentation of annual accounts to the Registrar of Trade Unions had always been a condition of certification. Despite this, few unions had ever submitted accounts within the required time limit and the GWU had failed to do so since 1973. Although various Gambian trade unions had in the past been deregistered for this offence (and four others were deregistered in 1977), all had been moribund and so the GWU was the first effective union to be banned.[35]

Trade unions in the later Jawara period: 1977–94

The PPP government responded in two ways to this new era in labour relations. First, it renewed its earlier half-hearted attempts to persuade union leaders to form a single trade union centre, which would exclude the banned GWU and could be expected to adopt a pliant pro-government line. Secondly, when this effort was thwarted by the personal rivalries of union leaders, it attempted to foster industrial unions to replace general workers' unions. When a dispute broke out in a particular sector, the GWU

34 See Perfect (1987), 'Organised Labour', 241–252; see also Ananaba (1989), *Trade Union Movement*, 20–21, although this contains some inaccuracies, and Saidy Khan (2004), 'Brethren', 253–254. On Bah and Ceesay, see also *The Independent* (2001), 'Veteran Trade Unionist'; Faye (2003), 'APRC Chairman'.

35 See Perfect (1987), 'Organised Labour', 253–256.

had often called all its branches out on strike in support, with damaging economic consequences. This would be avoided if unions were to represent workers in a single sector only. Since dockworkers, in particular, had often felt that their sectional interests had been ignored by the GWU, they were the first to receive official encouragement to form their own union. At first the leadership of the Gambia Dock Workers' Union (GDWU) formed in 1979 included pro-GWU dockworkers, but with at least the tacit approval of the Commissioner of Labour, these were later ousted by a rival faction.[36]

In the late 1970s and early 1980s, there was little labour unrest. But any government complacency was shattered when disaffected members of the paramilitary Gambia Field Force and self-styled Marxist civilians carried out a coup on 30 July 1981. This was initially successful, but Jawara was restored to power less than a week later following military intervention by Senegal. The coup leader, Kukoi Samba Sanyang, was rumoured to have received a scholarship from the GLU to study in Eastern Europe. But this seems to have been the extent of his contact with the labour movement, while the GLU was quick to denounce the coup (after the event) and to contribute to the government's Relief Programme Fund. Meanwhile, although the GWU resented its treatment by the government in recent years, it also opposed the coup that would have threatened its autonomy.[37]

Union leaders may not have supported the coup, but a number of individual workers, including dockworkers and taxi drivers, had clearly welcomed it. This had implications for the government's labour strategy suggesting that, in the absence of effective trade unions, workers might turn to violence to improve their conditions. Consequently, after the PPP had won the 1982 general election, reformist elements within the party persuaded the Cabinet to lift the ban on the only really effective union, the GWU, in January 1983.[38]

36 See Perfect (1987), 'Organised Labour', 273–276.

37 See Hughes and Perfect (2006), *Political History*, 210–220 on the coup and Perfect (1987), 'Organised Labour', 277–278 on the trade union response.

38 On the 1982 election and subsequent political reforms, see Hughes and Perfect (2006), *Political History*, 221–229.

At first, the GWU was only allowed to operate provisionally. Despite this, more militant union officials were determined to build up the membership as rapidly as possible and when workers at Jahally-Pacharr, a showpiece rice project, went on strike, their action was openly endorsed by Matarr Ceesay. Moreover, the GWU leadership actively encouraged their supporters on the docks in a power struggle with the GDWU. The government, which had hoped that the militant days of the GWU were over, responded by informing the GWU that it could not grant it a certificate of registration after all, on the dubious legal grounds that the names of de-registered unions could not be used.[39]

Well aware of the symbolic and historic appeal of the GWU name, Jallow refused to rename his organisation and instead became the first Secretary-General of a new organisation, the Gambia Workers' Confederation (GWC), in June 1985. The GWC, the first viable trade union centre established in The Gambia, was formed on the initiative of the Senegalese High Commission in Banjul and with the backing of the Senegalese trade union centre, the *Confédération Nationale des Travailleurs du Sénégal* (CNTS). Jallow became its Secretary-General and Daddy Sowe, the leader of the Gambia Motor Drivers, Mechanics and Allied Workers' Union, its President, but Bah and Ceesay remained aloof from the new body.[40]

The PPP government welcomed Jallow's return to the fold and after the GWC had remained neutral in the March 1987 general election, appointed him as a Nominated MP in May 1987 to serve the interests of labour. Unfortunately, he died two weeks later, at the age of only 58. Pa Modou K.B. Faal, the leader of the Gambia Industrial and Commercial Workers' Union, was appointed as the new GWC Secretary-General, a position he

39 See Perfect (1987), 'Organised Labour', 278–288. Jallow's account of why the GWU was re-registered is in *Africa Now* (1983), 'Workers Union'.

40 Perfect (1987), 'Organised Labour', 288–289; Hughes and Perfect (1989), 'Trade Unionism', 569; *West Africa* (1985), 'Trade union moves'; Bojang (2008), 'Daddy Sowe'. Touray (2007a), 'Post-1987 General Elections' suggests that Jallow was appointed because he supported the Senegambia Confederation (which operated between 1982 and 1989).

still holds in March 2011. Later in 1987, the government lifted the ban on the GWU (which resumed its place in the JICs). It also appointed Bah as a Nominated MP, after he had publicly expressed his support for the government's Economic Recovery Programme (ERP) even though this had led to cuts in public sector employment and the elimination of subsidies on rice and petrol, which had hit urban workers hard.[41] Relations between the government and both the GWC and the GWU remained generally good until 1994, with the unions apparently participating in, and welcoming, the 1990 Labour Act, even though it increased the notice period for strikes in essential services from 21 to 28 days.[42]

Trade unions under Jammeh: 1994–2010

In July 1994, the Jawara government was overthrown in a bloodless military coup organised by a group of junior officers in the Gambia National Army (GNA) who subsequently set up the Armed Forces Provisional Ruling Council (AFPRC) government.[43] The coup leader was Yahya Jammeh, a 29-year-old lieutenant, who subsequently became (and remains) the Gambian head of state. Faal cautiously welcomed the coup, but stated that this was conditional on the new regime maintaining the rule of law and subsequently

41 Hughes and Perfect (1989), 'Trade Unionism', 568–569 on the re-registration of the GWU; see also Touray (2007b), 'National Education Conference'. The GWU had certainly rejoined the JICs by 1989; see *Gambia Gazette*, 11 September 1989. On the ERP, see especially McPherson and Radelet (1995), *Economic Recovery*. Faal was dismayed at Bah's appointment; personal communication from John Stirling who interviewed him in 1990.

42 U.S. Department of State (1994), *Country Report*, comments favourably on the main provisions of the Labour Act. See also *Daily Observer* (2001), 'Pa Modou Faal', when Faal commented on government plans to amend the 1990 Labour Act, but expressed no criticism of its provisions.

43 On the 1994 coup and the Jammeh government, see Saine (2009), *Third-wave Democratization*; Ceesay (2006a), *Military and Democratisation*; Sarr (2007), *Coup d'Etat*; Perfect and Hughes (2006), *Political History*, 280–290; Perfect, 'Jammeh'.

criticised the AFPRC's initial decision that the transition period to civilian rule should last for four years. Matarr Ceesay, an old adversary of the PPP, also supported the military intervention (though also criticising the four year transition period) and remained a stalwart supporter of the AFPRC/APRC in Banjul North until his death in 2003. Even though he had joined the PPP in 1990 and lost his parliamentary seat on the abolition of the House of Representatives, Araba Bah endorsed the GNA's actions as well and even the four year transition period.[44]

Despite the labour movement's initial support for the new government, relations between the two soon cooled. Faal was detained for a short period in the run up to the 1997 National Assembly election.[45] The government may also have encouraged the formation in May 1996 of a new trade union centre, the Gambia National Trade Union Congress (GNTUC), as a rival to the GWC. By 2003, the GNTUC claimed to have 11 affiliates, including the GWU, and to represent a highly improbable 45,000 workers.[46] Its General Secretary at time of writing in April 2011 is Ebrima Garba Cham who claimed in 2010 that the GNTUC represented 16 unions, although a rival faction led by Ebou Faal, the leader of the Gambia Commercial Transport Union, disputed this.[47] A 2010 International Trade Union Confederation

44 Wiseman (1996), 'Military rule', 926–927; Faal (1994), 'Timetable'; Touray (2009), 'Decree no. 2'; Faye (2003), 'APRC Chairman'. The GLU's M.M. Ceesay also welcomed the coup; see Sowe (1994), 'Duration Matters'. *Gambia Weekly*, 26 October 1990 reported that Bah had recently joined the PPP.

45 Ceesay (2006a), *Military and Democratisation*, 168.

46 Saidy Khan (2004), 'Brethren', 270, Table 6.2, who also notes that the GWC claimed to represent around 30,000 workers at this time. See also Sanyang (2010), 'GNTUC Election'.

47 On the dispute within the GNTUC, see Sanyang (2010), 'GNTUC Election'; Janko (2010), 'Workers' Union'. Lamin Sanyang, the journalist who investigated the dispute, saw the registration certificates of 13 GNTUC affiliates. On Ebou Faal's union background, see also Ceesay (2006b) 'GTU'. Garba Cham was a former Secretary-General of the Gambia Transport, Food, Agriculture and Industrial Workers' Union and later held the same position for the Gambia Workers' Union; see *Daily Observer* (2000), 'GNTUC Scribe', Bojang (2008), 'Daddy Sowe'.

report claimed that the GWC represented 52,000 workers, an even more unlikely membership figure; an alternative view is that its sole affiliate is now Pa Modou Faal's Gambia Industrial and Commercial Workers' Union.[48]

Although the GNTUC has periodically called for substantial wage increases and the GWC has sometimes criticised government policies, neither has called any general strikes nor apparently encouraged their affiliates to strike.[49] A 2009 newspaper article, which condemned both the GWC and the GNTUC as 'one-man organizations' and criticised both Pa Modou Faal and Garba Cham for their individual failings, also asserted that 'The notion of collective bargaining has long been forgotten'.[50] The Dock and Maritime Workers' Union (DMWU), an affiliate of the GNTUC, has, however, been willing to threaten strike action against the Gambia Ports Authority (GPA), the employer of its members, notably in 2003 and 2007. However, on the latter occasion, the government showed that it would not tolerate serious labour unrest. Early in August 2007, the GPA dismissed 250 dockworkers without sending them termination letters; when the union threatened to strike in protest from 1 September (thus complying with the 28 days notice required), the government's internal security force, the feared National Intelligence Agency (NIA), warned the union leadership that the proposed strike threatened the peace and security of Banjul and would not be tolerated. When this did not prove a sufficient warning, the NIA arrested seven union leaders and held them for questioning; they were only released when they agreed to call off the strike.[51] The government's

48 International Trade Union Confederation (2010), *Core Labour Standards*, 2; personal communication from Kebba Ceesay, the Executive Secretary of the Gambia National Bureau of Trade Unions, April 2011. Unfortunately, it has not been possible to make contact with Pa Modou Faal.

49 See, for example, Sallah (2006), 'Workers'; Sowe (2007), 'Trade Unions'; Faal (2002), 'Trade Unionist'.

50 See *Gambia Journal* (2009), 'Micro-managing'.

51 On the 2003 strike threat, see Njie (2003), 'Dock Workers' and Fatty (2003), 'Dockworkers'; on the 2007 strike threat, see Keita (2007), 'Dockworkers'. The DMWU had been established in 1997; see *Gambia Daily*, 31 March 1997.

tactics worked; the union has been quiescent ever since. This was not the first time the NIA had arrested union leaders to forestall labour unrest; three officials of the Gambia Transport Union (including Ebou Faal) had been arrested in July 2006 over a threatened strike of taxi drivers.[52]

Concerned by the weakness and internal disunity of the Gambian trade union movement, the International Labour Organization (ILO) launched an initiative in the summer of 2009 to establish a new over-arching organisation. The eventual outcome was the foundation of the Gambia National Bureau of Trade Unions (GNBTU), which was officially launched on 29 October 2009. The GNBTU brought together the GWC and the GNTUC, as well as individual unions such as the Gambia Teachers' Union and the Gambia Labour Congress (GLC) (as the GLU now calls itself). Its aims are to build capacity through training and the sharing of experiences and best practices; to ensure that Gambian workers speak with one voice on a common platform; and to promote unity between workers. It also seeks to participate in socio-economic development in The Gambia and to promote ILO educational activities. The establishment of the GNBTU received the strong endorsement of Yusupha Kah, the then Minister of Trade, Industry and Employment, who made clear the APRC government's preference for dealing with one trade union organisation only.[53]

The GNBTU's first interim Chairman was Pa Modou Faal of the GWC. However, in 2010, following an internal dispute over union finances, Faal was replaced by Ebrima Garba Cham of the GNTUC, who holds the position in April 2011 (the GWC is still represented on the GNBTU's Executive Board through its President, Kebba Touray). The GNBTU's current Executive Secretary is Momodou Masaneh ('Kebba') Ceesay of

52 *Gambia Journal* (2006), 'Transport Union'.

53 See Baldeh (2009), 'Gambia National Bureau'; Ngum-Saidy and Jabbi (2009), 'National Bureau'; Jallow (2009), 'GLC, GNTUC Secretary Generals';. *Gambia Journal* (2009), 'Micro-managing'. Further information was supplied by the ILO's Faustina Mukazi Vanaperen and Kebba Ceesay of the GNBTU; personal communications, November 2009 and March/April 2011.

the GLC, who has been active in the trade union movement since the early 1970s, while the union's Treasurer, Sana Sonko, is also a GLC member. The Gambia Teachers' Union is no longer represented on the Executive, however. The other two members of the GNBTU's Executive have no particular trade union background. Churchill Bandeh has been a prominent APRC politician since the mid-1990s; he was MP for Upper Fulladu West between 1997 and 2007 and is a former Majority Leader of the National Assembly. The final member of the Executive, Tamsir Manga, who is acting as a consultant to the organisation, was formerly a senior civil servant.[54] Thus although the GNBTU's original backer, Yusupha Kah, is no longer in office, having been sacked in March 2011, it can be assumed that it remains a pro-government organisation.[55]

Although the formation of the GNBTU marks a new direction for the Gambian trade union movement, its achievements to date have been limited. Kebba Ceesay did manage to resolve the internal dispute within the GNTUC in 2010, although the losing Ebou Faal faction predictably criticised his intervention.[56] However, as noted above, internal disunity has already weakened the GNBTU, while its close ties to the ruling APRC means that it is unlikely to challenge government policies effectively in the future. It therefore remains to be seen whether it will be able to breathe new life into the largely moribund Gambian labour movement.

54 Information on the GNBTU's Executive in April 2011 and the removal of Pa Modou Faal was from Kebba Ceesay, personal communication, April 2011. On Ceesay's earlier career in the labour movement, see Perfect (1987), 'Organised Labour', 271–273, 292 (note 41). On Bandeh, see the 1997 and 2002 National Assembly election results at http://www.iec.gm/results [accessed 22 March 2011] and *The Gambia Daily*, 21 January 2002; see also *The Point*, 'APRC Names Candidates'. On Manga, see *Gambia Now* (2006), 'Public-Sector Heads'.

55 See *The Daily News* (2010), 'Two Ministers' on Kah's dismissal.

56 Sanyang (2010), 'GNTUC Election' discusses Ceesay's intervention. Additional information from Ceesay, personal communication, April 2011.

References

Africa Now (1983) 'Workers Union Official Discusses Future Plans' 27: 25–26.
Allen, C. (1970) 'African Trade Unionism in Microcosm: The Gambia Labour Movement, 1939–67', in C. Allen and R.W. Johnson (eds), *African Perspectives: Papers in the History, Politics and Economics of Africa Presented to Thomas Hodgkin*, Cambridge: Cambridge University Press.
Ananaba, W. (1979) *The Trade Union Movement in Africa*, London: C. Hurst.
Baldeh, P. (2009) 'The Gambia National Bureau of Trade Unions Inaugurated', *Foroyaa*, 2 November.
Bojang, M.B.O (2008) 'Alhagie Daddy Sowe Passes Away', *The Point*, 19 June.
Ceesay, E.J. (2006a) *The Military and 'Democratisation' in The Gambia: 1994–2003*, Victoria, BC: Trafford.
Ceesay, H. (2006b) 'GTU Fires Legal Threats', *The Independent*, 6 March.
Daily News, The (2011) 'Two Ministers Fired', 21 March.
Daily Observer (2000) 'GNTUC Scribe Hits at Houma', 7 November.
Daily Observer (2001) 'Pa Modou Faal Faults Labour Act Review', 2 April.
Faal, P.M. [K.B.] (1994) 'Timetable is Too Long', *Daily Observer*, 27 October.
Faal, P.M. (2002) 'Trade Unionist Urges Gov't to Revisit Budget', *Daily Observer*, 19 December.
Fatty, L.M. (2003) 'Dockworkers Renew Ultimatum', *The Independent*, 8 September.
Faye, P.M. (2003) 'APRC Chairman Dies', *Daily Observer*, 26 May.
Gambia Journal (2006) 'Three from Transport Union Detained and Released', 11 July.
Gambia Journal (2009) 'On Micro-managing Trade Unions', 4 November.
Gambia Now (2006) 'More Public-Sector Heads Roll', 22 November.
Grey-Johnson, N. (2002) *Edward Francis Small: Watchdog of The Gambia*, Kanifing: Book Production and Material Resources Unit.
Heintz, J., Oya, C. and Zepeda, E. (2008) *Towards an Employment-centred Development Strategy for Poverty Reduction in The Gambia: Macroeconomic and Labour Market Aspects*, Brasilia: International Poverty Centre.
Hughes, A. and Perfect, D. (1989) 'Trade Unionism in The Gambia', *African Affairs* 88(353): 549–572.
Hughes, A. and Perfect, D. (2006) *A Political History of The Gambia, 1816–1994*, Rochester, NY: University of Rochester Press.
Hughes, A. and Perfect, D. (2008) *Historical Dictionary of The Gambia*. 4th edition, Lanham, MD: Scarecrow, 2008.

Independent, The (2001) 'Tribute to a Late Veteran Trade Unionist: Amadou Araba Bah', 26 March.

International Trade Union Confederation (2010) *Internationally Recognised Core Labour Standards in The Gambia*. Report for the WTO General Council Review of the Trade Policies of The Gambia, Geneva, 14–16 September.

Jaiteh, S. (2001) 'Union Boss Calls for Round Table Dialogue', *The Independent*, 17 August.

Jallow, A. (2009) 'GLC, GNTUC Secretary Generals Reiterate Commitment for Sustainability', *Daily Observer*, 3 November.

Janko, S.S. (2010) 'Workers' Union Elects New Executive', *Today Newspaper*, 21 June.

Keita, A.J. (2007) 'Dockworkers Cancel Industrial Action', *Foroyaa*, 24 August.

McPherson, M.F. and Radelet, S.C. (eds) (1995) *Economic Recovery in The Gambia: Insights for Adjustment in Sub-Saharan Africa*, Cambridge, Mass: Harvard Institute for International Development.

Ngum-Saidy, M. and Jabbi, J. (2009) 'The National Bureau of Trade Unions Inaugurated', *Daily Observer*, 2 November.

Njie, M. (2003) 'Dock Workers Threaten Strike Action', *Daily Observer*, 9 January.

Perfect, D. (1987) 'Organised Labour and Politics in The Gambia: 1920–1984', unpublished PhD dissertation, University of Birmingham.

Perfect, D. (2010) 'The Gambia under Yahya Jammeh: An Assessment', *The Round Table*, 99(406): 53–63.

Point, The (2006) 'APRC Names Candidates', 27 December.

Saidy Khan, A. (2004) 'Brethren and Mother's Children: Developing an Industrial Relations Pluralism for African Realities: a Study of Industrial Relations and Personnel Management on the Gambian Docks', unpublished PhD dissertation, Loughborough University.

Saine, A. (2009) *The Paradox of Third-Wave Democratization in Africa: The Gambia under AFPRC – APRC Rule, 1994–2008*, Plymouth: Lexington Books.

Sallah, A. (2006) 'Workers Call for Salary Increase', *Daily Observer*, 2 May.

Sanyang, L. (2010) 'The GNTUC Election Controversy', *Foroyaa*, 13 October.

Sarr, S. (2007) *Coup d'Etat by the Gambia National Army*, Philadelphia: Xlibris.

Slater, J.E.D. (1966) 'Gambia: Labour and Social Affairs, October 1965', LAB 13/2451, 1 February.

Slater, J.E.D. (1967a) 'Gambia: Labour and Social Affairs, January 1967', LAB 13/2451, 2 February 1967.

Slater, J.E.D. (1967b) 'Gambia: Labour and Social Affairs, October 1967', LAB 13/2167, 31 October.

Slater, J.E.D. (1968) 'Gambia: Labour and Social Affairs, May 1968', LAB 13/2167, 21 May.
Sowe, B. (1994) 'The Duration Matters a Lot – M.M. Ceesay', *The Point*, 3 November.
Sowe, B.K. (2007) 'Trade Unions Call for 300 Percent Pay Rise', *Foroyaa*, 2 May.
Touray, S. (2007a) 'Post-1987 General Elections', *Foroyaa*, 5 October.
Touray, S. (2007b) 'The First National Education Conference', *Foroyaa*, 27 October.
Touray, S. (2009) 'Decree no. 2 Repeals NSS Act as ICRC's Attempts to Visit Military Detainees Rejected', *Foroyaa*, 24 March.
U.S. Department of State (1994) *U.S. Department of State Country Report on Human Rights Practices 1993 – Gambia*. Available at: http://www.unhcr.org/refworld/type,ANNUALREPORT,,GMB,3ae6aa4f0,0.html.
West Africa (1985) 'Trade union moves', 16 September.
Wiseman, J.A. (1996) 'Military Rule in The Gambia: An Interim Assessment', *Third World Quarterly* 17(5): 917–940.

AZIZOU CHABI IMOROU

Trade Unionism among Teachers in Benin since 1945

Recently in Benin (formerly Dahomey) trade unionism among teachers has undergone unprecedented growth. There are now more than thirty trade unions representing teachers. The evolution of trade unionism in this sector has been uneven, at times even turbulent, depending on the roles assumed by the actors involved. There have been at various times moments of hesitation, periods of cooptation, indoctrination, protest and alliances.

Much of the interaction between workers and the authorities flowed from periodic challenges that workers made to exiting authority. As will be seen, trade union challenges often preceded major political transitions, including the independence movement and the numerous coups d'état that have taken place in Benin. SYNEPDA, the Dahomey Primary School Teachers' Union, was created in 1945. It was the first teachers' union in Benin. It was dissolved in 1975 for encouraging its members to take strike action. Historians of African trade unionism often look at such examples to present a state-union dualism, in which the two actors represent diametrically opposing interests.[1] Such an analysis has proved very useful in the study of early African trade unionism, especially in the late colonial period when trade union struggles and the fight against the European presence ongoing. The post colonial trade union history does not lend itself to this kind of binary analysis; it shows the need to understand the complexity of social-political dynamics which characterise relationships between the authorities and oppositional groups. Although some studies have been carried which show the political role played by teachers in the colonial

1 Meynaud and Salah-Bey (1963), *Le syndicalisme africain*; Dossou (1981), *Le salariat et le développement des syndicats*; Fonteneau et al (2004), *Histoire du syndicalisme en Afrique*; and Paquelin (2005), 'Elliptiques historiennes autour de l'objet syndical'.

period,[2] or more recently the advent of new African democracies,[3] work on the socio-historical evolution of trade unions in different socio-political contexts remain rudimentary.

In many West African states, teachers are often the key actors in state development either as civil servants, or as political leaders or even as political leadership instructors. Therefore, their actions depend on each country-specific socio-political setting. In Benin, four major events of state development are considered in this study: independence, coups d'état, Marxist revolution and democracy. This chapter aims to determine the links that exist between these events and the activities of the teacher trade unions; explain the role played by the teachers in Benin's political history; explain links between political and trade union activity. The main focus of our analysis is teachers' collective activity and their trade unions. Reference will also be made to other professionals, civil servants and intellectuals since the activities of teachers often formed part of larger movements.[4]

Dahomean Teachers under Colonisation

In the early years of colonisation, educational duties in the AOF territories were carried out by metropolitan (i.e. French) teachers. These were relatively small in number, for the most part either religious missionaries or civilian volunteers. It was not until 1904 that the first local (i.e. African) graduates in teacher training from the William Ponty School of Dakar were recruited. During the colonial period, both black and white[5] teachers

2 Jézéquel (2002), *'Les mangeurs de craie'*; Jézéquel (2005) 'Les enseignants comme élite politique'.

3 Banégas (2003), *La démocratie à pas de caméléon*; Gbado Lalinon (1998), *En marche vers la liberté*; Granoux (2007), *La craie, l'urne et la banderole*.

4 Granoux (2007), *La craie, l'urne et la banderole*, 11–12.

5 While teaching was one of the least desirable professions for whites in West Africa, it was considered a highly prestigious job for Africans because it ensured proximity

served the interest of the French metropolis; they trained lower level civil servants and their lessons focussed on French political culture. Teachers were therefore allies of a colonial enterprise in which employment policies were discriminatory since French citizens and indigenous peoples were treated differently.

African teachers earned relatively low wages and were routinely given subordinate roles. Europeans earned relatively better wage and could be entrusted with administrative positions. Having been educated by Europeans, early African teachers recognised the disparity between the values taught by France (justice, equality, freedom and democracy) and its behaviour in the colonies. Louis Hunkanrin (1886–1964), for example, was a primary school teacher in Ouidah[6] who later became an important early figure in the history of Dahomean nationalism[7]. He taught for three years before being dismissed by the colonial administration for his refusal to accept an inferior status. He denounced forced labour and taxation, and as a result Hunkanrin spent twenty years of his life either in exile or prison. In 1918 and joined the French army but in 1923 he was accused of inciting rebellion in Porto-Novo and fled to Mauritania. In 1933 he was granted permission to return, and he continued to attack the administration in articles published in the journal *The Voice of Dahomey*. In 1941 he was arrested and imprisoned in Mali and was released only after World War II. His journey reveals a teacher determined to reform the colonial system, to criticise the abuse of the colonial administration without fear.

Less dramatically perhaps, but other intellectuals followed in the footsteps of Hunkanrin. Before 1944, small acts of defiance to colonial authority were not associated with trade unionism. They nevertheless constitute the first manifestation of intellectual challenges in the colony

---

to the 'master' and the feeling of belonging to a colonial elite. See Jézéquel (2002), *'Les mangeurs de craie'*.

6 Ouidah was an important slave trading centre in the south of Benin. The first missionary schools were erected in Ouidah in 1861 and in Porto-Novo in 1864. Education remained more widespread in this area than in other parts of the country.

7 Information on Louis Hunkanrin can be found in Jézéquel (2002), *'Les mangeurs de craie'*, 417–422, and Gandonou (1994), *Louis Hunkanrin ou la Grande France*.

of Dahomey and more generally in French West Africa.[8] The first trade unions appeared in Dahomey in the 1930s. 'Professional associations' and 'friendly societies' sprang up across the AOF, particularly among teachers, beginning in the 1930s. They provided arenas for socialisation, debate, and the building of a collective teacher identity.[9] In French West Africa the colonial administration considered these unions as potential fomenters of discord and therefore their appearance bred mistrust.

These professional associations provided future trade union leaders with their first experience of collective action. And such associations multiplied rapidly in the wake of the 1944 Brazzaville conference, which introduced significant reforms, such as the freedom of association and the end of discrimination in the recruitment of teachers. The 1946 constitution was founded on the principle that all inhabitants of France and its overseas colonies were French citizens, therefore instituting, on paper at least, equality of training courses, and equality in management structures.

The post Brazzaville period was marked by significant social, political and economic movements in the AOF territories, as Africans sought to have the colonial administration live up to the principle of equality. A principal example was the strike of railway workers on the Dakar-Niger railway from November 1947 to May 1948. African teachers took the advantage of the tense climate to advance to push for a fairer gradation of employment contracts, one that would grant equality of pay to Africans and Europeans. Their agitation was successful, leading to a simplified framework comprised of just three ranks, head teachers, teachers and assistant teachers.[10]

The *SYNEPDA* was the first legally recognised teachers' union in Dahomey. From its founding in 1945 it was heavily involved in politics. Its first general secretary, Valentin Djibodé-Aplogan, was also the general secretary of the Parti Républicain du Dahomey (PRD), the party of Sourou Migan Apithy. For years Djibodé-Aplogan directed both the political and

8 Bakary (1993), 'Système éducatif, stratification sociale'; Jézéquel (2002), *'Les mangeurs de craie'*; Jézéquel (2005), 'Les enseignants comme élite politique'.

9 Jézéquel (2002), *'Les mangeurs de craie'*, 374; Dossou (1981), *Le salariat et le développement des syndicats*, 12.

10 Jézéquel (2002), *'Les mangeurs de craie'*, 437.

trade union duties, and he also served as editor of the *L'école Dahoméenne*, the union's journal established at the fourth territorial congress in August 1954 at Cotonou. In 1957, his leadership role in the union did not prevent him to run for political office in the territorial assembly elections. In 1958, when he supported teachers' strikes in defiance of Apithy, he was excluded from the PRD.[11]

From Independence to the 1972 Coup d'Etat

The adoption of the 1946 constitution created new political offices that tempted many teachers: the National Assembly, the AOF General Council in Dakar, the territorial Assembly and finally the territorial governments from 1956. From this latter date, with the transfer of authority from Paris to Porto-Novo through the loi-cadre, trade unions throughout AOF became increasingly interested in territorial matters and politics in general. Because of their education and their spatial distribution, teachers were well placed to do well in territorial elections. Successful candidates could count on the support of their own union as well as that of the students' union, l'Union Générale des Elèves et Etudiants Dahoméens (UGEED). UGEED played an important role in shaping the nationalist agenda by stressing that the root cause of problems in the educational system was colonialism, and teachers were quick to push for a 'decolonisation' of education.[12]

From 1960, when independence was achieved, to 1972, the Republic of Dahomey experienced 12 coups d'état, of which five were successful.[13] Teachers and their unions played a critical role in shaping the country's

11 Granoux (2007), *La craie, l'urne et la banderole*, 35–36.

12 Ibid., 36; author interview with Léopold Dossou, Cotonou, 30 January 2006 and 14 February 2006.

13 There were successful coups in 1963, 1965, in 1967 in 1969 and 1972. Bio Bigou (1995), *Première révolution d'octobre 1963*.

turbulent early history. In October 1963, for example, there was widespread discontent over the proposed building of the presidential palace at the same time when workers had back wages due to them and when a member of the National Assembly (Christophe Bohiki) had been accused of murder and then released. In response, l'Union Générale des Travailleurs du Dahomey (UGTD), at that time headed by a teacher, Théophile Paoletti, called a 24 hour general strike. Mass street demonstrations took place in the main urban centres, Cotonou and Porto-Novo in response to the strike call. Unsuccessful negotiations between Paoletti and President Hubert Maga proved unsuccessful and the strike continued. In a process that would often be repeated, the army intervened. Headed by Colonel Nicéphore Soglo, the army disbanded the National Assembly, suspended the 1960 constitution, and ousted President Maga.[14]

In 1965 another general strike was called after the government's decision introduction of a solidarity 20 per cent tax along with a 25 per cent reduction in workers' wages. Teachers and their unions once again played a prominent role. The military intervened, dismissing the coalition government of Apithy and Ahomodegbe and entrusting authority to now General Soglo on 30 December 1966. This time, however, General Soglo was unable to restore calm. The general strike resumed in 1967. Ultimately, junior army officers forced General Soglo to resign and authority was entrusted to Emile Derlin Zinsou, who became the President of the Republic.

In May 1969 the regime of Zinsou also decided cut civil servants salaries, which represented a high proportion of government expenditures. Predictably, a general strike followed which weakened the Zinsou regime and facilitated the military overthrow in December 1969. The military retained authority until 7 May 1970, when a rotating presidency was adopted, a system that remained in place until the coup d'état engineered by Lieutenant-Colonel Mathieu Kérékou in October 1972.

The exact links between the coups and the teachers' trade unions have been a matter of speculation. According to Ahanhanzo Glèlè (1969), teachers consulted with the army during the general strike of 1963 and carried

14 Bio Bigou (1995), *Première révolution d'octobre 1963*.

signs that read 'Power to the Army'. Granoux found it significant that most coups took place in the weeks or months following the beginning of the school year; this revealed either the teachers' determination to involve the army or the army's readiness to exploit the teacher mobilisation.[15] Regimes that found themselves under attack from the teachers' unions routinely accused them of being under French influence. During the 1965 general strike, for instance, President Ahomadegbe made an appeal to the nation in which he claimed that the strike was nothing more than a 'political manoeuvre', one controlled by the 'enemies of the Government and the Dahomean people' in the interests of the French.

Political changes in the wake of the coups d'état influenced the trade union evolution. New regimes were intent on centralising trade unions in a single national confederation, one that could more easily be brought under state control, and to limit the right to strike and organise. The justification for such state control was that trade unions, in particular those of civil servants, were being manipulated for political ends. Politicians also sought to neutralize the trade unions by co-opting union leaders, especially teachers, and placing them within the ranks of the government.

Trade Unions under 'Revolutionary' Authority

With the 1972 takeover by Lieutenant-Colonel Kérékou, the relationship between trade unions and the state were redefined. In the beginning the teachers' trade unions supported the Kérékou regime. At first Kérékou represented a new generation of leaders who exhibited sufficient confidence to demand an end to all semblance of dependency on France, a goal

15 Ahanhanzo Glèlè (1969), *Naissance d'un Etat noir*; Granoux (2007), *La craie, l'urne et la banderole*. The school year typically begins in early October. The coups d'état took place in October 1963, November 1965, December 1967, December 1969 and October 1972.

with which the trade unions were in agreement. Kérékou then set about erecting a programme of 'New Schools', which were to be free from any foreign influence.[16] The new regime also won the support of teachers by nationalising a variety of industries to help pay for improved wage rates for Benin's large civil service. Kérékou also nationalised the Catholic schools, a long desired goal of the union representing teachers who worked in those schools, the Syndicat National des Enseignants des Ecoles Catholiques du Dahomey (SYNEECAD).

The honeymoon period was short lived, however. Friction between the regime and the teachers' unions, particularly over wages, led to strikes and strike threats even before Kérékou, on 30 November 1974, declared that Benin had now embarked on a path of Marxism-Leninism. With this radical departure and the formation of Kérékou's Parti de la Révolution Populaire du Bénin (PRPB), teachers and their unions adopted a highly critical stance toward the regime. Unions castigated the idea of a one-party state, and the regime openly attacked unions and their leaders. Organisations that had been active in the country for years were disbanded; the SYNEPDA was dissolved in 1975 because it incited teachers to take strike actions. In order to assert better control over trade union activities, the regime grouped together all unions in a single confederation, subservient to the state, called the l'Union Nationale des Syndicats des Travailleurs du Dahomey/Bénin. Since its inception, UNSTD represented 'a trade unionism opposed to conflict.'[17] By no means did the creation of UNSTD put an end to independent trade union activity or thought. But it did force independent trade unionism underground, and it did remove its institutional presence. Teachers who opposed the regime acted in secret and there were no mass opposition movements until 1985. In their classrooms and in anonymously published tracts, teachers in numerous subtle ways sought to undermine the regime and the idea of the one-party state.[18] Kérékou dismissed the

16 Granoux (2007), *La craie, l'urne et la banderole*, 64.

17 Touré (1986), 'L'UGTCI et le développement harmonieux', 81–83.

18 Author interviews with Paul Essè Iko, Cotonou, 20 January 2007; Léopold Dossou, Cotonou, 30 January 2006 and 14 February 2006; see also the interview with Léopold Dossou in Granoux (2007), *La craie, l'urne et la banderole*.

intellectuals who criticised the regime as 'crazy' and 'defective', educated in 'white schools' and threats to the revolution. For Kérékou teachers and intellectuals were 'enemies of the people, servile agents, and jacks of imperialism.'[19]

Fear of intellectuals led Kérékou in 1976 to create a variety of organisations designed to win the loyalty and defuse the threat of young teachers: Jeunes Instituteurs Révolutionnaires (JIR), Jeunes Professeurs Révolutionnaires (JPR) and Jeunes Bacheliers Révolutionnaires (JBR).[20] Through these organisations Kérékou sought to integrate young teachers into the military regime, inculcate the values of Marxism-Leninism, winning their allegiance, offering opportunities for promotion and thereby weakening the appeal of trade unionism. Many who participated in these organisations later gained influence in the regime and were appointed to important posts. Many of those who opposed the regime were hounded into exile or silence. During these years the only active opposition was found among student members of the Parti Communiste du Bénin.

Kérékou's stranglehold over political and trade union life began to weaken in 1985, when the country's debt problem began to spiral out of control, leaving the regime increasingly unable to pay civil servants. Protest after 1975 had been necessarily clandestine, but beginning in 1985 the poverty of the regime opened the door, however slowly at first, to those wanting to challenge its brutal suppression of opposition, its corruption and nepotism, or its failure to provide even modest economic advancement. Teachers and students of course played leading roles in an opposition that slowly began to make itself heard from 1985 onwards.

When the regime dissolved the executive of the student association, students at the Abomey-Calavi campus held a rally on 29 April that gained the support of their teachers.[21] The Parti Communiste du Bénin (Benin Communist Party) took this opportunity to strengthen its secret war with

19 Kérékou (1987), *Dans la voie de l'édification du socialisme*, 60.

20 Interview with Léopold Dossou in Granoux (2007), *La craie, l'urne et la banderole*.

21 Gbado Lalinon (1998), *En marche vers la liberté*.

the government by inciting the schools to revolt. Indeed, in their teaching activities, communist teachers had apparently been trained to encourage freedom of expression in the classroom. Paul Iko, a communist teacher, stressed that one strategy was to reawaken critical thought among students.[22] After 1985 teachers, in the face of harassment, dismissal of strikers and the withholding of wages, began creating informal organisations and holding street demonstrations. Their informal organisations were in many ways more representative of workers and their concerns than the party-controlled unions.[23]' The regime characterised the small revolts of teachers as emanating from 'small anarcho-leftist political extremist groups' of 'anti-revolutionaries' and traitors.[24] By 1988 the economic crisis was widespread and wages arrears had accumulated. At the end of that year teachers conducted a 24 hour strike, which they repeated several times. To make ends meet many teachers by this time had taken on work in the informal economy.[25]

Teachers and the Advent of Democracy

In January 1989 university students called a strike against the non-payment of their grants. By 6 May high school students had joined the university students and confronted the police in the street. The army was sent to meet the demonstrators and a high school student was killed.[26] This tragedy

22 Author interview with Iko, Cotonou, 20 January 2007.

23 Interview with Léopold Dossou in Granoux (2007), *La craie, l'urne et la banderole*.

24 Gbado Lalinon (1998), *En marche vers la liberté*.

25 Igué and Soulé (1992), *L'Etat-Entrepôt au Bénin*, 174–175, discuss the growing importance of the informal economy during this time as the state was simply too poor to pay the salaries of civil servants.

26 Banégas (2003), *La démocratie à pas de caméléon*; Gbado Lalinon (1998), *En marche vers la liberté*.

led others to join the strike and the opposition gained momentum. After a failed meeting with the Labour Minister, the teachers established ad hoc organisation which declared on 26 July that 'the schools are officially closed and the year 1988–1989 is declared null and void'.[27] Such defiance by an influential sector emboldened the oppositional forces, and crowds at street demonstrations grew ever larger.

In response, Kérékou ordered a cabinet reshuffle on 4 August 1989 and appointed several teachers to the government in an attempt to gain their acquiescence. Robert Dossou was appointed planning minister, Germain Kadja, minister of lower education, and Alidou Salifou, minister of higher education. Like their elders in 1970, these ministers supported the claims of the strikers and sought to improve communication between the regime and the teachers. By December 1989 the regime, bankrupt and illegitimate in the eyes of its citizens, abandoned Marxism-Leninism and announced a national conference of '*force vives*' to settle all national questions in open forum.

Teachers did not wait passively for the opening of the National Conference. In early February 1990 those in higher education took the initiative by convening a small conference, 'The democratic challenge'. Several participants at this conference would play important roles during the National Conference scheduled fifteen days later. After years of ridicule and disparagement from the Kérékou regime, teachers were keen to rehabilitate their image. The people of Benin have 'vowed to stop humiliating knowledge', they declared.[28]

The National Conference was a watershed even in the history of Benin, and a healthy part of the discussion during those heady days of change involved education. Condemnation was made of Kérékou's system of New Schools as well as the regime's centralised programme of teacher recruitment. A new recruitment policy, whereby communities as well as the state would play a role in teacher recruitment, was adopted. Teachers were also

27 Gbado Lalinon (1998), *En marche vers la liberté*, 37.

28 General Report of the conference submitted by Albert Tévoedjrè, General reporter, in Naumann (1994), *Les actes de la conférence nationale*, 49.

given greater freedom of association, and trae union rights were restored. Ultimately, the National Conference ended the eighteen year reign of the Kérékou regime, sent out a call for national elections, and set the country on the path toward far greater democracy and respect for civil liberties. But the National Conference could solve neither the ongoing economic emergency facing the country, nor could it resolve the myriad problems that beset the teaching profession.

In the wake of the National Conference, civic rights were rehabilitated and freedoms of expression and association were reinforced. At the same time, the integration of newly created categories of untrained teachers including the communitarians (those recruited by local communities) and the state contractors (those recruited by the state and often with little vocational training) considerably increased the number of teachers. The teaching profession had lost much of its prestige. Due to extremely low salaries, teaching came to be regarded as a stop gap job by many, a professional to be taken up only when other opportunities had fallen through. Moreover, teachers had come to be seen as habitual strikers and malcontents, as 'budget eaters' who depended exclusively on public funds during a period of extreme budget austerity, a point of view echoed by some economists.[29]

Teachers have responded, not through solidarity, but through fragmentation. Micro identities have developed within the profession, which have been reflected through a proliferation of trade union organisations. Sub categories of teachers have been formed based on seemingly small differences within the profession, such as differing attitudes about career prospects, teacher training and qualifications, and each of these has been institutionalised in trade union organisation.[30] There are currently far too many trade unions in the teaching profession. For example, there are thirty trade unions in primary education alone. The political threats that unions faced in the past have almost disappeared, at least in their most hostile form.

29 See, for example, Mingat et al (2000), *Les systèmes éducatifs africains*. For an opposing view, see Bierschenk (2007), 275–278.

30 Dubar (1992), 'Formes identitaires et socialisation professionnelle'.

Teachers have become so assertive that trade union action and striking are commonplace and form part of the daily life of Beninese education.

While the advent of democracy provided a ray of hope for the people of Benin, the ongoing economic crisis forced the new authorities to turn to the World Bank and IMF for loans. Structural adjustment in Benin, as in the rest of the continent, meant deep cuts in public expenditure, including mass layoffs, pay freezes, and a freeze on the hiring of new staff. In Benin the areas most affected by the demands of structural adjustment were the military and education. Labour market liberalisation under structural adjustment means, in effect, forced unemployment for graduates. At the same time a shortage of teachers meant that the new authorities resorted to non-permanent staff to maintain the educational system. The various teachers' unions decry this practice, yet the government continues to actively recruit lower paid contract teachers to meet its obligations both to the IMF and the educational needs of the country. In response, fully trained professional teachers feel compelled to strike in an effort to save their profession from further debasement. The unions seek an elimination of the practice of recruiting unqualified teachers. In late 2007 teachers conducted a largely unsuccessful six week strike toward this end.

Conclusion

Dahomean teachers were allies of the colonial administration in the teaching of civilisation. Yet they soon found themselves engaged in a struggle against the abuse and injustices of colonial authority. After independence this struggle continued as they pursued a complete 'decolonisation' of education and the establishment of links between their trade union and political activities. Their militant spirit and political tendencies led them repeatedly to intervene in the unstable political atmosphere of the early Republic, and it often led to their harassment and to restrictions on their rights to organise. Coupled with the economic crisis that descended upon

Benin in the mid 1980s, the defiance of teachers were at the vanguard in finally toppling the Kérékou regime. No other group in society has so effectively championed democratic rights. Since the fall of Kérékou, many teachers have been unable to abandon this longstanding opposition to authority, and relations between teachers and the state have often been tortuous. In the trilogy of Hirschman (exit, voice and loyalty),[31] teachers have been in a non-linear manner at the forefront of the challenge to authority, have participated in that authority, and at the same time have been the subject of estrangement by the authority (particularly at the beginning of the revolutionary regime).

Teachers and their unions have been far from monolithic in their thought and actions. Yet by and large, teachers have not hesitated to turn to their unions in order to assert their rights and maintain a constant dialogue with the authorities. Teachers and their unions therefore occupy a pivotal public space in Benin. They have made their collective voice heard in relation to the departure of colonial authority, to nation building, to the restoration of social justice, the equitable distribution of wealth, the establishment of democracy, and respect of individual rights. What the future holds in store for teachers and their unions is deeply problematic, but their contribution to Benin's past is of unquestioned value.

References

Adamon, A. (1995) *Le renouveau démocratique au Bénin: la Conférence nationale des forces vives et la période de transition*, Paris: L'Harmattan.

Ahanhanzo Glèlè, M. (1969) *Naissance d'un Etat noir. L'évolution politique et constitutionnelle du Dahomey de la colonisation à nos jours*, Paris: Librairie Générale de Droit et de Jurisprudence.

31 Hirschman (1970) *Exit, Voice and Loyalty*.

Bakary, T.D. (1993) 'Système éducatif, stratification sociale et construction de l'Etat', in C.D. Bach and A. Kirk-Greene (eds), *Etats et sociétés en Afrique francophone*, Paris: Economica.

Banégas, R. (2003) *La démocratie à pas de caméléon. Transition et imaginaires politique au Bénin*, Paris: Karthala.

Bayart, J.-F. et al (1992) *Le politique par le bas en Afrique noire. Contributions à une problématique de la démocratie*, Paris: Karthala.

Bierschenk, T. (2007) 'L'éducation de base en Afrique de l'Ouest francophone: Bien privé, bien public, bien global', in T. Bierschenk et al (eds), *Une anthropologie entre rigueur et engagement. Essais autour de l'œuvre de Jean-Pierre Olivier de Sardan*, Paris: APAD-Karthala.

Bio Bigou, L.B. (1995) *Première révolution d'octobre 1963. Massacre à Cotonou-Zongo et douloureux événements de Mars 1964 à Parakou et la question de l'unité nationale du Bénin*, Cotonou: Editeur inconnu.

Capelle, J. (1990) *L'éducation en Afrique noire à la veille des indépendances*, Paris: Karthala.

Codo, B.C. (1978) *La presse dahoméenne face aux aspirations des 'évolués'. L'exemple de la Voix du Dahomey (1927–1952)*, Thèse de doctorat de 3ème cycle d'histoire, Université de Paris 7.

Dossou, L. (1981) *Le salariat et le développement des syndicats au Dahomey (1937–1960)*, Thèse de doctorat de 3e cycle, Université de Paris VII.

Dubar, C. (1992) 'Formes identitaires et socialisation professionnelle', *Revue Française de Sociologie* 33(4): 505–529.

Engono, J.N. (2006) 'Les "déflatés" de la fonction publique au Cameroun: du rêve de la réussite sociale au désenchantement. Étude de cas sur l'itinéraire des "déflatés" du Minrest', *Le bulletin de l'APAD* 18.

Establet, J. (1997) *Mathieu Kérékou (1933–1996). L'inamovible président du Bénin*, Paris: L'Harmattan.

Fonteneau, G. et al (eds) (2004) *Histoire du syndicalisme en Afrique*, Paris: Karthala

Gandonou, A. (1994) *Louis Hunkanrin ou la Grande France*, Porto-Novo: JORB.

Gbado Lalinon, B. (1998) *En marche vers la liberté. Bénin: passage d'un régime autoritaire à un Etat de droit*, Cotonou: Ruisseaux d'Afrique.

Granoux, D. (2007) *La craie, l'urne et la banderole. Le rôle des enseignants dans l'émergence de la citoyenneté au Bénin*, Mémoire de master 2, Université de Paris 1.

Gupta, A. (1995) 'Blurred Boundaries: The Discourse of Corruption, the Culture of Politics, and the Imagined State', *American Ethnologist* 22(2): 375–402.

Habermas, J. (1974) 'The public sphere', *New German Critique* 3: 49–55.

Hirschman, A.O. (1970) *Exit, Voice and Loyalty. Responses to decline in Firms, Organisations and States*, Cambridge: Harvard University Press.

Igué, J.O. and Soulé, B.G. (1992) *L'Etat-Entrepôt au Bénin. Commerce informel ou solution à la crise?*, Paris: Karthala.

Iroko, A.F. (2001) *Le président Mathieu Kérékou. Un homme hors du commun*, Cotonou: Les Nouvelles Editions du Bénin.

Jézéquel, J.-H. (2002) *'Les mangeurs de craie'. Socio-histoire d'une catégorie lettrée à l'époque coloniale: les instituteurs diplômés de l'école normale William-Ponty*, Thèse de doctorat de 3eme cycle, Paris: EHESS.

Jézéquel, J.-H. (2005) 'Les enseignants comme élite politique en AOF (1930–1945). Des "meneurs de galopins" dans l'arène politique', *Cahiers d'Etudes Africaines* 178: 519–543.

Kérékou, M. (1987) *Dans la voie de l'édification du socialisme. Recueil des discours de notre Grand Camarade de Lutte le Président Kérékou*, Cotonou: Direction de l'Information et de la Propagande Société Yagoubi.

Mêtinhoué, P.G. (2006) *Les ministres du Dahomey et du Bénin*, Cotonou: CNPMS.

Mingat, A. and Suchaut, B. (2000) *Les systèmes éducatifs africains. Une analyse économique comparative*, Bruxelles: De Boeck Université & PED.

Meynaud, J. and Salah-Bey, A. (1963) *Le syndicalisme africain: Evolution et perspectives*, Paris: Payot.

Naumann, F.F. (1994) *Les actes de la conférence nationale*, Cotonou: ONEPI.

Noudjènoumè, P. (1999) *La démocratie au Bénin 1988–1993. Bilan et perspectives*, Paris: L'Harmattan.

Olivier de Sardan, J.-P. (2005) *De la nouvelle anthropologie du développement à la socio-anthropologie des espaces publics africains*, Texte de communication à conférence inaugurale du colloque APAD à Yaoundé.

Paquelin, S. (2005) 'Elliptiques historiennes autour de l'objet syndical', in V. Chambarlhac, V. and G. Ubbiali (eds), *Epistémologie du syndicalisme. Construction disciplinaire de l'objet syndical*, Paris: Logiques sociales.

RB/MEN (1990) *Actes des Etats Généraux de l'Education*, Cotonou: Ministère de l'Education Nationale.

Touré, I. (1986) 'L'UGTCI et le développement harmonieux: un syndicalisme anti conflits', *Politique africaine* 24: 79–90.

KWAMINA PANFORD

Trade Unions, Democratic Transition and Organisational Challenge: The Ghana Trades Union Congress, 1989–2009

The Democratisation Process in Ghana in the 1990s

Ghana has experienced a successful (if not one of the most successful) political transitions in Africa in the last two decades. As a result of the lifting of the ban on party politics by the military Provisional National Defence Council (PNDC) on 3 November 1992, Ghana held its first Presidential elections since 1979. That was followed on 29 December 1992 by Parliamentary polls, which were originally planned for 8 December 1992.[1] Rawlings won the Presidential elections of 1992 with 58.3 per cent of the vote. In the legislative contest, the opposition led by Professor A. Adu Boahen's New Patriotic Party (NPP) boycotted the elections, claiming that the PNDC had rigged the polls.[2] This led to a sweeping victory for Rawlings' coalition, the Progressive Alliance (with the Eagle Party and the National Convention Party) taking the vast majority of the 200 seats.[3]

1 Panford (1998), 'Elections and Democratic Transition in Ghana'; Haynes (1993), 'Sustainable Democracy in Ghana?'; Ninsin (1993), 'Some Problems in Ghana's Transition to Democratic Governance'.

2 Adu (1995), 'A Note on the Ghanaian Elections'; Oquaye (1995), 'The Ghanaian Elections of 1992'.

3 Haynes (1993), 'Sustainable Democracy', 462, 464.

On 7 January 1993 Rawlings was installed as President of Ghana's Fourth Constitutional Republic.[4] After over a decade of military rule, Ghana joined the list of African countries that commentators usually refer to as having undergone successful political transitions.[5] The parliamentary form of government established in 1993 was sustained in the Presidential and Parliamentary elections of 1996, which the NDC again won. The 1996 elections were crucial; it was the first time Ghana had back-to-back elections and a transfer of power from one civilian regime to another without military intervention. At the end of the 1980s the PNDC had implemented the International Monetary Fund's (IMF) and World Bank's policies called Economic Recovery programme (ERP) and Structural Adjustment programme (SAP), and Ghana had become a success story for the two Bretton Woods institutions in Africa.[6] Since an essential feature of the ERP and SAP is the liberalisation of the economy, Ghanaians entered the 1990s expecting to exercise freedom of choice not only in the market place but also in the political arena under the new Fourth Republic.

New expectations have arisen from the 1992 Constitution, which confers human, civil, political and even trade union rights on Ghanaians for the first time. Some examples are term limits on the Presidency, the right to demonstrate in public against government policies without a cumbersome police licensing process, and the right of individuals in police custody to appear before a judge within 48 hours. Freedom of association for workers is enshrined in the 1992 Constitution. The rapid growth in Ghana's press freedom which is also rooted in the 1992 Constitution is attested to by Ghana's rank as number one in press freedom in Africa and as one of the freest in the world. According to Reporters without Borders, Ghana ranked higher than France, Italy and South Africa in terms of its press freedoms.[7]

4 *West Africa*, 18–24 January 1993: 52–53.

5 Panford (1998), 'Elections and Democratic Transition'; Haynes (1993), 'Sustainable Democracy'.

6 World Bank (1991), 'Ghana: Progress on Adjustment'.

7 *Daily Graphic*, 28 October 2009, 3.

Table 1. Types of Government in Ghana since 1844.

Date	*Name of Regime*	*Type of Regime and Key Labour Trends and Activities*
1844	–	British establish administrative control over the southern Gold Coast.
1901–1904	British Colonial	Colonial rule is formally established. Exploitation of labour and natural resources for British economic development.
1951–1956	British Colonial	Kwame Nkrumah leads the CPP in the transition to independence.
1957–1960	CCP/Nkrumah Government	Parliamentary government. CPP launches an ambitious economic development plan.
1960–1964	CCP/Nkrumah Government	Parliamentary government and Ghana's First Republic.
1964–1965	CCP/Nkrumah	Ghana becomes a one-party socialist state with the TUC as the labour wing.
1966–1969	National Liberation Council (NLC)	First military-police junta, CIA-backed and anti-labour. Military decrees weaken public sector unions.
1969–1972	Progress Party (PP)/ Busia	Second Republic, anti-labour neo-liberal. The TUC is dissolved under a parliamentary Certificate of Urgency
1972–1979	National Redemption Council/Supreme Military Council I & II	Second Military intervention. Moderately left leaning, pro-TUC and pro-labour.
1979	Armed Forces Revolutionary Council/Rawlings	Third Military intervention, lasting just three months. First truly leftist regime that sought to 'cleanse Ghana of corruption' and social decay.

1979–1981	People's National Party (PNP)/Limann	Third Republic. PNP remained relatively inactive in labour sphere.
1981–1992	Provisional National Defence Council/Rawlings	Fourth Military intervention, at first radical. TUC is almost dissolved. After 1986 PNDC accepts western donor conditions that adversely impact workers while protecting the elite.
1992–2000	National Democratic Congress/Rawlings	Fourth Republic that saw the of Rawlings' term at the head of a centrist pro-IMF and World Bank government.
2000–2008	New Patriotic Party (NPP)/Kuffuor	Continuation of Fourth Republic and NDC's neo-liberal policies. Labour Act 2003 weakens TUC and labour movement.
2009–Present	National Democratic Congress/Atta-Mills	New civilian government under the NDC.

The Labour Movement and Politics in Ghana

This chapter assesses the role of the labour movement in Ghanaian politics from 1985 to 2009, when John Kuffour's NPP handed back power to the NDC led by John Atta-Mills. The labour movement is comprised of the seventeen national unions affiliated to the Ghana Trades Union Congress (TUC) (see Table 2), four labour associations and a new union not affiliated with the TUC. This first independent union in Ghana is the Textile, Garment and Leather Employees' Union (TGLEU).[8] The four other labour associations are the Civil Servants' Association of Ghana

8 TEGLEU is the first non-TUC affiliated union certified by the Registrar of Trade Unions to engage in collective bargaining since the promulgation of the 1965 Industrial Relations Act (Information from the Labour Department, Accra, 7 August 1995).

(CSAG), the Ghana National Association of Teachers (GNAT), the Ghana Registered Nurses' Association (GRNA) and the Judicial Services Workers Association of Ghana (JUSAG). These are public sector labour associations.

This chapter describes the activities and impact of Ghana's trade unions in recent efforts to establish democratic governance. As in other African countries, the political transition in Ghana has taken the form of the creation a multi-party parliamentary government. The TUC constitutes our focus because it remains the dominant central labour organisation (although the Ghana Federation of Labour was established in April 1999 as the second labour federation). The TUC represents Ghanaian workers at the ILO and is their leading advocate and main representative on public boards and institutions such as the Social Security and National Insurance Trust, the new National Youth Employment Programme, the Ghana Statistical Services and civil society organisations including Coalition of Domestic Election Observers. Under the Labour Act of 2003 (Act 651), the cornerstone of labour law in Ghana, the TUC continues to wield enormous influence over labour matters due to its roles in the Ghana Labour Commission, the statutory body that oversees national industrial relations.[9] The TUC is represented on this Commission and actively participates in the appointment of the Commission's chair in consultation with others.

Ghanaian industrial relations constitute contested terrain on which the two principal actors, the government of the PNDC and organised labour led by the TUC, pitched their strengths against each other to define and to protect their interests. The government has clearly indicated in numerous actions that it sought to implement IMF and World Bank policies by cutting labour costs to reduce the national budget and to make Ghana a haven for private investment that Western donors had advocated. The Ghanaian labour movement led by the TUC has in varied and significant fashion influenced the course of the nation's recent history. As a typical African trade union whose mode of operation is political unionism, the TUC has not confined its activities and programmes to purely economic matters.

9 Panford (2008), 'Ghana'.

Table 2. Ghana TUC'S 17 Affiliates.

1. Construction and Building Trade Workers' Union
2.* Union of Industry Commerce and Finance (UNICOF)
3. General Agricultural Workers' Union
4. Health Services Workers' Union
5. Local Government Workers' Union
6. Communication Workers' Union
7. Railway Workers' Union
8. Public Services Workers' Union
9. Mine Workers' Union
10. Teachers and Educational Workers' Union
11. Railway Enginemen's Workers' Unions
12. Maritime and Dockworkers' Union
13. National Union of Seamen
14. General Transport, Petroleum and Chemical Workers' Union
15. Ghana Private Roads Transport Union
16. Timber and Woodworkers' Union
17. Public Utility Workers' Union

* UNICOF replaced Industrial and Commercial Workers' Union after the latter broke from the TUC.

Table 3. Ghana TUC Membership (1984–1994).

Year	*Membership*	*Year*	*Membership*
1984	689,491	1990	707,610
1985	635,143	1991	645,472
1986	733,196	1992	551,477
1987	723,818	1993	554,503
1988	594,983	1994	560,978
1989	707,940		

Background and Historical Factors Shaping Political Unionism in Ghana

Although Ghana has been independent for well over 50 years, the role of unions has been deeply influenced by both colonial rule and the nature of the colonial economy. We might add that Ghanaians have failed to change fundamentally the neo-colonialist state to which colonialism gave rise.[10] The British labour relations legacy is substantial and has endured.[11] Examples of the British legacy in terms of the lack of the institutionalisation of trade unionism are numerous. Institutionalisation refers to the use of labour statutes and practices to enhance the growth and effectiveness of workers' associations. It also entails the existence of bona fide workers' organisations that are treated by public authorities and private employers as legitimate social institutions which are allowed to operate freely in the interest of workers. In practice, it would have meant the English allowing unions to grow and being accepted as necessary and socially useful organisations. It also would have meant unions being permitted to operate without administrative impediments and even being able to strike without massive retribution from the state or private employers.

Rather than creating conditions conducive to union growth and stability, as several authors have shown,[12] one crucial outcome of British policies in Ghana (then the Gold Coast) was the emergence of weak unions often threatened with dissolution by the authorities. These emaciated unions faced chronic problems, including but not limited to inadequate funding, membership and leadership. The weak state of unions at the time Ghana gained independence was one of the major factors leading to the turn

10 Panford (1994a), 'Structural Adjustment' and (1996b), 'Evolution of Workers' Rights'; Tetegah (1958), *A New Chapter*; Gray (1981), *Unions and Leaders*; Jeffries (1978), *Class, Power*; Arthiaba and Mbiah (1985), *Half a Century*; and Cowan (1960), *Evolution*.

11 Panford (1988), 'State-Trade Union Relations'; Panford (1994a), 'Structural Adjustment'.

12 Ibid; Ziskind (1987), *Labor Provisions*; ILO (1958), *African Labour Survey*.

toward political unionism. An essential aspect of political unionism is reliance on state power to resolve work-place issues. Hence in the Ghanaian context, the TUC forged numerous alliances with regimes, starting with the CPP even before independence.

The nature of colonialism and especially the under-developed economy inherited from the British also profoundly shaped the economic programmes launched by the first Ghanaian government. Because colonialism impoverished Ghana by imposing an exploitative economy, the Nkrumah government sought to overcome the vestiges of underdevelopment by resorting to 'African Socialism'. Nkrumah stated his desire to accelerate Ghana's development to catch up with other industrialised societies by attempting to develop Ghana at what he called a 'jet propelled' pace.[13] Because Nkrumah and his CPP perceived that Ghana lagged behind other societies in economic development, they sought to play catch up by practising statist socialism.[14] That required using state power to marshal resources that were poured into state-owned commercial and manufacturing enterprises. By the time the CPP was overthrown, Ghana had as many as 600 public commercial concerns that made an assortment of items ranging from cement, steel and shoes to vehicle assembly and an aluminium smelter.

The large state sector has had a lasting impact on the role of unions in politics, as recent developments show. In October 2009 workers of the state-owned Tema Oil Refinery (TOR) hoisted red flags (signs of danger or mourning) because in their view by not procuring adequate supplies of crude oil, the country was creating an acute shortage of vehicle fuel. Upon meeting the President, John Atta-Mills, workers alleged that TOR managers who are NPP supporters may be undermining the new NDC government by creating public disaffection through artificial fuel shortages.[15]

Throughout the history of Ghana's industrial relations, from the colonial to the present time, because the state is the largest employer of wage labour, it has remained extremely sensitive to trade union activities. At the

13 Nkrumah (1971), *Autobiography*; Padmore (1953), *Gold Coast Revolution*.

14 Lofchie (1971), *State of Nations*.

15 *Daily Graphic*, 12 October 2009, 31.

peak of public sector growth, the state employed as many as 70 per cent of those who worked for wages. Hence strikes and demands for higher wages invariably attract the attention of all Ghanaian governments. Threatened industrial action by the Teachers and Educational Workers (TEWU) of the TUC at the end on the first semester of the 2009–2010 academic year demonstrated the relative clout of trade unions in contemporary Ghana. The Ghana government, the Ministry of Education and the nation's six public universities averted a massive interruption of university final examinations and the entire public education system only when the government quickly released funds for salaries owed to workers.[16]

In addition to the state owned sector, the important role of the trade unions in the independence movement led to a close alliance with Nkrumah's CPP from 1951 to 1966. Until the military coup of 1966, the TUC and the CPP engaged in collaborative state-trade union relations under the theme of 'Work and Happiness'. The TUC was designated the Labour Wing of the party. The state benefitted from relatively peaceful industrial relations and the state passed pro-labour laws including the 1958 and 1965 Industrial Relations Acts. Most of the policies of the CPP led to substantial improvements in the social wage in the form of free or heavily subsidised social services – education, health, housing, electricity, water and even transport and hot meals at work. According to Ernest Ako Adjei (Labour Minister under Nkrumah), Joe Fio-Meyer (chair of TUC's executive board and Nkrumah's last Ambassador to China) and John Tettegah (the first TUC General Secretary), the TUC was so powerful that it initiated and drafted both the 1958 and 1965 Industrial Relations Acts which were approved by the President's Cabinet and passed by the Ghanaian Parliament. According to these sources, the CPP's role was limited largely to passing these laws in Parliament.[17]

16 Observation by the author at Cape Coast University, Cape Coast, November 2009; see also *Daily Graphic*, 19 November 2009, 55.

17 Interviews with the author, August–September 1991.

The NLC and PP Eras

After the overthrow of Ghana's socialist and one-party experiment in 1966, relations between the TUC and the two subsequent administrations soured as both the military NLC and its civilian counterpart regime, the PP, feared the TUC would be used by Nkrumah's supporters to subvert them. The TUC operated in a hostile atmosphere as the military sought to control organised labour. One obvious attempt was appointing B.A. Bentum as TUC General Secretary due to his personal ties with a member of the NLC and the Inspector General of Police, J.W.K.Harley. When this and other attempts to bring the TUC under its influence failed, the NLC resorted to outright coercion and for the first time since independence, striking workers were shot or dismissed en masse.[18] The government also passed The Trade Unions (Amendment) Decree 1966 (NLCD 110) with the pretext of enhancing civil servants' freedom of association. In fact the NLC wanted to emasculate unions by allowing public employees to opt out of membership. The NLC and TUC failed to collide head-on only because the former handed over power to a new civilian PP regime in 1969.

Although the PP declared it respected workers' and other civil rights, the labour tensions that emerged by the end of this short-lived government were unmatched.[19] The PP's anxiety over the TUC as the only surviving Nkrumahist institution, the elitism of the party's leadership and its unabashed pro-business biases, its attempts to liberalise the economy under terms imposed by the IMF and World Bank, coupled with labour's opposition to liberalisation – all these factors led to repeated clashes between the TUC and the PP. Confronted with what PP leaders deemed an untenable situation, one in which the TUC literally became 'the unofficial opposition party', the PP resorted to harsh violations of workers' rights. In September 1971, under a Certificate of Urgency, the PP-led Parliament abolished the TUC and declared it an illegal organisation.

18 Arthiabah and Mbiah (1995), *Half a Century*.

19 Ibid; Panford (1994a), 'Structural Adjustment'.

As a result of the second military coup, the dissolution proved temporary. On 13 January 1972 the NRC toppled the PP and re-established the TUC. The labour relations situation under the NRC and SMC were similar to those with the CPP because they were cordial. The TUC regained its stature as the most important workers' organisation in Ghana, and its leaders were once again appointed to the boards of public corporations. The relations were sealed with the appointment of A.M. Issifu, the TUC General Secretary, as an Official Advisor to the Head of State, Col. Acheampong. In reciprocating the kindness of the NRC and SMC, the TUC openly showed unflinching loyalty by supporting the bogus Union Government proposed by Acheampong.[20] The support the TUC gave to both the corrupt and inept NRC and SMC and the failed Union Government concept had devastating effects on the TUC from 1982 to 1985.

In the case of the SMC, for the first time in Ghana, a military administration was successfully overthrown by another. The overthrow of the SMC by the Armed Forces Revolutionary Council (AFRC), led by Flight Lieutenant Jerry Rawlings, led to the 'First Coming of Rawlings' from June 4 to 24 September 1979. This was followed by Limann's PNP being installed as the government of the Third Republic. Incidentally, like its predecessor civilian administration (the PP government) the PNP lasted exactly 27 months when the 'Second Coming of Rawlings' booted it out of power. The PNP's rule was relatively uneventful on the labour front with only one exceptional event – the dismissal of 2,000 Ghana Industrial Holding Corporation employees who stormed the Parliament to protest working conditions.[21]

On 31 December 1981 Rawlings led a small section of the Ghana Armed Forces and some civilians installed a military government, the Provisional National Defence Council (PNDC). The PNDC governed until January

20 Ibid; Union Government was proposed by Acheampong in 1978 under pressure from students, professional bodies and the Catholic and Christian Churches to hand over power to a civilian government. Union Government was perceived as a ploy by Acheampong to cling to power.

21 Yankah (1986), *Trial of J.J Rawlings*.

1993 and handed over power to another Rawlings-led regime, the National Democratic Party (NDC) government. The difference this time was that Rawlings shed his military uniform for civilian clothes.

The TUC's Leadership Crisis of 1982–1985

1982 to 1985 were years of tumult in labour affairs as the TUC and its affiliates faced perilous internal leadership crises which stemmed from several causes. Among these was the failure of the TUC to protect workers during the reign of Acheampong. This regime not only bankrupted the nation's economy and social institutions but also created policies which led to exceptionally high inflation and thereby undermined workers' purchasing power.[22] With the PNDC's declared intent to 'House Clean' all public institutions in order to rid them of corruption, radical labour activists organised as the Association of Local Unions (ALU) seized the TUC's headquarters in Accra and installed their own Interim Management Committee (IMC). ALU declared its intent to democratise the TUC and make it responsive to the needs of workers.[23]

This and other leadership crises paralysed the TUC and other sections of the labour movement at the time when the PNDC began adopting policies which had adverse consequences for workers. Significant among these were the rise of Workers' Defense Committees (WDCs), and the PNDC's decision to negotiate with the IMF and World Bank from April to May 1983. Prior to 1983 Rawlings and his colleagues denounced these two institutions as imperialist, exploitative and irrelevant to Ghana's development.[24]

22 Panford (1994a), 'Structural Adjustment'; Ray (1986), *Ghana, Politics, Economics and Society*; and Pellow and Chazan (1986), *Ghana*.

23 Adu Amankwah (1990), 'The State, Trade Unions and Democracy'.

24 Hutchful (1989), 'From Revolution to Monetarism', explains why the PNDC turned to these international financial institutions for assistance.

Contacts between the PNDC and the Bretton Woods institutions culminated first in an ERP from June 1986 and second, a more potent version, the SAP which continued even after the transition of 1992.

The Rawlings Revolution and Organised Labour

Paradoxically, despite attempts to dismember the TUC, no other government except the Nkrumah regime raised the expectations of workers as much as Rawlings' PNDC. From 1981 to 1985 the PNDC and Rawlings especially, enjoyed considerable support from workers. He was not only charismatic, but he was also perceived as the champion of workers and other socially disadvantaged groups. The PNDC won the sympathy of such groups by inflicting heavy penalties on elites who exceeded price controls for goods and rent. Rawlings often stressed the intentions of the '31st December Revolution' to transform Ghana into a country in which workers' interests were supreme. He assured workers and his supporters that he was prepared to die if his revolution failed.[25]

Workers responded by expressing their loyalty for the PNDC and by demonstrating their support through street marches (called 'demos' in Ghana). In addition they worked voluntarily on a massive scale to clear Accra and other municipalities of rubbish while evacuating cocoa to the ports for export.[26] Rank and file workers expected good relations with the PNDC government, in sharp contrast with the acrimonious relations they had with the NLC and PP. After all, the PNDC touted itself as the protector of the working poor and the disadvantaged in the society.

Workers initially had other reasons to be optimistic about the PNDC. Some factions of the labour movement including ALU and the New Democratic Movement (comprising radical operatives, academics, labour

25 Yankah (1986), *Trial of J.J Rawlings.*

26 Tutu (1994), *Structural Adjustment programmes.*

leaders and lawyers) shared the PNDC's openly anti-colonialist tendencies. Instead of relying on 'imperialist sources of finance,' 'People's Power' was to be harnessed for Ghana's nation-building. Significantly, until 1985, when radical activists were purged from the PNDC, several members of the PNDC and their operatives were individuals closely linked to a left-leaning wing of the labour movement. Some PNDC members held official positions in trade unions. These included Eboe Tawiah and D.S Boateng. The latter as the Principal of Ghana's Labour College and became Ghana's longest-serving labour minister.

The PNDC initially created a new dawn in industrial relations reminiscent in some respects of the Nkrumah, NRC and SMC eras. As Kwakyi has shown, the government openly acknowledged the essential role of labour and created new avenues for their involvement in national policy.[27] In fact, the PNDC took the position that only workers produced the wealth of the nation and therefore deserved better living and working conditions. It appeared from events from 1981 to 1985 that Ghana had entered a radical phase of government-worker relations.

WDCs and the Challenge to the Hegemony of the TUC

An important feature of the PNDC's revolutionary days (especially from 1981 to 1983) was the creation of Workers' Defence Committees (WDCs) by certain revolutionary groups. The spontaneous nature of the WDCs is attested to by the fact that no official decree was passed to establish or to legalise them. They were powerful expressions of discontent with the status quo on the eve of the December 31st coup. They were so radical that they forced the management of some state enterprises to flee.[28]

27 Kwakyi (1988), 'A Study of Social and Political Struggles'.
28 Adu Amankwah (1990), 'The State, Trade Unions and Democracy'.

With the PNDCs tacit approval, WDCs sprouted in public organisations to spearhead a mass-based national movement that sought economic and political democracy. The WDCs focused on workers' participation in management to protect the nation's interest in state-owned-enterprises. The WDCs linked up with the People's Defence Committees (PDC) to launch the National Defence Committee which coordinated revolutionary activities including curbing corruption which became so widespread that a new label – 'Kalabule' – emerged in the Ghanaian lexicon. It meant utter graft and the plunder of public assets for private gain. While the PNDC was encouraging mass-based organisations such as the PDCs and WDCs, relations between the government and the TUC were rapidly deteriorating.[29] Even the forced resignation of Issifu, the General Secretary, in 1982 did not improve relations. From 1982 to 1983, numerous social institutions such as the army, police, judiciary and the TUC, were not spared spontaneous revolutionary actions by WDCs.

The ejection of the TUC's leadership and the imposition of an IMC by PNDC backed-operatives led the TUC and other international labour organisations to file a case at the International Labour Organisation (ILO) against the PNDC. The crux of the complaint was that the WDCs had replaced the TUC in representing workers. The TUC's position was that the WDCs were sanctioned by the state to supplant the TUC. According to one PNDC operative, only the intervention of the ILO and the PNDC's concerns about protests by labour and civil rights groups deterred it from repeating what the PP did – dissolve the TUC.[30]

The intervention of the ILO and a turn of events in Ghana led to the restoration of the TUC in 1985 when it was able to elect freely its own leaders. Moreover, after facing enormous economic problems and repeated attempts to overthrow it by foreign-based dissidents, the PNDC began to tone down its revolutionary rhetoric and abandon various revolutionary activities by April 1983. The WDCs were dissolved and replaced by Committees for the Defence of the Revolution (CDRs) which were tame

29 Arthiabah and Mbiah (1995), *Half a Century*.

30 Yeebo (1991), *Ghana: The Struggle for Popular Power*.

compared to the WDCs and the PDCs. CDR membership was open to chiefs, landlords, lawyers and other elites previously branded reactionary. The abandonment of the original goals of the PNDC and subsequent actions linked to the December 31st Revolution coincided with the launching of what became in over a decade, a much lauded relationship between the PNDC, the IMF and the World Bank. This relationship began in June 1983 when the Rawlings-led PNDC formulated the Economic Recovery Programme (ERP) with many anti-labour components.

The ERP, SAP and the End of the Workers' and Peoples' Revolution

Three events led to the virtual end of the December 31st Revolution of the PNDC.[31] These were bush fires set by farmers and hunters for planting crops and trapping 'bush meat', which led to catastrophic food shortages exacerbated by one of the severest droughts. While the fires were raging, the Nigerian government repatriated over one million Ghanaians back to Ghana. As if these calamities were not enough, from 1982 to 1985 the PNDC was subjected to bloody counter coups by foreign based dissidents. This helps to explain why Rawlings and the PNDC capitulated by reversing its revolutionary stance and turned to the IMF and World Bank.

The PNDC desperately needed financial assistance, and western donors took the opportunity to create political and economic conditions favourable to them. One of the first issues the World Bank and IMF repeatedly requested the PNDC to clarify was the status of private property rights in Ghana. They also urged the government to curb the so-called excesses of revolutionary bodies including the WDCs and PDCs.[32] The PNDC

31 Yankah (1986), *Trial of J.J Rawlings* provides a good summary of PNDC revolution.

32 Hutchful (1989), 'From Revolution to Monetarism'.

thus abandoned its power base in the labour movement and other mass-based organisations.

The ERP contained anti-worker and anti-poor policies such as steepest currency devaluation and trade liberalisation without mechanisms to protect socially disadvantaged groups. Plans of the PNDC to dismiss workers in the public sector in conjunction with unprecedented lay-offs in the private sector (due to the devaluation of the cedi, trade liberalization and the high cost of credit) and the withdrawal of subsidies for many social services resulted in workers and the TUC opposing the PNDC. In fact since 1985, the TUC has not changed its initial rejection of the ERP and its twin, the SAP. Commenting on Ghana's 2007 National Budget, Akwasi Adu Amankwah, the Secretary General of the TUC remarked that, 'The decision by government to end the neo-colonial relationship with the IMF should give meaning to our sovereignty as a society after half a century of independence and Ghana, hopefully, should no longer allow itself to be treated as if it were a corporate entity'.[33]

By 1986, due to the impact of the ERP and the SAP on workers and the poor in Ghana, Rawlings, who used to be affectionately referred to as 'Junior Jesus' or 'J.J' by the masses, had become 'Junior Judas' because they felt he had betrayed them and the December 31st Revolution by implementing IMF and World Bank policies.

The labour pains associated with the ERP and its twin, the SAP, shaped the relations between organised labour and the PNDC and the political roles of trade unions from the mid 1980s to the present. The ERP and SAP severely polluted Ghana's industrial relations climate and deeply influenced even NDC-TUC relation until the NDC was replaced by the NPP government in 2001 (see Table 1). Hence, since 1985 the context in which workers and their representative organisations have operated to defend their interests through political actions and other trade union actions has been influenced by the SAP. That was the case in the 1992 transition to civilian and constitutional government as demonstrated in this study.

33 Adu Amankwah (1990), 'The State, Trade Unions and Democracy', 4.

The Role of Labour in the 1992 Transition to Civilian Governance

Although the TUC resolved at its 1988 congress that it 'found it prudent to distance itself from party politics', it was fully committed to ensuring Ghana's return to civilian rule. According to the TUC's representatives, they chose to be neutral in the 1992 elections by not endorsing or sponsoring candidates because they 'learnt from past experience the adverse implications of direct involvement in partisan politics'. They alluded to the retribution the NLC and PP meted out to the TUC for its Nkrumahist tendencies and how involvement in the Union Government fiasco negatively affected workers. The TUC thus took measures to maintain its neutrality and required officials interested in contesting national elections to resign from the TUC. These measures differed remarkably from what happened in 1979 when the TUC sponsored the Social Democratic Front Party that won only three out of 200 seats in Parliament and lost the Presidential election by a huge margin.

In spite of the resolution and declared intentions to remain above the political fray during the transition, the TUC added its voice to public debates that preceded and led to the 1992 transfer of power from the military PNDC to a civilian NDC. Dennis Vormawor, the first Deputy Secretary General of the TUC articulated precisely why the TUC and other sections of organised labour supported democratic types of regimes and human rights: 'Trade unions ... cherish the observance of fundamental human rights, as by the very nature of work that unions do, they are easy prey to regimes that violate human rights.'[34]

The TUC explicitly set the tone for its participation in Ghanaian politics after the PNDC declared its intentions to allow a transition to non-party politics by declaring its unwillingness to compromise on 'the fundamental right of the people of Ghana to decide democratically on the political system of the nation and by whom they would be governed at all

34 Mayer and Vormamor. (1995), *TUC and Human Rights*.

levels of the structures created'.[35] Therefore, the TUC showed that it was opposed to a system of government that was not multi-party. The TUC restated its earlier position that any new constitution should guarantee all Ghanaians equal participation in all public affairs including significantly, the right to determine the form of government.

In order to achieve its goal of a return to constitutional rule, at its Third Annual Congress in 1988, the TUC urged the PNDC to take measures to recognise 'fundamental democratic rights including the right to free expression and publication of views; the freedom to associate and to assemble around social, economic and political issues'.[36] In addition to asserting the right of Ghanaians to determine the type of government they preferred, the TUC nudged the PNDC to promote conditions to permit the exercise of this crucial right. Specifically the TUC urged the government to stop widespread arbitrariness on the part of PNDC officials and operatives, in particular, security agents; to repeal PNDC Law 4 (Preventive Custody) which allowed indefinite detention and without due process; and to grant a speedy trial or immediate release of prisoners held under PNDC Law 4.

Together with many resolutions it passed, on several occasions, the TUC persisted in demanding that the PNDC should transfer power to an elected regime. In relevant resolutions, policy papers and public pronouncements, the TUC laid out systematically what it considered key ingredients to ensuring democratic rule in Ghana. Prime among these were: respect for the rule of law and fundamental human, civil and political rights, especially, freedom of association, expression, movement, religion and trade union rights; the full separation of powers through the establishment of an independent judiciary buffeted from executive and legislative interference; and all members of the executive and legislative branches of government being elected solely through universal adult suffrage.

35 Ghana TUC (1992), Fourth Quadrennial Congress, Report to the Executive Board.

36 Ghana TUC, Third Quadrennial Congress (1988), to the Executive Board; Fourth Quadrennial Congress (1992), Report to the Executive Board.

The TUC then laid out two steps it considered necessary for a sustainable multi-party system. First, was the creation of a Constituent Assembly to collate public views on the country's political future. Second, in addition to the Constituent Assembly being the sole representative of the will of the people on the nature of future government, the labour federation insisted that the Draft Constitution crafted by the Constituent Assembly should be ratified by a national referendum. The PNDC met the two conditions stipulated. The PNDC created a Consultative Assembly whose draft constitution was approved in a referendum. This was crucial to Ghana's relative success in transitioning from the military PNDC to the civilian. Thus events following the TUC's demands and the subsequent flurry of activities suggest that most of the political objectives of the TUC in relation to the return to civilian rule met. These depict the TUC was effective in championing Ghanaians' political rights.

Many interest groups including the Christian Council, the Catholic Secretariat, the National Union of Ghanaian Students, Recognized Professional Bodies (mostly lawyers, medical doctors and engineers) together with organised labour, led by the TUC, were largely responsible for the PNDC putting in place mechanisms and legislation that led to the successful transition of 1992. These included PNDC Law 253 (Consultative Assembly) of May 1991 which made the Consultative Assembly responsible for drawing up a constitution based on the work of a Committee of Experts. The Consultative Assembly's Draft Constitution led to the presidential and parliamentary elections of 1992.

Representatives of the TUC were instrumental in the successful work of the Consultative Assembly. Using the ten seats allotted to it by the PNDC, labour's representatives took the initiative to facilitate the Assembly's deliberations. It was the first time since the Second Republic that the TUC officially participated in drafting a Ghanaian Constitution. The TUC group, led by the then Secretary General Yankey elaborated effectively during the proceedings of the Assembly its position on the nation's political future.[37] The labour federation utilised its Political Committee, Executive

37 Arthiabah and Mbiah (1995) *Half a Century*.

Board and Political Department to mobilise the views of Ghanaian workers for the Assembly's deliberations.

From 1991 to the time of the transition, through seminars and workshops, sponsored independently or jointly with human rights organisations and the revived District Councils of Labour, the TUC collated the views of workers in the entire nation.[38] Out of the different public fora, the Political Committee of the TUC prepared documents which the TUC's Executive Board submitted to the Consultative Assembly.

Working documents submitted by the TUC facilitated the timely completion of the responsibilities of the Constituent Assembly which allowed the PNDC to meet benchmarks involved in the transition. Two aspects of the transition illustrate further the significant contributions of the TUC. The labour federation's uncompromising views on the formation of political parties and a provision that the Executive should have a maximum of two four-year terms were incorporated into the 1992 Constitution. This is why Rawlings stepped down as head of state after the 2000 elections. Article 66 (2) of Ghana's 1992 Constitution stipulates that: 'A person shall not be elected to hold office as President of Ghana for more than two terms.'

The fact that even though Rawlings and his PNDC were in power and yet promulgated the 1992 Constitution is partly responsible for Ghana's reputation as a beacon of stability in Africa. This particular constitutional provision and Ghana's capacity to hold successful presidential and parliamentary elections which on two occasions led to power being transferred from the government to the opposition party have remained crucial to Ghana being viewed as on its way to one of Africa's full-fledged democracy. Ghana's situation contrasts sharply with conditions in many African countries which are struggling with elections and political instability such as Niger, Cote d'Ivoire, Angola and Guinea.[39]

38 Ghana TUC (1988), Third Quadrennial Congress to the Executive Board; and Fourth Quadrennial Congress (1992), Report to the Executive Board.

39 'Ghana's Democracy Lauded,' *Daily Graphic*, 19 November 2009, 16; 'Trade Unions Call for Strikes in Guinea,' *Daily Graphic*, 12 October, 2009, 5; 'Niger Hits Back at ECOWAS,' *Daily Graphic*, 22 October, 2009, 5 and 'Ghana Condemns Atrocities in Guinea,' Daily Graphic, 1 October, 2009, 3.

Additional proposals submitted by the TUC were incorporated into the 1992 Constitution. Significant among these are: the founding of a Press Commission (a Media Commission, as it is called today) and universal free education to enhance citizens' political participation and national human capital plus the establishment of an autonomous Electoral Commission (EC). With respect to both the Media Commission and the EC, these bodies, especially the autonomy of the latter, have remained essential to Ghana's relatively flourishing democracy.

An Assessment of the Role of the Ghana TUC in Ghana's Transition

Unions fill important social and political voids resulting from no-party or military rule.[40] Ghanaian unions, led by TUC, have substantially fulfilled their potentials by not only demanding a return to civilian rule but also through concrete policy recommendations, facilitated the transition from the military to a civilian government. Thus in word and deed as Gray anticipated, trade unions: 'have made the urban wage worker a part of the debate on national priorities and have served as a channel through which the nation articulates its hope.' They worked with bodies such as the National Union of Ghana Students and Professional Bodies to oppose and nudge the PNDC to hand over power to a constitutional regime.

The TUC has fulfilled crucial roles in not only the transition, but also in other critical economic and political areas such as educating workers and the public about civil, political and economic rights. It also assumed a leading role in the NDC's withdrawal of the unpopular Value Added Tax system in 1995.[41] The political controversy sparked by the failed VAT

40 Gray (1981), *Unions and Leaders*, p. 201.

41 On the NDC's problems leading to the withdrawal of VAT see Panford (1996a), 'IMF/World Bank', and Economist Intelligence Unit (1995), *Ghana: Country Report*.

when it was first introduced is attested to by the fact that it caused Ghana's longest serving Minister of Finance, Kwesi Botchwey to resign.

The significance of the TUC becomes even more apparent when one bears in mind that it has experienced much turbulence and operated in a hostile industrial relations and economic climate due to the ERP and SAP. In spite of these organisational constraints, the TUC launched at a steady pace, many new educational and political initiatives such as seminars, workshops and other public *fora.* An example is District Councils of Labour educating workers and the general public about their civil and political rights. In light of deteriorating living and working conditions, it called for a national forum involving labour, other groups and the government to discuss the future of the economy of Ghana.[42] Other recent trade union challenges include but are not limited to public sector massive downsizing which has severely eroded unions' strong hold which has in turn contributed to diminished finances. It is estimated that the Ghanaian public sector may have shed at least 300,000 jobs within the last two decades.

The accomplishments described in this chapter were made in an industrial relations and political climate tantamount to being under siege. The relatively low profile adopted during the actual presidential and parliamentary elections of 1992 and the declaration of neutrality were not caused by selfish organisational reasons per se but by the necessity to avoid being dragged into highly contentious partisan politics. Also as the TUC indicated to this author, it sought to re-affirm its status as a non-partisan organisation. The latter was to ensure that the TUC preserved its integrity and avoided the backlash experienced after the fall of the CPP and the Acheampong regime. As we have noted, both the NLC and the PP were extremely hostile to the TUC because of its affiliation with the CPP.

As to the question of why it demanded that the PNDC hand over power to a civilian regime, the TUC explained that with a civilian/democratic government, restrictions which the PNDC had imposed on collective bargaining and other trade union activities would be lifted and the rights of the citizen would be fully restored. As D. Vormawor, a Deputy

42 Author's interview with TUC leaders, September, 1995, Accra.

TUC Secretary General put it, civilian or constitutional regimes tend to tolerate collective bargaining and other trade union rights, especially those that involved political rights such as freedom of expression and the right to protest publicly policies unfavourable to labour.[43]

According to the TUC, it has been reaping the benefits of the struggles it waged to press the PNDC to institute Ghana's transition. A representative of the TUC acknowledged that 'civilian rule under the NDC Government improved the situation of workers with respect to collective bargaining' (Ibid). This representative added that the harsh effects of the ERP and SAP have been less since the transition. In the opinion of the TUC, although workers were still reeling from the pains of structural adjustment, they have been able to secure relatively better wages through collective bargaining. Raises in the official minimum wage may support the TUC's position. In 1995 the minimum wage was increased to 1,200 (old) cedis and in April 1996, to 1,700 (old) cedis. In subsequent interviews with the author, the TUC's leadership noted that their relations with the Kufour government were even more cordial than with the NDC under Rawlings as a civilian head of state. Thus developments in the post-transition period have led the TUC's leadership to remark in 1995 that:

> It is relatively optimistic about ... relations with the government. The TUC sees this as a departure from the situation under the PNDC in which policies affecting workers and the nation were unilaterally formulated and implemented ... The TUC believes that as long as the newly-created industrial democracy and harmony are not disrupted, Ghana may continue to enjoy the kind of peaceful industrial relations that has prevailed since 1993.[44]

Besides its optimism concerning Ghana's political future, the TUC expressed the view that it sought to promote 'a permanent constitutional order to foster national integration and social progress. In diverse and concrete ways, the TUC has demonstrated an enduring commitment to the success of constitutional rule.

43 Ibid.

44 Ibid.

The SAP and a Labour Movement under Siege in Ghana

Except the temporary dissolution of the TUC by the PP government, the PNDC's ERP and SAP constitute the most daunting external threat that the Ghana labour movement has faced. The ERP and SAP did not only disrupt the industrial relations climate, but may also have contributed to dwindling trade union membership as illustrated in (Table 2). That in turn, led to rapidly shrinking organisational resources including cash from union dues.[45] The pressure to beef up the TUC's finances could be heightened by Labour Relations Act 2003 (Act 651) abolition both union shop and automatic of union dues check off.

Whatever the intentions attributed to the PNDC and NDC's ERP and SAP, abundant evidence from Ghana indicates that these IMF and World Bank economic packages have contributed one of the longest and most acrimonious government-labour relations in Ghana. With major emphasis on rolling back government expenditure, especially on payroll, social services, and subsidies for petrol and state-owned companies, the ERP and SAP exacerbated relations between workers in general, but the TUC in particular, and the PNDC and NDC from 1983 to 2001 when the NPP assumed power.

One way in which the ERP and SAP contributed to worsening PNDC-TUC relations is that they exerted tremendous pressure on the government to resist demands for increased wages and benefits to counter mega rates of inflation. The latter was due partly to the high interest rates and the declining value of the cedi.[46]

K. Botchwey, the PNDC's Minister of Finance revealed the enormous pressures the two Bretton Woods institutions put on the government to

45 'The TUC's Cash Crisis', *West Africa*, 18–24 October, 1999.

46 The PNDC allowed the selling and buying of foreign currencies by individuals at forex bureaus which were privately owned. This together with other economic factors resulted in Ghana's currency experiencing precipitous falls in value. For example, the cedi's record decline led to a fall of 1,200 cedis to one US dollar in June 1995 to over 1,500 cedis by April 1996.

pre-empt salary increases. He openly stated at a press conference that both the IMF and World Bank expressed concerns about the PNDC yielding to demands for more wages. He added that, increased wages, especially for non management personnel would ruin the economy and derail the economic programmes multi-lateral financial institutions favoured. Thus even the PNDC's leading advocates acknowledged the role the ERP and SAP had in polluting Ghana's industrial relations. Some of the tactics the PNDC used to avert 'the path to economic ruin' included unilateral abrogation of collective bargaining agreements especially, terms on end of service benefits. After failing to use collective bargaining to extract wage concessions, the TUC resorted to a complaint at the ILO accusing the NDC of refusing to pay workers their end of service benefits.[47]

Together with frequent lay off of workers, trade liberalization made unions lose members rapidly. This was particularly the case in the large and union stronghold – the public or state-owned sector. As shown in (Table 3), the TUC lost approximately 40 per cent of its members by 1994. Job losses in the public sector resulted from the PNDC's outright closure, sale of companies or shares in companies owned by the state. In February and March of 1996 this author witnessed in Ghana, the sale of 60 per cent of shares in the nation's premier state owned bank (The Ghana Commercial) to private investors. Another factor inducing unprecedented levels of unemployment is unmitigated and instant trade liberalization. Because the productivity of local enterprises were not boosted before imports were liberalised, Ghanaian enterprises faced stiff foreign competition, closed shop and laid off workers.[48] Besides, high rates of inflation (over 40 per cent to 50 per cent per annum) coupled with rapid decline in the value of the cedi, severely put local industries at a competitive disadvantage. These

47 *Africa Report* (1995), March–April: 39; Panford (2001), *IMF-World Bank and Labor's Burdens in Africa.*

48 Mkandawire (1989), 'Structural Adjustment and De-Industrialization in Africa', shows how ERAs and SAPs led to the de-industrialisation of Africa and Panford (1994b) and (1996) deal with the resulting labour pains under the PNDC. See also Ghana TUC and Friedrich Ebert Foundation (1995), *The Effects of Trade Liberalisation on Industry and Labour in Ghana.*

external threats had a chilling effect on the ability of the TUC to lead workers and to protect them.

An irony of Ghanaian labour history is that just at the time organised labour, should have celebrated its fiftieth anniversary, it faced an almost intractable dilemma. While operating in one of the most hostile environments with membership and revenue losses, more was expected of it in terms of protecting workers.[49] On top of the external threats alluded to, organised labour had to grapple with one more ominous challenge – unprecedented fiercely competitive international economy that thrives on cheap and unorganised labour. Pressure from globalisation has induced governments not excepting Ghana governments to abandon labour practices based on respect for workers' rights.

Challenges Facing the Ghana Labour Movement

There are a number of institutional challenges the TUC and other organised labour groups have to overcome to enhance their legitimacy in future. Firstly, the TUC, GNAT, CSAG, GRNA and the newly-formed JUSAG and Ghana Federation of Labour need to engage in systematic public relations and educational campaigns to make more Ghanaians fully aware of their broad social functions. Currently, most non-labour experts are not aware of the many non-collective bargaining services of unions. This is due in part to the relevant documentation not being circulated widely and not being featured in the popular media. The public's perception is that unions are about strikes and unreasonable demands for wages. It might be asserted rightly that the TUC seems to be on the right path by stepping up publicity of its work in Ghana. These include publications, seminars and other activities some of which have been cited in this study.

49 Alkalimat (1995), 'Note on the Origins of a New Class in Africa'.

Secondly, like most labour groups in the Third World facing high unemployment, Ghana's organised labour has to grapple with the Herculean task of organising large numbers of workers in the informal sector. One national union was on the verge of meeting this unique challenge. The Timber and Wood Workers' Union began in 1995 to organise small-scale chain-saw operators. This programme was launched to assist indigenous and resource-poor operators to survive in an industry dominated by big multinational companies. Successfully organising low-scale operators would not only help to sustain jobs in the informal economy but also yield an additional benefit of preserving local saw-mills. Unions could even enhance their positive impact by ensuring that tree logging practices they promote incorporate steps to preserve Ghana's fast dwindling forests.

A third and a more daunting task is organising more women to raise gender issues in the work place. The unions should resist attempts to use pure public relations with no substance when it comes to gender matters. The TUC appeared poised to demonstrate its commitment to meeting the needs of women by assuring them more leadership roles and decision-making power. The last two decades have brought important changes in women's status as the following developments attest to. The Women's Section of the TUC was revamped into the Women's Desk headed by a Deputy Head of Department.[50] The new Desk was responsible for increasing the percentage and actual numbers of women in leadership positions. It was also mandated to provide services such as crèches (day care centres) to support women and parents. On top of all this, it was made responsible for translating into action one of the TUC's ambitions: 'to educate and offer skills to women members to be more active in their unions, to acquire professional and occupational advancement … communication skills and to overcome the fear of victimisation'.

To demonstrate its commitment to improving the status of women within its ranks and in leadership roles, in January 1991, four Women's Organisers were hired and in March, 1991, they were authorized to organise more women in the various regions of Ghana.

50 Ghana TUC (1992), Fourth Quadrennial Report of the Executive Board.

It may be early to ascertain the impact of the TUC's new initiatives with respect to gender but documents from the labour federation show that even in the short-term, these women's programmes are yielding desired outcomes. The Women's Desk reported that the Garment Workers' Union (GAWU), the Teachers and Educational Workers' Union (TEWU) and Public Service Workers' (PSWU) have women assuming significant leadership positions. These unions for the first time have women as Regional Chairs, Vice Chairs and Trustees. Besides, with the support of the Organisations Department of the TUC, District Councils of Labour in the Accra-Tema area elected five women into important executive positions.

A consensus among current TUC leadership is that more efforts should be made to ensure increased representation of women within the entire trade union movement. For instance, the TUC plan's to implement a new policy to boost by 40 per cent the roles of women in leadership and the activities of its unions and to collaborate with other groups that seek to enhance gender parity in all spheres of Ghanaian life.[51]

As more African nations are thrust into relations with China, the Ghana TUC is taking measures to mitigate the undesired outcomes of the Chinese presence. As part of a network of African trade unions – African Labour Research Network (ALRN) – the Ghana TUC has assessed and recommended policies and actions to shield workers from any adverse effects of businesses operated by new Chinese companies. TUC and ALRN have issued a report that deals with how they the unions are preventing the abuse of workers, especially non-union and temporary labourers employed on two projects financed and managed by Chinese companies in Ghana: The Bui Dam and Sekondi-Takoradi Sports Stadium.[52]

There are a few more newly-emerging challenges that the TUC must face. Two of these emanate from both the 1992 Constitution of Ghana and Labour Relations Act, 651 of 2003. They are closely connected. The first is

51 Ghana TUC (2012), *Policies*, pp. 62–64; 'Three Decades into the Gender Equality Struggles and the Way Forward' (2005), *TUC Policy Bulletin* 1(1): 9–11.

52 'TUC Identifies Human Rights Abuses on Chinese Projects', *Daily Graphic*, 19 November 2009, 46; and TUC/ALRN (2009), *Chinese Investments in Africa*.

trade union plurality. Contrary to their de jure and de facto monopolies over organising workers, the TUC and its affiliates now must compete with other unions and the Ghana Labour Federation. New opportunities to create non-TUC unions have led to conflicts within the labour movement some of which have ended in the law courts. An example is Napoleon Kpoh, the General Secretary of the ICU that broke away from the TUC being jailed for contempt of court in September 2007.There is also the issue that it is now possible to have multiple unions vying to represent workers employed by a single enterprise. Labour Relations Act 2003 has in addition abolished union or closed shop and automatic check off of union dues. The latter has led to the problem of free riding by workers who benefit from unions but do not pay any dues. As Yaw Baah, the TUC's Deputy Secretary General stated: 'Only those who are members of a union pay dues through check off and non-members do not pay although they benefit from union activities. Previously, non-members paid agency fees but that is no longer the case'.[53] In discussing the new quandaries the TUC faces, Baah indicated that the TUC was fully cognizant of the need to organise more workers in the informal sector and also assume a more proactive role in training workers to allow them to compete in a knowledge-intensive global economy but he also pointed out that the unions are torn between meeting the needs of current members and taking on costly widespread and complex skills training.[54]

Lastly, the US Diplomatic Mission to Ghana alludes to how Ghana's 'Labour relations and policies are generally favourable to business.' Clear evidence of this is the High Court's ruling of 18 January, 2008 that an employer can terminate employees without reasons (Ghana High Court, *National Labour Commission v. Ghana Telecom*, 18 January 2008). The TUC protested this as an anti labour ruling which could set new precedence that discards traditional labour practices which could in turn plunge the

53 Correspondence dated 14 January 2007.

54 Observation by the author at Cape Coast University, Cape Coast, November 2009; see also *Daily Graphic*, 19 November 2009.

country into a chaotic labour climate. Although the Court's decision was deemed provocative, the TUC acted calmly by expressing respect for the 'rule of law' under Ghana's new democratic dispensation.

Conclusion

Assessed against a back drop of mounting hostility from the PNDC and the debilitating effects of the ERP and SAP, the TUC has proven to be resilient by not only outliving most institutions established in the Nkrumah era but also rebounded from a leadership paralysis in the 1980s. The TUC has not only been restored, but also even while facing severe constraints, is making steady progress in meeting new and difficult challenges including organising women and informal sector employees and assisting Ghanaian employees of new Chinese companies. An additional exceptional achievement of the TUC is offering trade union protections to workers in the Export Processing Zones in the Accra-Tema industrial area. Usually enterprises and governments seek to exclude workers in such export enclaves from trade union protections and thus subject them to fierce exploitation. The TUC's record of social services, including a positive political role, may have been better had it not faced some serious set-backs.

References

Adu Amankwah, K. (1990) 'The State, Trade Unions and Democracy in Ghana, 1982–1990', MA thesis, The Hague: Institute of Social Studies.

Adu, B. (1995) 'A Note on the Ghanaian Elections', *African Affairs* 94(375): 277–280.

Alkalimat, A. (1995) 'Note on the Origins of a New Class in Africa', unpublished paper.

Arthiabah, P.B and Mbiah, H.T. (1995) *Half a Century of Toil, Troubles and Progress: The History of the Trade Union Congress (1945–1995)*, Accra: Gold-Type Publications.

Cowan, E.A. (1960) *Evolution of Trade Unionism in Ghana*, Accra: TUC Ghana.

Ghana TUC and Friedrich Ebert Foundation (no date) *Policies 2008–2012*.

The Economist Intelligence Unit (1995) 'Ghana: Country Reports'.

Ghana TUC and Friedrich Ebert Foundation (1995) *The Effects of Trade Liberalization on Industry and Labor in Ghana*, Accra: Gold-Type Publications.

Ghana TUC and Friedrich Ebert Foundation (2004) 'Policies of the Ghana Trades Union Congress Adopted at the Seventh Quadrennial Delegates Congress', Kwame Nkrumah University of Science and Technology, Kumasi.

Ghana TUC and Friedrich Ebert Foundation (2005) *Policy Bulletin* 1(1): 9–11.

Ghana TUC and Friedrich Ebert Foundation (2007) *Policy Bulletin* 13(1): 11–18.

Ghana TUC, Friedrich Ebert Foundation and African Labour Research Network (ALRN) (2009) *Chinese Investments in Africa: Opportunity or Threats for Workers?*, Accra: ALRN Secretariat and Ghana TUC Labour Research and Policy Department.

Gray, P. (1981) *Unions and Leaders in Ghana*, New York: Owerri and Conch Publishers.

Gyimah-Boadi, E. (1991) 'Notes on Ghana's Current Transition to Constitutional Rule', *Africa Today* 38(4): 5–17.

Haynes, J. (1993) 'Sustainable Democracy in Ghana? Problems and Prospects', *Third World Quarterly* 14(3): 451–467.

Hutchful, E. (1989) 'From Revolution to Monetarism: The Economics and Politics of Adjustment programme in Ghana' in B.K. Campbell and J. Loxley (eds), *Structural Adjustment in Africa*, New York: St. Martins.

ILO (1985) *Freedom of Association, Digest of Decisions and Principles of the Freedom of Association Committee of the Governing Body of the ILO*, Geneva: ILO.

ILO (1958) *African Labour Survey*, Geneva: ILO.

Jeffries, R. (1978) *Class, Power and Ideology in Ghana: The Railway men of Sekondi*, Cambridge: Cambridge University Press.

Kwakyi, S.K. (1988) 'A Study of Social and Political Struggles in Ghana Since 31st December 1981: A Case Study of TUC and Government Relations', unpublished essay, Legon: University of Ghana, Department of Political Science.

Lofchie, M. (1971) *The State of the Nations: Constraints on Development in Independent Africa*, Berkeley: University of California Press.

Mayer, P. and Vormamor, D. (1995) *TUC and Human Rights*, Accra: Friedrich Ebert Foundation.

Mkandawire, T. (1988) 'Structural Adjustment and De-Industrialization in Africa', *Africa Development* 8(1).

Ninsin, K.(1993) 'Some Problems in Ghana's Transition to Democratic Governance', *Africa Development* 18(2): 5–22.

Nkrumah, K. (1971) *Ghana: The Autobiography of Kwame Nkrumah*, New York: Industrial Publishers.

Oquaye, M. (1995) 'The Ghanaian Elections of 1992: A Dissenting View', *African Affairs* 94(375): 259–275.

Padmore, G. (1953) *The Gold Coast Revolution*, London: Dennis Dobson, London.

Panford, K. (1988) 'State-Trade Union Relations: The Dilemmas of Single Trade Union Systems in Ghana Nigeria', *Labour and Society* 13(1): 37–53.

Panford, K. (1994a) 'Structural Adjustment, the State and Workers in Ghana', *Africa Development* 19(2): 71–95.

Panford, K. (1994b) *African Labor Relations and Workers' Rights: Assessing the Role of the ILO*, Westport, CT: Greenwood Press.

Panford, K. (1996a) 'IMF/World Bank's Structural Adjustment and Labour/ Industrial Relations and Employment in Ghana', in *Towards Active Labor and Employment Policies*, Bremen: African Development Perspective Yearbook, University of Bremen.

Panford, K. (1996b) 'The Evolution of Workers' Rights in Africa: The British Colonial Experience', *International Law Journal* (Boston University) 14: 55–79.

Panford, K. (1998) 'Elections and Democratic Transition in Ghana: 1991–96' in J-G Gros (ed.) *Democratisation in Late Twentieth Century Africa*, Westport CT: Greenwood Press.

Panford, K. (2001) *IMF-World Bank and Labor's Burdens in Africa: Ghana's Experience*, Westport, CT: Praeger.

Panford, K. (2008) 'Ghana' *International Encyclopaedia of Laws*, Alphen aan den Rijin: Kluwer Law International.

Pellow, D and Chazan, N. (1986) *Ghana*, Boulder, Colo: Westview Press.

Ray, D.I. (1986) *Ghana, Politics, Economics and Society*, London: Frances Printer.

Rodney, W. (1982) *How Europe Under-developed Africa*, Washington: Howard University.

Rothchild, D. (ed.) (1991) *Ghana: The Political Economy of Recovery*, Boulder, Colo: Lynne Rienner Publishers.

Tettegah, J.K. (1958) *A New Chapter for Ghana Labour*, Accra: Ghana TUC.

Tutu, K. (1994) *Structural Adjustment programmes and Their Effects on Ghanaian Workers*, Accra: Friedrich Ebert Stiftung.

World Bank (1991) 'Ghana: Progress on Adjustment', Report No. 9475-GH, Washington D.C.: World Bank.

Yankah, K. (1986) *The Trial of J.J Rawlings: Echoes of the 31st December Revolution*, Accra: Ghana Publishing.
Yeebo, Z. (1991) *Ghana: The Struggle for Popular Power*, London: New Beacon.
Ziskind, D. (1987) *Labor Provisions in African Constitutions*, Los Angeles: Litlaw Foundation.

OUSMANE OUMAROU SIDIBÉ

Political Pluralism and the Trade Union Movement in Mali

Introduction

In many respects the Malian trade union movement is typical among French-speaking African nations in its relationship with political parties. This was true during the colonial period and after the 1991 transition pluralist democracy, the events of which trade unions were significantly involved. Although France established the principle of freedom of association in 1884 in French West Africa, it was not until 1920 that Africans with French citizenship (i.e. only citizens of the four municipalities of Senegal) were granted the right to organise trade unions. With a decree on 11 March 1937, the French government extended the provisions of the metropolitan code of trade unions. To be eligible for trade union membership, however, one had to possess a certificate of primary education, and thus the scope of the decree was very limited. The French finally removed this requirement after the Brazzaville Conference (30 January–5 February 1944) and the action of the International Labour Organisation (ILO). The decree of 7 August 1944 at last gave freedom of association to the workers of French West Africa.

Employment policies in French West African work sites were discriminatory and humiliating. Wage rates for the so-called indigenous workers were derisory and subject to heavy taxes and arbitrary levies. It was in response to these conditions that the first trade unions were created in Mali (at that time known as French Soudan). The Soudanese trade union movement became autonomous in 1951, and it developed through its affiliation to metropolitan organisations. This is the case of the Union Régionale des

Syndicats du Soudan Soudanese Regional (URSS), a union confederation established in 1947 and affiliated to the French Confédération Générale du Travail de France (CGT). Subsequently the URSS became the Union Territoriale des Travailleurs du Soudan (UTTS), and then the Union Nationale des Travailleurs du Mali (UNTM) in July 1963. Since 1991, with the establishment of a multiparty political system, the trade union landscape has changed. The new politics has had a significant influence on the practice of freedom of association, and real achievements can be seen in areas where struggles have taken place.

Mali's Trade Union Landscape

The national trade union confederation, the Union Nationale des Travailleurs du Mali (UNTM), consists of twelve national unions. It has always had a very close relationship with the the ruling party, called the Union Soudanaise, Rassemblement Démocratique Africain (USRDA), which had led the country to independence. This UNTM held its meetings in the Parliament with the elected members whose names were on the party list, and who were also members of the government and part of the various joint commissions. Furthermore, leaders could be found in all areas of Malian life, such as cultural associations, public service and the diplomatic corps, who had risen from the ranks of UNTM.

After a 1968 coup d'etat the USRDA regime collapsed and UNTM became the object of harassment. Its officers were arrested and the organisation was temporarily dissolved. Beginning in 1978 its relationship with the new single party system, called the Union Démocratique du Peuple Malien (UDPM), was standardised in a policy framework called 'responsible participation'.[1] In Africa, there has traditionally been cooperation

1 See Dicko, Sidibé, and Touré (1985), *Participation des travailleurs et des organisations syndicales*.

between trade unions and political parties through their leaders. This cooperation developed during the struggles for independence after World War II and continued in many countries for years thereafter. In Mali it was not until the agitations for democracy in 1990 that UNTM ever challenged responsible participation. During the UDPM congress in May 1990 UNTM for the first time questioned this long standing policy, and by March 1991 UNTM was pushing for regime change.

With political democracy came trade union pluralism. The unity imposed through the state-sponsored UNTM gave way to infighting and leadership rivalry on a scale previously unthinkable. Throughout the 1990s, two rival sets of leaders vied for control of UNTM. Such rivalry had never existed in Malian trade union history and it was regarded as a crisis of the highest magnitude. A wide variety of civil actors intervened in an effort to heal the split, including the employers' federation. Several years of failed negotiations led at last to a special unitary congress in August 1997. This, too, failed to bring about unity and ultimately, in December 1997, Hammadoun Guindo of the Syndicat National des Banques and his supporters created the the Confédération Syndicale des Travailleurs du Mali (CSTM). CSTM held its constitutional congress on 27 and 28 April 1998, and it now rivals UNTM in terms of number of affiliates and overall membership, although precise membership figures are unavailable.

The main conclusion that can be drawn from the birth of CSTM is that trade union pluralism in Africa was not based on ideological or strategic differences. Trade union pluralism in Africa typically resulted from personal conflicts, or even conflicts involving personal interest, or lack of democracy within the trade unions. This is also true for African political parties which have also undergone unprecedented growth since the advent of pluralist democracy in the 1990s.

Spaces of freedom were created in Mali after March 1991. Paradoxically, there was a lack of democracy in the functioning of trade unions which promoted the proliferation of independent trade unions that were unaffiliated to either confederation. These independent unions often competed with existing union for the same workers in many sectors. Professional workers in particular felt that the confederations failed to consider the concerns related to their specific occupations. In Mali today the longest strikes have been carried out by independent trade unions. Their mobilisation is facilitated by their relatively small number and keen awareness of their professional interests. Independent trade unions tend to consult with the confederations in order to develop action plans without establishing binding institutional ties. This is particularly the case for the teachers' union, the Fédération de l'Education Nationale (FEN) and the magistrate's union, Syndicat Autonome de la Magistrature (SAM), both of which cooperate with CSTM but do not belong to it.

The most significant trade union issue since the advent of pluralistic democracy in March 1991 has been the development of voluntary and self-help associations. While unions represent the general interest of workers in a defined branch or sector, workers in various occupations who face similar problems have organised themselves and formed associations in order to make their claims heard. One of the first and most effective voluntary associations was that of civil servants seeking early retirement. Their organisation, the Association des Travailleurs Partants Volontaires à la Retraite (ATVR), has a high capacity for mobilisation and its freedom to act is not encumbered by involvement in the big confederations. It has been highly successful in making sure that those who took early retirement from the civil service would enjoy their full pension benefits.

Other successful voluntary associations involving a wide range of workers are the 'victimes du PAS' or the 'victims of structural adjustment programmes' (SAPs). The trade union confederations routinely attribute responsibility for the failures of SAPs to government ineptitude. According to the unions, SAPs are poorly designed and poorly implemented by the government. In trade unions speeches, it is the government, far more than the IMF or World Bank, which is condemned for the dislocation caused by privitisations and labour liberslisation, and for the failure of these programmes to bring about any sustained economic growth in return. UNTM has regularly advocated a comprehensive assessment of privatisation involving all social partners and a renegotiation of ongoing structural adjustment policies carried out in the best interests of the parties involved. Far more effective in coping with dislocation, however, have been the voluntary associations, 'victimes du PAS'. These associations bring suit against corporations and the government for compensation for dismissal, retraining, and the creation of a labour exchange. As a result of many cases brought against it, the government has paid out a considerable amount of money in compensation to workers who have been laid off on economic grounds.

Two decades after the advent of pluralist democracy and trade union pluralism that followed in its wake, and the labour movement finds itself in decline. This is in part because many other forms of voluntary association have been more effective. But it is also due to the fact that current trade unions have often failed to address the problems facing many categories of workers. Labour realities in Africa have fundamentally changed, as they have in the rest of the world, and trade unions have yet to come to grips with the problems which beset the majority, such as chronic underemployment, declining wages, the downsizing of the public sector, the vast expansion of the informal sector, and the high cost of living. Unions must incorporate these new realities in their fighting strategies in order to avoid losing their legitimacy and their memberships.

The Era of Trade Union Pluralism

It is generally acknowledge that in many countries trade union fragmentation and proliferation are often counterproductive and do not always serve the interest of the workers.[2] In 2008 the government of Mali sought a wide ranging discussion of issues with all the social issues in an effort to renew social democracy and establish a pact, the Pacte de Solidarité pour la Croissance et le Développement, committing all partners to a development agenda. The exercise foundered on the continued animosity between UNTM and CSTM. Government efforts to arrange a truce between these

2 On this question in Africa, see Bio (1993), 'La querelle des centrales syndicales'; Barret (1994), 'Trade unions in Nigeria.'

two confederations proved impossible due to the enduring bitter legacy, and it could not assemble all parties for a frank discussion of issues. According to the leaders of CSTM, any international or national attempt to create a consultation framework with UNTM since its creation had failed.

In Mali, having union representation on state agencies has been and contiunues to be very important to the union movement. Unions traditionally have used such representation to influence government decisions at the highest level. Since its inception CSTM has been excluded from such representation, even excluded from consultative meetings of the social partners, and this has been one of the most sensitive issues in the relationship between the government and the unions. From the beginning CSTM has brought grievances to the Labour Ministry about its lack of representation in such agencies as the office of social planning (Institut National de Prévoyance Sociale, INPS), the national employment agency (Agence Nationale pour l'Emploi, ANPE) and the economic, social and cultural council (Conseil Economique Social et Culturel, CESC). The claims of CSTM were rejected by the Labour Ministry because, at the time, most of the advisors and administrators in the ministry were UNTM representatives. Furthermore, in accordance with labour legislation the right of CSTM had to provide proof of its spatial distribution in the country. CSTM argued that the government and the employers' association had the authority to accept its entry to these Boards, against the will of UNTM.

In September 2000 the Malian Labour Ministry suggested to the two confederation secretary-generals that national union elections be held to determine their respective representativeness. However, as could be anticipated, even in the absence of any principled opposition to the idea, the attempt failed due to their persistent rivalry. In the absence of consensus, any attempt to organise these elections was deemed to be doomed to failure. Denied access to governmental boards and social partnership, and denied even the right to prove its representativeness among the workers of Mali, CSTM would do little but complain about its plight to the ILO and international trade unions. Thus, the secretary-general of CSTM submitted a complaint against Malian Government to the ILO for 'systematic violation of the Convention (No. 87) on the freedom of association and protection of right to organise and of the Convention (no 98) on the right to organise and collective bargaining' on 14 February 2001.

Among CSTM's complaints are its exclusion from all joint commissions and tripartite bodies and the lack of rela and permanent frameworks for social dialogue. CSTM also complained that it was denied offices at the state-provided union headquarters, long occupied of course by UNTM. It became obvious soon after the creation of CSTM that the co-existence of two rival confederation headquarters in the same building was problematic. This explains why, one month after its creation, citing article L-252 of the Labour Code on the granting of accommodation to union headquarters, CSTM requested state reiumbursement for all accommodation costs for his headquarters. After several rounds of negotiation, the government in 2004 agreed to assume the rent of CSTM headquarters, as well as to pay the rental arrears from 1998 to 2003.

Furthermore, following a protest made by CSTM regarding the composition of the national delegation sent to the 89th ILO session in Geneva, the ILO declared that it was the 'responsibility of the government to collect reliable information that should enable its assessment of the representativeness of workers' organisations based on sound and objective criteria'. Until such information was collected, the ILO concluded, the government must consult with all worker organisations 'likely to be among the most representative of the country'.

The division between UNTM and CSTM currently remain unresolved and is often to principal subject of discussion in the relationship between the government and the social partners. This is not a problem unique to Mali. Indeed, in francophone Africa, only Benin has definitively solved this question of representiveness through nationwide elections. In other countries trade union organisations have agreed to define criteria or to define unions' representations that are used by consultative bodies. With regards to this issue, the Malians case appears isolated and should be resolved.

Trade Union Legitimacy

The perceived legitimacy of Malian unions in the eyes of workers is difficult to estimate due to lack of an adequate research. During strike orders in a specific sector, there is great mobilisation by all existing unions (across the board) in the specific sector, and this is a prominent feature of the Malian trade union landscape, one which can best be explained by cultural factors. In effect, if a trade union member does not comply with or participate in a strike action, this act is regarded as a form of treason. He is ostracised and could be subject to discrimination which could have a negative impact on his reputation, on his work place relations, and even on his social standing. However, participation in strike action does not necessarily give any legitimacy to trade unions.

Members of trade unions view trade unions leaders with mistrust and suspicion, especially when their leaders prove subservient to administrators (ministers and other heads of services) and to entrepreneurs. It should also be emphasised that African trade unions are not divided along lines of ideology or political party as observed in many Western countries. With the advent of pluralist democracy, because political parties are not based on real ideologies as reflected in the electorate, trade union cannot take ideologically based positions either.[3]

The legitimacy and credibility of the union is often undermined due to a lack of financial autonomy. Malian trade unions often resort to employers (public or private employers) in order to fund some trade unions activities, in particular for training purposes. While between 15 and 57 per cent of the budgets of French trade unions, and between 80 and 90 per cent of trade union budgets in Europe are provided by member contributors,[4]

3 See Akwetey (1994), 'Trade Unions and Democratisation', Muase (1989), *Syndicalisme et Démocratie en Afrique noire*.

4 Report, Raphael Hades-Lebel to the French President of the Republic, May 2006. On the problems of trade union funding see Borenfrend, G. (2008), 'Le financement des syndicats'; and Ray (2008), 'Sur le financement des syndicats'.

trade unions in Mali depend on the financial aid of employers, the government or Western trade unions to conduct most of their activities. Trade unions leaders therefore compete for these subsidies and this competition constitutes a cause of union destabilisation and at times a loss of legitimacy. Another factor of trade union delegitimisation is without doubt the lack of transparency in the management of the small available resources that is observed in many trade unions. Unions in several countries are required by law to maintain strict records of their financial accounts and supervise in a transparent fashion the management of their affairs, but this is not the case in many African countries, including Mali.

In Mali, the State does not provide grants to any trade union organisation, because the national budget does not make provisions of this nature. UNTM which was the single central union until 1998 did receive financial support from government agencies (the INPS and ANPE). When CSTM applied for similar grants, it was denied. The government recognises the problem. This explains why the government pushes for unity within the labour movement and now insists that all grant applications must be addressed directly to the agencies concerned, while expressing its willingness to support and help unions in their training, information, and trade union education missions. The position of the government and that of employers remains potentially discriminatory in that these agencies were theoretically considered to be tripartite, but are exclusively represented by UNTM.

Trade Union Freedoms

Freedom of association is a fundamental public right guaranteed both on the international and national level. On the international level, the 1948 Universal Declaration of Human Rights, and ILO convention No. 87 of 1948 remain the principal documents. The first stipulates that 'any person has the right to associate with others to form trade unions or the right to join trade unions in order to defend their interests' (art. 23 paragraph 4). The ILO convention, which is related to freedom of association and protection of the right to organise, raises three fundamental principles: the right to establish and join organisations of one's own choosing; that public authorities shall not restrict this right; that workers' associations had the right to form federations and confederations, and that these bodies had the right to affiliate with international organisation. On the national level, the Malian labour code stipulates in its article L256 that 'any worker or employer may freely join a union of his choice within the framework of his profession'. The general manager of company or his representatives should not use any means to pressurise in favour or against any trade union organisation'.

Thus, on an individual level, freedom of association is defined as the right of employees to join a trade union of their choice, while collectively it means the right to form unions that operate independently and freely. Therefore in accordance with ILO Convention No. 87, which was ratified in Mali, the creation of trade unions is free and not subjected to any prior administrative authorisation. Unions develop their own staff regulations and procedural guidelines; they freely elect their own representatives freely; they manage their own activities and formulate their own action plans. Public authorities must not engage in any action that is likely to limit these prerogatives or impede the legal exercise of trade union rights. Trade union organisations cannot be dissolved or suspended by administrative means. However, they must respect the law in their activities.

Article L234 of the Malian labour code prescribes that a trade union must submit its statutes and the names of the responsible officers at the district council headquarters where the union is established. A copy of the statutes must be sent to the labour inspector who verifies compliance with the law. Although criticised by CSTM this provision does not appear to be against the spirit of ILO convention no. 87, which stipulates that the creation of trade unions should not be subjected to any administration authorisation.

Article L257 of the labour code prohibits discrimination of any employee on the ground of his trade union activities or his membership to any trade union. The involvement of workers in trade union activities should not influenced any decisions with regards to the hiring, the performing and the distribution of work tasks, vocational training, promotion, remuneration and the granting of social benefits, disciplinary measures, etc. Furthermore, company managers or their representatives must not use any form of pressure in favour or against trade union delegates because of their affiliation to trade union organisations. A breach of the provision of article L257 by any employer will be deemed improper and give rise to damages, including fines and /or imprisonment of one to four months.

When considering the law, the proliferation of trade union organisations and the extraordinary development of voluntary associations, it is clear that since the advent of democracy in March 1991, the obstacles to the formation and establishment of trade unions at the national level have been insignificant. Protecting the right to organise has also led to an unprecedented increase in labour conflicts both in firms and in the public service sector since the advent of democracy in March 1991. The proliferation of associations for the purpose to defending the rights of workers and the adoption in 1992 of a new labour code which made conciliation optional has meant that the labour courts have become overwhelmed with labour disputes. In the public sector in particular, but also for the private sector in general, most of the conflicts remained unsolved. Workers who are faced with increasing poverty, misery and the concentration of wealth in the hands of a few of individuals have made ever more and increasingly radicalised claims in the labour courts.

One of the weak points of trade unionism in French African countries in general and Malian trade unionism in particular is that claims are usually based on wages, and very little attention is paid to conditions of work. Currently in Africa, the use of temporary, casual labour intended to reduce the cost of staffing has reached alarming levels with little counter action from the unions. Casual labour considerably reduces overall labour cost because the company does not pay benefits that are guaranted to those on permanent employment contracts. Furthermore, potential labour conflicts are more easily avoided because these workers can be summarily dismissed. Considerable corporate wealth has been extracted from casual labour in French-speaking Africa. Unions have by large ignored this growing category of worker, who are the most vulnerable, often the least educated, and who feel unable to to challenge power employers or their own. The lack of support for casual workers within the labour community is undoubtedly one reason why trade unions currently lack legitimacy.

In contrast, there is invariably a great deal of mobilisation when the union representatives are fighting dismissal. In recent years, following the denunciation made against the dismissals of trade union leaders, various parties (government, employers and trade unions, in this case UNTM and CSTM) have put in place tripartite commissions to discuss and deal with the cases of the alleged violation. Can we say that there is a major trend of unfair dismissals of workers' representatives that aim to silence trade unions activities in companies? What about the respect of the right to strike which remains one of the major aspects of the freedom of association?

The Malian labour code has in place specific rules (Articles L 263, 277 and 281) dealing with the dismissal of workers' representatives. By law these union representatives are described as 'protected employees', and they can only be dismissed by hand written authorisation from the Labour Inspector. It is true that the so-called protected workers may, like all other employees, be dismissed for disciplinary reasons (for 'a real and serious mistake' committed in the course of employment) or on economic grounds (economic difficulties of the company, or technological change), or even for incompetency. Administrative authorisation is thus intended to protect these individuals from unfair dismissals based on their role as workers' representatives. Any protected employee who is subjected to unfair dismissal must be reinstated or the employer faces fines and possible imprisonment.

Despite these legal provisions, UNTM and especially CSTM have often claim that trade union officials are arbitrarily dismissed or transferred, sometimes for taking part in strike actions, or because the firm is undergoing some restructing. Following these persisting complaints, the government, the employers and the unions had organised tripartite commissions in order to investigate. The following paragraphs discuss two current cases involving questions of dismissal, and they serve to highlight some of the present trade union concerns in Mali.

SOMADEX[5] was a subcontractor of the Society of Gold Mines in Morila-Sa. Its workers struck on 5 July 2005 for 72 hours, and they then declared an unlimited strike. The workers demanded the dismissal of three company managers, namely the director of human resources, the financial director and the head of staff services. Subsequent attempts at conciliation by the labour inspector, the commission of local mediation, and the unions (Union Régionale des Travailleurs and the Section Nationale des Travailleurs des Mines) failed one after another. The managing director of SOMADEX ordered a return to work, giving a deadline of 1 August 2005. Failure to return to work, he added, would be considered an act of voluntary resignation on the part of the employee. On 1 August 283 of the 525 workers had returned to work. Letters were sent to the absent 242 workers accepting their resignation, and the company at once sought replacements. During the strike, some workers were guilty of assault. Shots were indeed made by the factory security agents and a local police vehicle was set ablaze. After an investigation carried out by the authorities, suspects were arrested. Has there been obstacle to freedom of association? Were the redundancies abusive and unfair?

The strike aimed to obtain the resignation of decision makers in the company, and it therefore was not regarded as professional in nature thus illegal by the comapny. From an exclusively legal point of view, it is difficult to prove or speculate on any breach of the freedom of association. However, in order to understand the issues behind the strike, an awareness of the poor environment in which mining in carried out in Mali is imperative. These mines are managed by multinationals whose organisational culture has not been adapted to specific conditions in Mali. All the mines operating in Mali have been subjected to strike movements with violence of various magnitudes. Although unfair and illegal dismissal of workers cannot be established, the untimely interventions of the police during strike actions and especially their indirect support to the mining company without any

5 SOMADEX is a subsidiary of Bouygues BTP, responsible for mineral extraction in the mines of Morila.

guarantee of their neutrality is however surprising and questionable.[6] Furthermore, it should be noted that, despite being financially healthy, mining companies frequently carry out dismissals on the ground of economic crisis in other to increase their profits, or they over-exploit the mines in the course of the first five years during which they benefit from tax exemptions.

In 2006, in response to redundancies carried out in March by TRANSRAIL-SA (the company working on the Dakar-Niger railway connecting Dakar to Bamako), two strikes occurred, one in June lasting 48 hours and one in July for 72 hours. Due to a lack of communication between TRANSRAIL-SA management and its workers, company managers dismissed 18 Malian workers, including eight trade unionists. Two representatives of the Senegalese union were also suspended. These layoffs caused significant deterioration in social relations. In order to restore a social climate necessary for the prosperity of TRANSRAIL, a meeting of conciliation with the Malian and Senegal ministers of transport, the company's managers, as well as trade union leaders, was held at Bamako on 18 and 19 September 2006.

At the end of their discussions, the parties agreed to rehire eight workers, who according to the employer had extenuating circumstances. The case of the ten other workers was also reviewed by a tripartite commission (government, UNTM, TRANSRAIL). The dismissed workers and company officials were heard and provided proof of their allegations. Other witness whose testimonies were necessary in order to find out the truth was also interviewed. The Commission found that TRANSRAIL had not respected the procedure provided in the labour code when dismissing the union representatives and the ordinary workers. The labour inspectorate had never recived a request of dismissal from the employer. The Commission therefore concluded that the ten TRANSRAIL workers had been dismissed in violation of the labour code.

6 In a context of austerity and meagre government budgets, mining companies often provide transport to the police.

A far different picture of unfair dismissals would be gleaned if one looked at the informal sector where workers are almost left to themselves, without help from trade unions. In the informal sector, both workers and employers feel from the relevant labour codes. In Mali as elsewhere in Africa few provisions of modern codes infiltrate the informal sector. Martin Kirsch has written that 'each Francophone African country holds a modern legislative tool which is of great value in the field of labour law. Certainly, these tools are not used appropriately in all companies, because although the right to work is generally well applied in large and medium size companies and by those located in urban areas, it is not always applied in the same way in local areas or in small businesses, especially those of a family nature'.[7]

Trade Union Prospects in Mali

Ever since the transition to pluralist democracy in 1991, the Malian trade union movement has been searching a second breath. Trade union fragmentation was one of the first and most notable effects of the new political order. The creation of CSTM as a rival to UNTM dominates discussion in labour circles, and the rivalry between these two confederations has been at best a mixed blessing for the movement as a whole. The creation of powerful independent professional trade unions, in the judiciary, policy and education for example, while adequately serving the needs of the workers in these occupations, has led to a distinct decline in solidarity among working people as a whole. Trade union fragmentation has unfortunately thus far not led to a democratisation of trade union practices. Workers often beome disillusioned by the seemingly endless personal quarrels and selfish games of self interest played by union leaders. Such infighting has little to do with the real concerns of working people and often serves to delegitimize trade unions in the eyes of their members.

7 Kirsch (1979), *Droit du travail en Afrique*, 9.

In an era of labour liberalisation and privitisation, one of the key challenges of the tade union movement is to address the concerns of the new vulnerable classes of workers who have not traditionally been trade union members. Trade unions must act more vigorously in their leadership, training and support of these disadvantaged workers (women, young unemployed graduates, the unemployed, the disabled, and the self-employed in the informal sector). Such workers need to be trained in order to participate effectively in discussions on major national socio-economic problems.

In francophone African countries, social dialogue has been for too long been confined to 'responsible participation'. Although the mechanism by which trade unions gained representation in government agencies, responsible participation largely meant government control of unions and the silencing of demands put forth by working people themelves. Trade unions are only slowly beginning to realise that in an era of political democracy, social dialogue can become far more meaningful. Trade unions have the capacity to become effective social partners, participating fully in decisions that impact the nation as a whole. They must consider social dialogue as a dynamic process of change, as a renewal of labour relations and as a system that enables information, authority and income sharing which takes into account all the parties involved. Social dialogue should be seen in effect as a process of fundamental transformation of labour relations enabling workers to strengthen their influence beyond wages and working conditions.[8]

On 14 August 2001 the government of Mali has concluded with employers and traded unions, as well as some voluntary associations, a solidarity pact for growth and development, le Pacte de Solidarité pour la Croissance et le Développement. The real challenge remains the best way to make this pact more effective and more significant. Although all social partners have more or less agreed on the importance and effectiveness of social dialogue (trade unions and the governments apparently more that

8 On social dialogue, see Kester and Sidibé (1997), *Syndicats Africains*; Kwasi and Kester (1999), *Comment réussir la participation démocratique en Afrique*; and Lorino (1991) 'Être citoyen dans l'entreprise'.

employers), its content has yet to be clearly defined. In order to meet this challenge, four conditions must be met.

First, greater tolerance between trade union confederations (UNTM and CSTM) is essential if labour is to act as a true social partner able to hammer out accords with the government and employers. Second, a new legal framework is necessary to establish formal structures of viable social dialogue and to provide the necessary financial and administrative support to carry on negotiations. Third, trade unions require intensive training to avoid the passivity they often display in social dialogue. Traditional trade union seminars are insufficient; real programmes of trade union education are required if trade unions are to discuss economic conditions and formulate viable alternative proposals during discussions with social partners. Fourth, greater cooperation between trade unions and universities could greatly assist the former in preparations for fruitful social dialogue. In Mali the potential of university research for social dialogue is underexploited. Profound changes are taking place in the labour relations and union have been unable to make their opinion heard and to propose alternatives which take into account the needs of workers. Trade unions must possess a clear vision that addresses workers's concerns with regards to new labour legislation, and collaboration with universities could be beneficial.

References

Akwetey, O.E. (1994) 'Trade Unions and Democratisation: a comparative study of Zambia and Ghana', unpublished PhD thesis, University of Stockholm, 1994.

Barret, J. (1994) 'Trade unions in Nigeria: the temperature is rising', *South Africa Labour Bulletin*, 18(4): 84–88.

Bio, G. (1993) 'La querelle des centrales syndicales profite-t-elle aux travailleurs béninois?', *Forum de la semaine* 114: 9.

Borenfrend, G. (2008) 'Le financement des syndicats sous l'emprise de l'autonomie collective', *Droit Social* 1: 106–112.

Dicko, O., Sidibé, O.O., and Touré, T. (1985) *Participation des travailleurs et des organisations syndicales en tant que stratégie de développement*, Bamako: Fondation Friedrich Hébert/UNTM.

Kester, G. and Sidibé, O.O. (eds) (1997), *Syndicats Africains: A vous maintenant! Pour une démocratie durable*, l'Harmattan.

Kirsch, M. (1979) *Droit du travail en Afrique*, Paris: EDIENA.

Kwasi, A.-A. and Kester, G. (1999) *Comment réussir la participation démocratique en Afrique*, Paris: l'Harmattan.

Lorino, P. (1991) 'Être citoyen dans l'entreprise', *Le Monde Diplomatique*, Septembre.

Muase, C.K. (1989) *Syndicalisme et Démocratie en Afrique noire: L'expérience du Burkina Faso*, Paris: Karthala.

Ray, J.E. (2008) 'Sur le financement des syndicats', *Droit Social* 2: 139–150.

Sidibé, O.O. (1997) 'Le Mali: l'évolution comme gageure', in G. Kester and O.O. Sidibé (eds), *Syndicats Africains: A vous maintenant! Pour une démocratie durable*, l'Harmattan.

Sidibé, O.O. (2005) 'Quels modèles d'inspiration pour le droit du travail malien depuis le Code de 1952?', *Bulletin de droit comparé du travail et de la sécurité sociale*.

AKUA BRITWUM

Trade Unions and the Informal Economy in Ghana

Trade Unions and Informal Employment

The increased informalisation of labour representation presents both challenges and prospects for organised labour.[1] Shrinking formal economy work and expanding informal employment means that trade union claim to representing working people is being seriously contested. Closing what Webster calls 'the representation gap' demands that trade unions develop capacity to articulate the concerns of their informal economy members and devise strategies to pursue these concerns. However, the unique features of informal work act as barriers to the organisational efforts of trade unions.[2] Barriers to trade union organisation of informal economy workers include the extreme heterogeneity of the workforce and the corresponding multifarious forms of labour relations that arise. Informal economy workers are less bound by the known traditions of formal employment and their concerns far removed from issues of collective bargaining.[3] 'Their immediate concerns are related to threat of eviction …, and access to inputs for their productive activities in the form of credit, and market access for their products'. Informal economy workers can be 'individualistic or communalistic in orientation' depending on the nature of their productive activity.[4] Informal economy labour relations do not follow traditional work relations

1 Munck (2002), *Globalization and Labour.*

2 Webster (2005), 'New Forms of Work and the Representational Gap'; Munck (2002), *Globalization and Labour.*

3 Philip (2005), 'Rural Enterprise'; Munck (2002), *Globalization and Labour.*

4 Munck (2002), 117.

within the capitalist production relations. Workers are not in the traditional relations with an identifiable owner of capital. This results in an absence of an identifiable negotiating partner or counterpart.[5] Daily struggle to earn a living is waged more within sites of contestation with government policy and the traditional exploitative social norms and practices.[6] Relations with capitalist exploitative systems appear remote, but all are agreed that the final beneficiary is capital even in its globalised form.[7]

Organising informal economy workers presents opportunities like strengthening union legitimacy as a way of securing better grounding for trade union revitalisation.[8] Some recommendations for realising the benefits of informal economy organisation include a re-conceptualisation of trade unionism as social movement, broadening union constituency and forming alliances with groups outside the traditional fold of unions.[9] Social movement unionism, Munck explains, operates on two assumptions: one that workers have multiple identities and, secondly, that labour politics extends beyond the workplace.[10] These assumptions suggest a serious engagement of the union with informal economy workers. The nature of informal employment incorporates forms of production relations very different from formal employment that has shaped trade union form and structure. Informal economy workers organisation will be meaningful only to the extent that it leads to a restructuring of union and a re-definition of union functions. This will involve an understanding of the informal economy as a production form that embodies relations of exploitation in direct relations with the formal and not as separate.

The traditional focus on trade unions and informal economy workers has been on organisational difficulties in extending union membership. Whether within the informal economy workers or in the nature of their

5 Webster (2005), 'New Forms of Work'.
6 Philip (2005), 'Rural Enterprise'.
7 Colás (2002), *International Civil Society*.
8 Webster (2005), 'New Forms of Work'.
9 Webster (2005); Munck (2002); Von Holdt and Webster (2005), 'Work Restructuring and the Crisis of Social Reproduction'.
10 Munck (2002), 149.

work, what Webster captures as the axes of bargaining discord.[11] Webster's framework for identifying factors constraining and promoting organisation is useful for unions which are considering the task of informal economy organisation.

The Ghana Trade Union Congress (GTUC) and its national unions have organised different forms of informal economy workers with varying degrees of success. However for the GTUC and its national unions that have overcome the barriers of informal economy organisation, the main challenge has been how to maintain their membership in union structures once organised. Informal economy workers have shown an intense interest in union affiliation. However, their membership has produced tensions in existing union structures. Granting union membership in ways that offer meaningful union membership has been a serious challenge to trade unions. This is an area seldom investigated and little is understood about the tensions that informal economy membership imposes on traditional trade union structures. The rest of this study examines the experiences and the accompanying challenges to union internal democracy that have emerged. This study explores the experiences of all the 17 union affiliates of the GTUC as well as the Industrial and Commercial Workers' Union (ICU).

Information was first gathered from national officers about union work in the informal economy. Where they existed informal economy desk officers of the national unions were also interviewed. Once identified the leaders of informal economy groups of the national unions were then interviewed in groups. The interview data was supplemented with information from union documents on the informal economy as well as existing research reports. The findings were later shared with representatives of informal economy groups, trade union leaders and informal economy desk officers in January, 2008. The next section gives an overview of the Ghanaian economy and the place of the informal economy within it.

11 Webster (2005).

The Informal in Ghana's Economy

Ghana's economy can be broken into three main sectors: the formal, rural agriculture and urban informal.[12] The rural and urban informal sectors are dominated by informal employment types and the formal has varying degrees of informalisation as discussed above. Rural and urban informal employment are made up of own account or self-employed workers, independent service providers, waged and non-waged employees. Self-employment dominates the informal economy making up 66 per cent of the working age population. Non-waged employees are either family or household members like wives, children, poor distant relatives or apprentices. The informal economy has been expanding in recent years. In 1991 for example the proportion of the Ghanaian workforce in informal economy was 80 per cent this increased to 86 per cent in 2007.[13] Informal economy also serves as the main employment provider recording a growth rate of 5.6 per cent in 2000, whilst the formal economy grew at one per cent.[14]

Ghana's pre-colonial economy was largely subsistence with local and international trade in agricultural products, gold, salt and cloth.[15] Of course there was also the callous trans-Atlantic human trade in slaves that lasted over four hundred years, whose impact on the development of African countries such as Ghana has yet to be estimated. The existing land tenure system lent itself to support entrepreneurship in cash crop production for export without recourse to plantation production forms. Direct access to free land made plantation agriculture uncompetitive and the production levels within small holding of peasant farmers were able to meet the demands of European industry.[16]

12 Britwum and Martins (2008), 'The Challenge of Globalization, Labor Market Restructuring and Union Democrarcy in Ghana'.

13 Britwum et al. (2006) *Organising Labour in the Informal Economy* A.Y. Baah (2007), *Organising the Informal Economy*.

14 Baah (n.d), 'Trade Unions and Working Conditions in Ghana'.

15 Hymer (1970), 'Economic Forms in Pre-Colonial Ghana'.

16 Ibid.

Colonial rule changed the largely unwaged employment forms. The need for labour to support the colonial system began with the introduction of formal sector employment. These forms of employment were found in the colonial civil service, construction and rail transport, retailing outlets and the extractive mining concerns. Cowan states that in 1952 the colonial service employed 37 per cent of the 250,000 waged labour force and mining 16 per cent.[17] Not all waged forms of employment were formal employment. The emerging urban spaces in towns and mining enclaves served as the location for formal economy workers. Social services like healthcare and education also provided avenues for formal employment. These forms of employment however were limited to few Ghanaians who were mainly men.[18]

Formal employment received a boost after independence (1957–1965) with the adoption of import-substitution industrialisation and 'Africanisation' policies. These translated into the expansion of the civil service, infrastructure and social services such as education and healthcare.[19] The post independence economic policies increased public sector employment by 198 per cent. Over a period of eight years the number of workers employed directly by the state in various positions was 184,000, and grew to 397,000 in the early 1980s.[20] These impressive increases however, were unable to absorb the Ghanaian labour force and informal employment still remained the dominant employment form. The rate of expansion in formal employment suffered a decline with the first military coup that overthrew the Convention People's Party (CPP) regime. The military junta (National Liberation Council) that took over power and its civilian successor, the Progress Party, worked to overturn the economic policies of the CPP and halted the industrialisation and expansion in physical and social infrastructure.[21] Subsequent governments' efforts at reversing this

17 Cowan (1960), *Evolution of Trade Unionism in Ghana.*

18 Ibid.

19 Ibid; ISSER/DPPC (1996), *Women in Public Life in Ghana*, Accra: DFID.

20 Britwum and Martins (2008), 'The Challenge of Globalization, Labor Market Restructuring and Union Democrarcy in Ghana'.

21 Ibid.

trend were submerged by general mismanagement, including corruption that caused the total collapse the Ghanaian economy in the 1970s.[22] The introduction of economic reforms in 1983 set out to entrench the growth of the informal economy as the major employer in Ghana.

Davies' assertion of a base consensus that the 1980 crises inverted the relative structural positions of the formal and informal sectors largely reflects events in Ghana.[23] Ghana was second to Tanzania in terms of the number of pre-reform public enterprises. Ghana had an estimated 300 state owned enterprises in the mid 1980s. By 1991 however, over 200 of these enterprises had been divested.[24] The introduction of World Bank and IMF economic reforms in 1983 led to the expulsion of workers from the public and state owned enterprises, causing a reduction in public sector based formal employment from 397,000 to 156,000 from 1985 to 1991.[25] These workers found refuge in the informal economy. Presently informal employment dominates agriculture, manufacturing, and trade. The loss of formal employment in the 1980s and 1990s caused a sharp fall in union membership by 40 per cent.[26] Out of an estimated workforce of over nine million, 1.5 million are employed in the formal economy. The GTUC covers 350,000. By the mid 1990s union membership representativeness of the Ghanaian worker was severely threatened by the rapid expansion of the informal economy and the contraction of the formal. Unions had to respond and they did. The next section explores the forms of informalisation that the GTUC and the national unions' have had to confront.

22 Ibid; Britwum (2007), *The Ghana Trades Union Congress: Sixty Years of Promoting Workers' Rights*.

23 Davies (2004), 'Planet of Slums: Urban Involution and the Informal Proletariat', *New Left Review* 26.

24 Aryeetey and Goldstein (2000), 'Ghana Social Reform in Africa'.

25 Britwum and Martins (2008); Fine and Boateng (2000), 'Labour and Employment under Structural Adjustment'.

26 Panford (1996), 'The Labor Movement, Politics and Democracy in Ghana (1985–1996)'; Adu-Amankwah and Tutu (1997), 'Ghana: Going Beyond Politics'.

Unions and Informalisation

Workplace and enterprise restructuring have been constant features of the Ghanaian employment scene since economic reform began. Public sector reforms resulting in privatisation and externalisation have been the major precursors (See figure 1). Corporate and employment restructuring take the form of mergers, takeovers, downsizing, sub-contracting or outsourcing. Accompanying enterprise restructuring is labour informalisation through casualisation, and indirect employment which generates short term labour forms like casual, contract, seasonal and temporal workers. Both private and public enterprises meet some of their employment needs through contract employees supplied by employment agents or casual and seasonal workers. In a similar manner both private and public enterprises have carved out peripheral tasks to medium and small scale enterprises through sub-contracting or out sourcing. The main forms of formal sector informalisation causing the erosion of formal employment in Ghana and expanding the informal are captured in figure 1 (p. 204).

Informalisation elongates the production process by carving out tasks to workers who, although serving the production needs of one company, occupy different positions within the production chain. This consequently allows the company to renege on its responsibilities to its workers. The more informalised the employment type the more distant the positioning of workers in relation to the formal enterprise that benefits from the exploitation of their labour. The characteristic features of such employment forms are their precariousness and total absence of employment rights and security. Wages come in the form of piece rates which are sometimes below the national minimum wage of GH¢2.25 (€1 = GH¢1.5) with cases of envelope wages. Workers have no social security or leave, and they work long hours. In the case of contract workers like the Ghana Dock Labour Company, working hours have been submerged by the work contract rule.

Figure 1. Informalising the Formal.

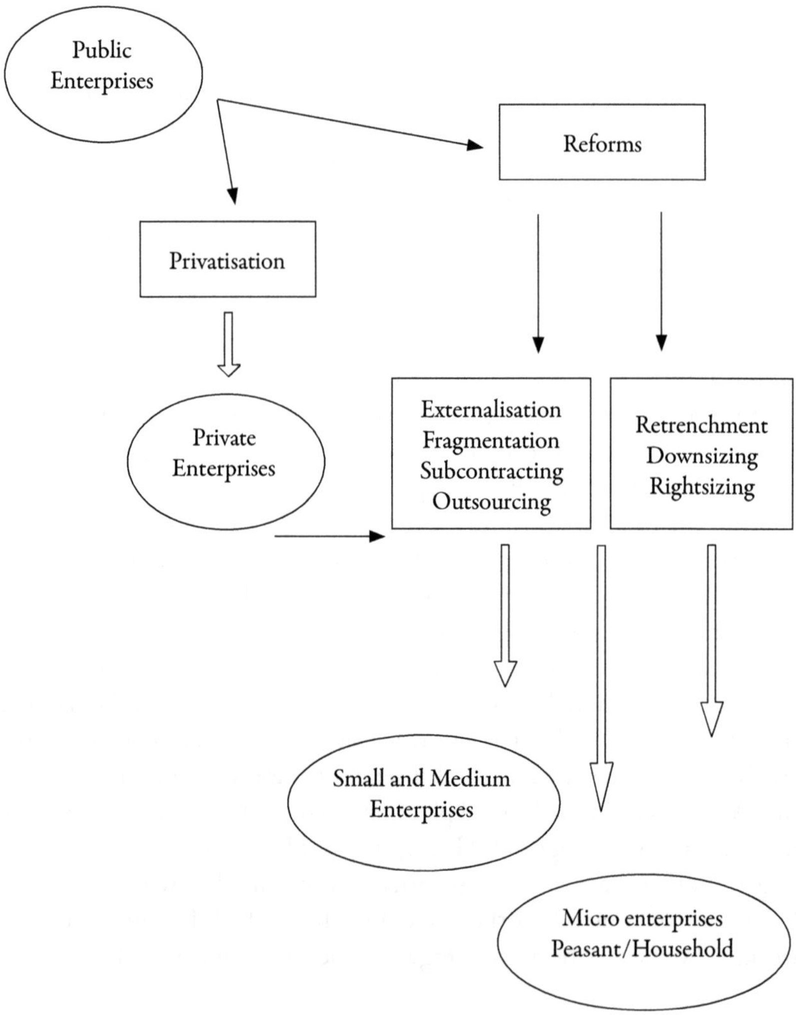

Formal employment informalisation de-concentrates workers by spreading and repositioning them in different forms of aggregation along the elongated production chain. The workplace is re-configured and loses its association with a particular space and a common employer, a key ingredient in building worker solidarity. When spread over a long space in different forms of aggregation diverse interests develop along the production chain. Casuals, temporary and seasonal workers as well as small holders in plantation agriculture have a more direct contact with a common employer even though employment concerns might differ. Contract workers however have more diffused relations with the final beneficiary of their labour. De-concentration and re-positioning workers along an elongated production chain undermines the principles of trade union organisation based on solidarity and mobilisation around a common agenda. Employment informalisation also removes workers from the organising ambit of trade unions impacting union finance. Organising trade union meetings can be frustrating in areas of poor communication and transportation and collecting union dues a near impossibility in a system of envelope wages where the check-off system cannot function.

Work informalisation constitutes new ways of robbing unions of membership and eroding gains in workers' rights thereby cheapening formal economy labour. Trade unions are constrained by the coverage of labour legislation in Ghana which provides coverage for formal employees in permanent employment. This situation reveals government's attitude to informal employment creating the impression that informal employment is less important than formal. In a country where 86 per cent of the working population are in the informal employment the intention of the Labour Act can be called to question. Its legitimacy for promoting the rights of working people in Ghana remains doubtful if only a small fraction can call on its protective powers to secure employment rights. Unions need to address what form to adopt to deal with the challenges posed by the process of informalisation. The changing parameters of work and workplace organisation through informalisation call for a redefinition of the margins of workers' rights and a re-conception of collective bargaining. All stages of production call for some measure of bargaining and workers irrespective of where they are placed in the production chain have to undertake various forms of bargaining. It is in this way that workers' movement can begin to engage securing workers irrespective of where they are located. The GTUC and its national unions are aware of the implications of this trend on union organisation and workers rights. The next section examines the modes of organising, approaches adopted by trade unions to offer union coverage to informal economy workers and the relative strengths and weaknesses of these approaches.

Organising in the Informal Economy

In the late 1990s and early 2000s, the GTUC began more concerted efforts to coordinate the expansion of its affiliates into the informal economy. The 1996 the 5th Quadrennial Delegates' Conference (QDC) of the GTUC adopted a policy to set up a coordinating desk to direct union informal economy organisational work. The Informal Economy Desk situated within the Organisational Department of the GTUC began work in 2000.[27] In August 2004 the 7th QDC adopted a policy to allow more informal economy groups to be directly affiliated to the GTUC as associational members. The GTUC's 4-year policies set the framework for union engagement in the informal economy. National unions are expected to identify and organise informal economy workers that fall within their jurisdiction. Informal economy groups who yearn for union affiliation and have no identified jurisdiction are given direct affiliation to the GTUC first as associational members and later as national unions.

The medium term goals in the latest policy (2004–2008) of the GTUC include extending union coverage to the informal economy and ensuring the

27 Britwum (2007), *The Ghana Trades Union Congress: Sixty Years of Promoting Workers' Rights*.

application of minimum labour standards.[28] Strategies included, developing links with existing informal economy associations, designing programmes and activities to respond to the identified needs of informal workers and encouraging the unorganised to form associations. Other policy strategies were to develop a network of national unions' informal economy Desk Officers and enhance their informal economy organisational skills. A final strategy was to advocate for a National Informal Economy Policy.

In terms of levels of intensity and enthusiasm deployed in organising informal economy workers, national unions of the GTUC fall into six groups. The first group is made up of wholly informal economy unions like the GPRTU, Makola Traders' and Union, Madina Traders' Union. The second group consists of formal economy based unions like the General Agricultural Workers' Union (GAWU), Timber and Woodworkers' Union (TWU), Local Government Workers' Union (LGWU), Public Services Workers' Union (PSWU) and Industrial and Commercial Workers' Unions (ICU) with active engagement with informal economy workers as members. The third group of unions, the Construction and Building Materials Workers' Union (CBMWU), and the Communications Workers' Union have lost contact with groups they previously organised. The fourth, the National Union of Seamen and the General Transport, Petroleum and Chemical Workers' Union are unions whose earlier initiatives at organising in the informal economy failed. The prospecting unions, the fifth group of unions have only identified informal economy groups; they are yet to embark on organisational drive to offer union coverage. These unions, the Maritime and Dockworkers' Union, Health Services Workers' Union and the Public Utility Workers' Union doubt their capacity to effectively provide meaningful union coverage to the informal economy groups that they have identified. The last group the Teachers' and Educational Workers' Union do not have any plans for venturing into the informal economy. Union leaders explained that education in Ghana has no informality and

28 See the GTUC policy document entitled 'Meeting the challenges of the Quadrennial: 2004–2008 – Medium Term Policies of the Ghana Trades Union Congress; August 2004'.

that in addition the demands of their traditional members do not allow the union space to take on informal economy groups.[29]

The GTUC's direct engagement with informal economy workers began with the affiliation of the Ghana Private Road Transport Union (GPRTU) in 1967. The GPRTU, originally the Motor Drivers Union, was set up in 1935 to mobilise private road motor transport operators in the then Gold Coast to regulate their operations and provide a system for social and employment welfare (Britwum, 2007b). It is a distinctive affiliate because its members are a mixture of employers and employees (owners, owner drivers and employee drivers). The main union concern is the viability of the sector not collective bargaining. The focus of the GPRTU underscores Philip's explanation that amongst informal economy groups, enterprise viability tends to override democratic systems of internal organisation (Philip, 2005). Work regulation is achieved through rules and conventions that guide the conduct of drivers and porters at the loading points where members bring their vehicles to pick passengers. The GPRTU had an elaborate system of union guards (a paramilitary organ) who monitored the adherence of drivers to union rules and road traffic regulations. This unit was proscribed by the government of the New Patriotic Party (NPP) in 2001.[30] Membership welfare is served through a fund from which contributions are offered in times of high income need like, marriage, child naming, ill health and bereavement. Various branches operate credit schemes for the vehicle purchases or maintenance. Various forms of retirement or unemployment schemes exist for retired or out-of-work drivers. Variable income levels means that only 15,000 of the 80,000 members of the union regularly pay dues.[31]

Two other informal economy groups affiliated to the GTUC are the Makola Traders Union which was passed on from the Public Services Workers' Union (PSWU) in 2002. The second the Madina Traders' Union formed in 1999 was affiliated to the GTUC in 2005. In August 2008 the

29 Britwum (2007), *Review of GTUC's Work in the Informal Economy.*

30 Interview with National union executive, November 2007.

31 Interview with National union executive, November 2007.

two graduated from associational members to full national union status.[32] These groups operate under conditions very similar to the GPRTU stressing welfare support and regulation of trading practices among members. They are however smaller in comparison to the GPRTU with members only based in Accra, the national capital.

The PSWU was the first formal economy based national union to sign on informal economy members when in 1968 the Lotto Receivers' Union's request for union affiliation was granted. Lotto receivers are contract workers attached to the state Department of National Lotteries who earn as income 30 per cent of the sale of lotto coupons. This affiliation ended in 1996 when the Lotto Receivers' Union broke away from the PSWU. In 1987 PSWU granted the Ghana Union of Photographers' request for affiliation which is still holding. GAWU was the second formal economy based national union to admit informal economy members in 1979. Unlike PSWU the effort was initiated by GAWU prompted by two coinciding national and international factors to organise rural self-employed agricultural workers. Private plantation agriculture began informalising in the 1960s through small holders and out-growers' schemes that enabled the oil palm, rubber and cotton plantations to expand production whilst reducing labour costs. There emerged an expanding group of informal agricultural workers who, though self-employed, retained formalised contractual work relations with the nucleus plantations. The plantations provided agricultural inputs, seedlings, agro-chemicals, equipment and extension services on credit deducting input costs through check-off from payments for crops received from farmers. The determination of produce costs was the prerogative of the plantation companies which used a punitive system of fines and withholding payments for crops supplied to compel farmers to sell their products to them.[33] The flip side the loss of members through retrenchment pushed GAWU to extend coverage to the out-growers and small holders.

The ILO's determination to promote and extend the fundamental rights to organise to all workers subsequently backed by the adoption of

32 See *Ghanaian Times*, 28 August 2008, 'GTUC Admits 4 New Unions'.

33 Britwum et al. (2006), *Organising Labour in the Informal Economy*.

Convention 141 on the organisation of rural workers provided the internal motivation for GAWU. GAWU's enthusiasm for organising rural workers waned in the 1980s and later revived in 1996. Rural self-employed members of GAWU are either community or socio-economic groups of farmers within a given farming community with or without specific relations with a formal enterprise. The second the socio-economic groups, are farmers in special relations with an enterprise like small holders and out-growers or farmers on irrigation schemes. GAWU also covers a wide range of rural self-employed workers like beekeepers, food and fish processors, pito brewers, local soap manufacturers and charcoal burners. The membership profile of GAWU has undergone transformation from a formal worker dominated union to an informal worker dominated membership. In 1980 GAWU's membership was made up of 5 per cent rural self-employed by 2005 this proportion had increased to 53 per cent.[34]

ICU's encounter with the informal economy workers began in 1990 when the leaders of Ghana Hairdressers' and Beauticians' Association (GHABA) asked for affiliation. GHABA, a female dominated trade association of professional hairdressers with a nationwide membership spread, was formed in 1972. In November 2007, only 40 out of its 6,000 members were males.[35] GHABA and Ghana National Association of Barbers and Barbering Saloon Owners (GABBSO), the latter male dominated, formed an umbrella organisation the Ghana Federation for Professional Hair Dressers, Cosmetology and Barbers (GHAFEB) which is dormant owing to the dwindling membership of GABBSO. Other hairdresser groups affiliated to ICU are the Ghana Progressive Hairdressers' and Beauticians' Association, and the United Hairdressers' Association of Ghana. They are splinter groups which emerged during the six-year leadership crisis that plagued GHABA in the late 1990s and early 2000s (ICU-LO/FTF, 2008). The Domestic Workers' Union (DWU), BATMAG, the Bolga Weavers'

34 Britwum (2007), *The Ghana Trades Union Congress: Sixty Years of Promoting Workers' Rights*.

35 Interview with ICU informal economy desk officers and national leadership of GHABA.

Association and the Traditional Caterers' Association are groups that ICU organised after 1999. The informal economy organisation by ICU received a boost from the funding support of the LO/FTF Denmark.

The TWU began organising informal economy workers in 1996 with chain saw operators and later Small-Scale Carpenters (now Woodworkers' Association of Ghana). Other informal economy groups organised by the TWU are wood carvers of the Aburi Industrial Centre and the Cane and Rattan Weavers. The TWU lost its small-scale carpenters, Charcoal Producers of Kintampo, Canoe Carvers and Lumber Sellers members to state policy and micro-credit schemes. The ban on chainsaw ostensibly enacted to protect Ghana's rainforests killed the chain saw operators' association, as members were driven out of job or turned to operate underground. The LGWU began covering informal economy workers in 2001 with the Global Handicraft Association as an affiliate. The second group, the Darkuman Artisans' Association, joined in 2006. Both groups were moved to seek union affiliation under threat of ejection from the local government authorities. Efforts to organise the butchers' group failed when the members split along ethnic lines.

A series of obstacles tend to dampen union enthusiasm for organising informal economy workers despite the recognition of the potential benefit to union strength, credibility and political influence. These include maintaining contact with highly dispersed or iterant workers with no fixed place of work, complicated by jobs insecurity and employer hostility.[36] Organisational work demands funding for meetings, between union organisers and informal economy groups as well as informal economy and union leaders low and irregular income constrain informal economy groups from paying dues to cover investments for their organisation. A significant part of the organisational drives of formal economy unions have been sustained by funding from counterpart European and international trade union partners like the FNV, the ILO, IWF, LO/Norway and LO/Denmark and NGOs like Action Aid Ghana and Business Sector and Advocacy Challenge Fund (BUSAC). Organising enthusiasm has usually

36 Britwum (2007), *Review of GTUC's Work in the Informal Economy*.

been high with regular union activities during the project cycles, follow-up and contact with informal economy groups usually wane on the cessation of project funding. During interview sessions, informal economy group leaders made constant almost nostalgic references to foreign counterparts attached to such funded projects pointing out that regular contact with unions were achieved during such periods.

Other funding related constraints come from NGOs who have monetised support to informal economy workers through investments in social projects and micro credit schemes. In some communities politicians have hi-jacked informal economy groups organised by unions through co-opting their leaders with cash. Such practices create the impression amongst some informal economy workers that contact with formal sector or urban based organisation should provide easy access to money. The inability of unions to deliver cash or worse still demand for dues have served to discourage union affiliation.

Despite these constrains there is adequate enthusiasm for the unionisation of informal economy workers especially on the side of the informal economy workers themselves who initiated union coverage long before the GTUC instituted strategies. Such groups remained vibrant trade union members. The desire to maintain union affiliation by informal economy groups was sometimes unmatched by trade union aspiration to extend union coverage. In such situations the axes of commonalities identified by Webster as constraining unionisation of informal economy workers far outweigh the discordant ones. Discordant factors lie more within the GTUC and its national unions.

Organisational Approaches

The unionisation of informal economy workers have either been through direct incorporation into existing unions through individual recruitment or broadening union jurisdiction. In other instances existing informal economy groups have been granted affiliation to national unions or the union confederation.[37] The approaches adopted have been determined by the nature and levels of intra group organisation within the sub-sector where informal economy workers are based. Where group organisation is strong and intra group regulatory mechanism effective, informal economy associations have themselves initiated trade union affiliation after they had formed their own groups. In Ghana the first two approaches have been the preferred modes for extending unionisation to informal economy based workers. GPRTU the largest informal economy based national union and the oldest to be affiliated to the GTUC as well as the Traders' Unions of Makola and Madina had in place effective internal systems for membership recruitment and organisation prior to union affiliation.

GAWU and TWU to some extent organised informal economy workers through direct recruitment. GAWU recruited individual rural self-employed members through contracted canvassers who mobilise farmers within the community and report on the work of the group once organised. GAWU uses service provisioning such as training and skills development, pre-cooperative, savings and credit schemes, community forestation programmes and agricultural technology as organisational entry points and group maintenance tool. These services are mostly built around programmes like the Right to Work, Sustainable Agricultural and Rural Development Programme and involve trade union education, gender sensitisation, violence against women, and the promotion of children's rights. Groups mobilised around such programmes are considered project partners and later offered union membership.

For ICU, LGWU and PSWU, recruitment is done through the contact person and snowball approach usually facilitated by identifying and training a key person within an existing informal economy group on group mobilisation. The contact person has to convince group members of the benefit of union organisation and persuades the group to seek affiliation. Union officers, usually the Informal Economy Desk Officers and informal economy group leaders, plan for a first meeting with all members of the

37 Ibid; Webster (2005).

group. The first meeting discusses the feasibility of union affiliation, group needs, how union coverage can address such needs and possible challenges. This meeting is used to set up structures for addressing identified needs. Group leaders are given trade union education for strengthening group cohesion and internal democracy.

National unions find the contact person and snowball approach cost effective and time saving. It allows the organisation of large numbers of informal economy workers with little funds over a short time with little effort. Unions do not have to locate dispersed informal economy workers. This approach facilitates easy entry into existing informal economy groups without the need to secure group confidence. Membership expansion remains the responsibility of the group. The contact person approach however tends to restrict interaction between informal economy members and the union to contact persons, a situation which has been exploited in some instances for personal benefit.[38] Organisational strategies appear to influence the nature of membership unions grant informal economy workers generating a crisis of union representation. The specific representational problems and functioning of informal economy members within union structures that emerge from the different forms of recruitment is discussed in the next section.

Representation in Union Structures

Meaningful union membership that fulfils the aspiration of workers depends on avenues for participation in union decision making and procedures for expression of concerns. Strategies for recruiting informal economy workers into trade unions define their union membership and differentiate them from their formal economy based counterparts. The ensuing definition of union membership circumscribes their space within union structures

38 Britwum (2007), *Review of GTUC's Work in the Informal Economy*.

and shapes how unions respond to their needs; or they utilise their union membership to address their concerns. The nature of membership offered is explored in terms of access to union governing structures, the right to hold union office and determinants of union membership and the limits of union membership.

National unions utilise different arrangements to provide informal economy members space within union structures. The ICU, GAWU and the TWU, to some extent, are altering union structures to provide meaningful space for informal economy members. The union constitutions of GAWU and ICU grant informal and formal economy members equal membership. They have representation on the National Executive Boards (NEC) of these unions, attend the union Quadrennial Delegates Conferences (QDC) as full delegates with the right to vote and be elected to union office. These constitutional provisions notwithstanding, no informal economy worker had ever been elected to national office, a few however held union offices in regional and district structures of ICU and GAWU. In fact one area dominated by informal economy members within ICU was the Women's Wing where members of GHABA held positions in the Regional Women's Wing of ICU in Northern Region. TWU limits representation in union governance to the QDC as full delegates informal economy members of TWU have no positions on the NEC that takes day to day decisions in between the four-yearly QDC.

Another area of representation investigated was the type of union activities that informal economy members were engaged in. The major trade union activities that informal economy members were involved in were educational workshops and seminars and May Day parades. Informal economy groups found educational programmes valuable for promoting their businesses. Participation in such programmes, owing to their high costs, was restricted to group leaders and contact persons. For most informal economy members interaction with their unions was reduced to visits by Informal Economy Desk officers or field officers of unions. In one instance (the case of the Aburi Industrial Centre), members, unaware of group affiliation, had assumed that the contact person was participating in the activities of TWU in his own right. It was the field work for this study that unveiled this posturing of the contact person revealing the inherent danger of the contact person approach. GAWU and ICU however have been able to expand participation in educational seminars to larger numbers of their informal economy members giving union officers better contact with informal economy group members beyond contact persons and canvassers.

One factor that limits the membership status of informal economy workers in formal economy based trade unions is the role of dues in qualifying union membership. Finance remains central to union existence, for pursuing union goals, supporting trade union education, paying salaries of union officers and maintaining infrastructure for union administration. Union membership size and mobilisation capacity underscore its presence and are important factors giving it credibility and shoring up its political power. Good financial standing helps to maintain membership and enhance mobilisation capacity. In fact membership expansion has been designed to correct dwindling union finance. The level and regularity with which informal economy workers pay union dues restrain unions from granting them full membership that affords the right to attend union meetings and vote, attend QDC as delegates, elect union officers and most importantly hold union office. Any mode of dues payment that does not measure up to that prescribed for formal employees is considered inadequate to grant full union membership.

Informal economy members are constrained by their low and irregular incomes and the manner in which they access their incomes to pay regular union dues like the formal members whose dues are paid by check-off. Low and irregular incomes mean that it is not feasible to demand dues from some self employed informal economy workers. Where informal economy members are in a position to pay dues, determining levels of dues to pay, the modalities for collecting these dues and whether they pay dues as individuals or as groups are challenges yet to be resolved. Most unions have weak dues collecting mechanisms and are dependent on the check-off system which is convenient for collecting dues from waged employees who earn regular income that is paid through some formalised system. Most informal economy groups have in place some mechanism for collecting dues and levies to finance their various welfare schemes and it is this that trade unions have relied for collecting dues. The preferred strategy is for informal economy groups to pay yearly dues. The size, regularity of dues paid by union members raises issues about nature of union membership to grant informal economy workers, whether as individual members, an affiliate group, as full members or associational members. Failure to resolve this problem cost the PSWU an organised and vibrant informal economy group of 5,000 members. The Lotto Receivers' Union disaffiliated from PSWU in 1996. Its member who stood for national union office during the QDC of the PSWU was disqualified. They objected to size and regularity for paying dues as basis for discriminating membership.

Some informal economy groups questioned the need to pay dues in the light of their dissatisfaction with support offered by their national unions. Others insist that factors such as union numerical size are more important for securing union influence. Being self-employed allows them to participate in demonstrations and parades more than their formal employment based counterparts who require their employers' permission for participation. The time invested in such activities is as important as dues since membership mobilisation gives a positive image of union's political presence. The relative importance of dues and union mobilising capacity remains unresolved. Organising informal economy workers, it appears is not a viable avenue for replenishing dwindling union dues.

Granting full union membership is the first step for true representation next is how union space can be utilised to voice livelihood concerns. The knowledge of their low subscriptions and the nature of their relations with their unions constrain the capacity of informal economy members to utilise union space to further their interests. GAWU and ICU, as mentioned earlier, grant their informal economy members full union membership. This makes them eligible to hold union office and vote on all union decision making structures. This notwithstanding, leaders of some informal economy groups acknowledged that the quality of their participation was compromised by the strain of low subscriptions for union resources. Overwhelmed by the amount of funds unions were spending on training activities, they were hesitant to make further demands that would impose financial obligations. In a situation of low union and dwindling union finances the reminders of their low contributions were several and produced some element of discomfort tempering their demands on unions to pursue their concerns.

The Informal Economy Desk is the organ used by formal based unions to secure the institutional anchoring of informal economy groups headed by an officer who coordinates union relations with its informal economy members. This arrangement impacted the tabling of informal economy members' concerns in union structures. Desk Officers report to their administrative heads who are ex officio members of the NEC. The Informal Economy Desk Officer of the GTUC for example served under the Head of Organisation, an ex officio member of Executive Board, who had additional responsibility for Regional and District Councils of Labour, as well as the Gender and Youth Desks. The concerns of the informal economy members were usually submerged by the heavy responsibilities of the Organisation Department and the absence of vote. The need to set up a special administrative unit also suggested that informal economy members were considered typical trade union members sufficiently mature to pursue their interests within mainstream union structures. The Desks were under resourced and in most cases dependent on the largesse of their foreign partners.

Informal economy members impacted internal dynamism of unions in ways that threatened the grip of formal economy workers on their unions through their superior ability to mobilise intra group solidarity to support members who stand for office. This slowed down processes for granting them access to national union structures and dues served as a useful alibi for preventing informal economy members from changing union power dynamism in unions such as the PSWU. ICU and GAWU had to confront opposition from their formal economy members who opposed the idea of sharing union leadership positions on the burden of informal economy groups on union finance reduced union ability to deliver meaningful services to those who made the largest contribution. There was in addition a resentment of new entrants crowding out 'true' and 'legitimate' union members.

Meaningful representation through trade union membership should be empowering offering informal economy members the occasion to develop and apply their political capacity independently. Service provisioning however, appears to be dampening the spirit of informal economy workers especially rural self-employed community groups to do things for themselves and to place them in a receiving position. Unions seem to rely more on service provisioning to retain their informal economy members away from the lure of cash enticement from foreign funded NGOs and corrupting influence of politicians. Unions are providing occupational inputs like tools, raw materials, skills and entrepreneurial training. The implications of the organisational costs of this method on union finances have already been discussed. It is important here is the diversionary and demobilisation impact when unions allocate to themselves the function of making up for state lapses instead of granting citizens the capacity to make demands on the state to fulfil its responsibilities. GAWU for example usually utilise service provisioning as an organisational entry and group mobilisation tool. However, under the easy availability of foreign funding, unions lose sight of the goal of using service provisioning as mobilising instrument. GAWU's project evaluation documents and regional officers' reports revealed that most group meetings were preoccupied with discussions on credit access, provisioning of infrastructure for day care centres and clinics and income generating activities. One GAWU report laments the lack of capacity for self-help and the dependence on union to supply basic needs.[39]

Despite inadequate representation and inadequate union structures, informal economy groups found that union membership was relevant. The benefits of union affiliation cited included access to a mediator to lead their negotiations with formal authorities. Such groups had identified negotiating partners but felt constrained by their lack of negotiating skills and clout to back their demands. For GHABA, it was the negotiations of modalities collecting taxes and levels of taxes to pay. Global Handicraft Association and Darkuman Traders' Associations joined the LGWU to secure the land on which they traded their wares. Union affiliation strengthened bargaining position with state and local authorities and helped to insulate some groups from harassment and ejection by local government authorities during so-called city beautification or decongestion exercises.

39 Regional industrial relations officers' reports, 1997–1999; End of Project Report, 2003.

The greatest benefit of union affiliation is improved group image and political clout which provides access to previously inaccessible formal institutions like banks and the national pension scheme Social Security and National Insurance Trust (SSNIT). Union affiliation also facilitates access to formal micro credit schemes and raw materials on credit. Trade union education has enhanced group organisation and internal cohesion through alternative avenues to arbitration and conflict resolution. Union affiliation had helped to enhance production by strengthening the rules and adherence to group regulations. GHABA and the Woodworkers' Association used union affiliation to erect platforms for regulating professional practices, standardise apprenticeship training and professional certification. Union affiliation was not only addressing group coherency and internal democracy within informal economy groups but was making the connection between strong group structures and enterprise survival. It is in making this connection that informal economy groups remained eager for continued trade union membership despite the challenges outlined.

Conclusion

The fact that various unions have began to address the question of meaningful representation within union structures suggests some awareness by unions that true representation for informal economy workers in trade unions is important if unions are to benefit from their membership. What remains to unravel is the event that triggers this realisation in unions and factors that serve to motivate unions to address such issues on a continuous basis. It appears that as informal economy membership increases within national unions their ability to impact change in union structures increases as the case of GAWU and ICU show. Separate and independent organisation gives better representation and voice and the experience of the GPRTU as one of the strong national union that is consistent and focused on work related problems of its members is a clear example. But

GPRTU's success is also dependent on the proportion of informal economy workers within the sector from which it draws its members. It is perhaps in this light Makola and Madina Traders' Unions have less influence and political presence than the GPRTU.

The discussions so far have shown that union approach for organising informal economy workers has implications for the demands informal economy group members make on union resources, their confidence, group cohesion and identity, group independence which in turn impact the nature of informal economy representation and ability to voice concerns within union structures. The shortcoming in the organisation of informal economy workers reflects several things. The first is union conceptualisation of the informal economy and its relations with the formal. Inability to grant meaningful representation on union structures and provide equality in institutional anchoring suggests that unions see the informal and formal economies as separate and unrelated. There is also a disconnection in trade union discourse about the links between levels of informalisation within formal employment and informal economy workers and as a result little effort is invested linking the two sites that threaten union existence. These problems account for the choice of strategies that seek to address immediate needs and not the structural economic imbalances that impact informal economy work. The choice of union projects to 'service' informal economy members appear to stay clear off challenging the status quo and getting their members to make demands on the state, or local government to address their needs. As a result the potential benefit of the successes of GTUC and its national affiliates in organising informal economy workers is being submerged by failure to make the connection between what Van Holdt and Webster believe is the solution for true union revitalisation, the ability of trade unions to utilise the energies of core workers based in secure formal economy employment to organise non-core temporary workers and link with informal economy workers at the margins of formal economy.[40]

40 Von Holdt and Webster (2005), 'Work Restructuring and the Crisis of Social Reproduction: A Southern Perspective'.

Organising informal economy workers has pushed unions to redefine their operating terrain both spatially and conceptually. Spatial alterations appear easy to overcome for unions which are actively engaged in organising in the informal economy. The problematic is unions understanding of the link between formal and informal work and the process of work restructuring and how work informalisation provides the link between the two seemingly discrete sectors. Organising informal economy workers should provide the opportunity to address union revitalisation within the political and membership dimension and eventually impact their economic power. Union internal democracy has to provide the means for unions to realise this potential.

References

Adu-Amankwah, K. and Tutu, K. (1997) 'Ghana: Going Beyond Politics' in G. Kester and O.O. Sidibé (eds), *Trade Unions and Sustainable Democracy in Africa*, Aldershot: Ashgate.

Aryeetey, E. and Goldstein, M. (2000) 'Ghana Social Reform in Africa' in N.T. Morales-Gomez and N. Tschirgi (eds), *Reforming Social Policy: Changing Perspectives on Sustainable Human Development*, Dakar: International Development Research Centre.

Baah, A.Y. (2007) *Organising the Informal Economy: Experiences and Lessons from Africa and Asia*, Accra: ICU-LO/FTF-Denmark.

Baah, A.Y. (n.d) 'Trade Unions and Working Conditions in Ghana' unpublished report.

Britwum, A.O. (2000) 'Female Representation and Participation in Trade Unions', in P. Agbesinyale, *Democratic Workers' Participation for Economic and Social Development: The Case of Ghana*, Accra: TUC Ghana/APADEP.

Britwum, A.O. et al. (2006) *Organising Labour in the Informal Economy: The Case of. Rural Agriculture in Ghana*, Accra: Ghana Universities Press.

Britwum, A.O. (2007a) *Review of GTUC's Work in the Informal Economy*, Accra: GTUC-LO/FTF-Denmark.

Britwum, A.O. (2007b) 'The Gender of Trade Union Democratic Participation', in G. Kester, *Trade Unions and Workplace Democracy in Africa*, Aldershot: Ashgate.

Britwum, A.O. (2007c) *The Ghana Trades Union Congress: Sixty Years of Promoting Workers' Rights*, Accra: Ghana Trades Union Congress.

Britwum, A.O. (2008) *Review of ICU's Work in the Informal Economy*, Accra: ICU-LO/FTF-Denmark.

Britwum, A.O. and Martens, P. (2008) 'The Challenge of Globalization, Labor Market Restructuring and Union Democracy in Ghana'. *African Studies Quarterly* 10(2–3).

Colás, A. (2002) *International Civil Society: Social Movements in World Politics*, Cambridge: Polity Press.

Cowan, E.A. (1960) *Evolution of Trade Unionism in Ghana*, Accra: TUC Ghana.

Fine, B. and Boateng, K. (2000) 'Labour and Employment under Structural Adjustment', in E. Aryeeter, J. Harrigan, and M. Nissanke (eds), *Economic Reforms in Ghana: The Miracle and the Mirage*. Accra: Woeli Publishing Services.

Hymer, S.H. (1970) 'Economic Forms in Pre-Colonial Ghana', *The Journal of Economic History* 30(1): 33–50.

Munck, R. (2002) *Globalization and Labour: The New 'Great Transformation'*, London: Zed Books.

Panford, K. (1996) 'The Labor Movement, Politics and Democracy in Ghana (1985–1996)', *Methodological Seminars and Special Studies on Social Movement in Africa*, Dakar: CODESRIA.

Philip, K. (2005) 'Rural Enterprise: Work on the Margins' in E. Webster and K. Von Holdt (eds), *Beyond the Apartheid Workplace: Studies in Transition*, Natal: University of KwaZulu-Natal Press.

Von Holdt, K. and Webster, E. (2005) 'Work Restructuring and the Crisis of Social Reproduction: A Southern Perspective', in E. Webster and K. Von Holdt (eds), *Beyond the Apartheid Workplace: Studies in Transition*, Natal: University of KwaZulu-Natal Press.

Webster, E. (2005) 'New Forms of Work and the Representational Gap: A Durban Case Study', in E. Webster and K. Von Holdt (eds), *Beyond the Apartheid Workplace: Studies in Transition*, Natal: University of KwaZulu-Natal Press.

MOHAMED SALIOU CAMARA

Trade Unions and Politics in Guinea since Independence

Introduction

In February 2007, union-led strikes brought down the cabinet of President Lansana Conté and resulted in the formation of a new, more representative cabinet under a prime minister selected from a short list of technocrats proposed by a coalition of trade union and civil society leaders. Arguably, this was the first time in the country's postcolonial history that a legally and systematically organized mass movement succeeded in imposing the will of the population upon an entrenched autocracy. The mass movement that triggered this 'mini regime change', as Guinean commentators called the dismantling of the cabinet, was in fact the culmination of a long crisis punctuated by several strikes of varied magnitude.

The events of 2007 attracted the attention of Africa and the world, due to the brutality with which the Conté government attempted to suppress the mass uprising and to the perseverance with which the union leadership stood up to the government. And yet, most accounts seem to treat the crisis as a 'Grand Premier' in Guinea's history on the ground that trade unionism had been co-opted under Sékou Touré and marginalised during most of Lansana Conté's reign. In retrospect, one can concur with the authors of such accounts on the premise of their inference but not on the inference itself. Indeed, under the rule of the Democratic Party of Guinea (PDG) trade unionism had been made a social instrument of the party-state, and it was not until the late 1980s that it began to fully reawaken from this long period of political co-optation and marginalisation and started to adjust to the new challenges facing Guinea's labour force.

What has not been sufficiently addressed in the accounts is the historical dimension of the interrelations between trade unionism and the state in conjunction with the development of a discernable Guinean political culture. That is an important gap which historians ought to fill, and the present study seeks to contribute to that endeavour by exploring the historical dynamics of the union-state-society nexus in Guinea's socio-political history since independence.

What caused trade unionism to lose its institutional independence vis-à-vis the Guinean state, despite the fact that the latter's birth owed much to the actions of trade unions during the last decade of colonialism? How did Sékou Touré, a trade unionist turned politician and once among the most influential union leaders in French Africa, justify the political co-optation of trade unions thenceforth turned into one of the institutional organs of the PDG machinery? To what extent is the combination of Marxist unionism, Leninist monopartyism, and a strong Pan-Africanist worldview in Touré's political philosophy responsible for the encroachment on the independence of trade unions in the name of national unity and state sovereignty? What is the driving force behind the renaissance of plural trade unionism under Lansana Conté? In what ways has this renaissance influenced the struggle for political liberalization and good governance in Guinea? These are the central questions addressed in the chapter.

Trade Unionism and the Party-State System under Sékou Touré

At the time of Guinea's independence, Sékou Touré and much of the PDG leadership were deeply involved in the struggle for the establishment of a Pan-African trade union independent of French organizations, including the General Confederation of Labour (CGT). The founding of the General Union of Black Africa's Workers (UGTAN) in January 1957 and the establishment of French Guinea's semi-autonomous government with

Touré as vice president in May 1957 had placed Touré at the epicentre of the collision between trade unionism, party politics, and state centrality. Frederick Cooper contends that the enactment of the *Loi-Cadre* in 1956 and the exacerbation of the so-called autonomist movement in French West African trade unionism in 1957 came as a peculiar and unintended convergence of the two connected but conflicting ways of thinking about colony and metropole.[1] As a result of this, Cooper further argues, the assimilationist model of labour, which the CGT had been advocating, lost its appeal.

Additionally, African politicians were given the opportunity to enter the halls of government, while the labour movement, 'already caught up in the political ambitions of much of its leadership, was not in a position to challenge the administrative decentralization that was the concomitant of political devolution'.[2] In other words, with the balkanisation of French West Africa and the establishment of territorial governments with budgetary powers, the storm of unionist challenges to state administration was no longer the French officials' to weather. It was henceforth the responsibility of the territorial governments to either make concessions or resist demands.[3] More often than not, the newly formed territorial governments resisted the demands of the trade unions, arguing for a united African front to be formed by political parties and unions behind the Loi-Cadre semi-autonomous governments.

Such was the case in Senegal where Mamadou Dia told UGTAN representatives that their grievances were secondary 'compared to the great struggle of the Government to bring about genuine autonomy from France'.[4] In fact, both in Senegal and in Côte d'Ivoire the governments tried to force trade unions to merge into a single national organisation. In both countries, union strikes were severely suppressed in the early independence years.

1 Cooper (1997), 'UGTAN, the Loi-cadre and the Breakup of l'AOF'.

2 Ibid.

3 Ibid.

4 Ibid.

Such was also the case in Guinea where Touré seized every opportunity to remind union leaders that the labour movement was but one front among many in the national liberation struggle and that it would fail in its historical mission unless its action was intimately tied to the broader struggle of the Guinean people for freedom and development. This vision of trade unionism as a part and parcel of Guinea's political struggle was first expressed as the official policy of the PDG in that party's third Congress in January 1958. The vision was enunciated as follows:

> Some trade unions would impose the view that the labour movement is an entity in itself and should be independent of the political movement in its orientation and action. This is wrong ... What we must support, encourage and develop is trade unionism conceived as a means in the service of African progress, while we should overtly combat any trade unionism aimed at dividing Africans among themselves. In so doing we may rest assured that we are true to our programme, in line with the trend of general progress.[5]

The Resolution of the Congress concluded: 'This Congress should put an end, once and for all, to any hesitation or confusion as regards the relationship between the PDG and trade unions; our sub-sections should denounce and openly combat any trade union activities which might jeopardize the completion of our programme for progress'.[6]

This pronouncement calls for a few remarks if the political treatment of trade unionism under the PDG regime is to be adequately understood. Firstly, by January 1958 the PDG had dominated the Territorial Assembly since the elections of November 1956. It had also held executive power since Touré's election to the vice presidency of the Territorial Government Council in May 1957. Therefore, it was no longer the minority party of the early 1950s, the urban-based elite that had been using the dynamic labour movement to build a truly national political base. Secondly, as the secretary-general of the PDG (since 1952) and now the top African political and executive leader of French Guinea, Touré appeared to be positioning his party for a future single-party rule on the ground that only such a

5 Touré (1967), *Doctrine and Methods*, 241.
6 Ibid., 241.

system could ensure national unity and promote development in a newly decolonized nation-state.

To that end, and this is the third remark, the PDG leadership had launched a strategy whereby all spheres of power situated outside the realm of the party were to be either incorporated into the party apparatus or eliminated. Such had been the fate of ethnically-based political organizations in the 1940s and, most remarkably, that of the canton chieftaincies the disbanding of which the PDG had orchestrated in December 1957 with the secret blessing of the French district commanders. By accomplishing this latter manoeuvre the PDG had killed two birds with one stone: eliminating a major obstacle to the party's desire to gain ground in the Futa and Mande regions and seriously undermining its key rivals, the African Bloc of Guinea (BAG) and the Socialist Democracy of Guinea (DSG), whose political base rested upon the aristocratic clout of the Canton chiefs in Futa Jallon.

As regards trade unions in this wider political project, Touré wrote in 1967: 'In its struggle to satisfy the aspirations of the working masses the trade union movement should constantly have regard to the character and nature of the measures adopted by the state for satisfying these aspirations.'[7] He went on to specify: 'These measures should never go against the nation's sovereignty or the fundamental rights of free human being; in fact, any step that would improve welfare, while weakening the bases of the nation's independence and the popular, democratic nature of the regime, would be a dangerous set-back in terms of history.'[8]

It is against this background that the status of trade unionism under the PDG regime ought to be examined, with the understanding that the labour movement was only one of the social strata that the PDG had reengineered into complementary organs of the party-state. The other spheres were the national youth movement, which was organized into the Youth of the African Democratic Revolution (JRDA), and the women's movement, which was organized into the Revolutionary Union of Guinean Women

7 Ibid., 142–143.
8 Ibid., 143.

(URFG). As for the labour movement, it was reconstituted in 1960 into the National Confederation of Guinean Workers (CNTG) from the old Labour Alliance of Guinean Workers (USTG).

While the restructuring of the women's movement and, to a lesser degree, that of the youth movement happened with relative ease (the integration into the JRDA of students residing in France and pro-French countries posed serious problems), the actualisation of a national workers' union proved harder to accomplish. There were many reasons to that. For one thing, not all unions co-opted under the CNTG had given up their determination to fully defend the interests of their constituencies, especially since Guinea's Constitution recognized them the right to do so. As such, those unions constituted what Touré termed 'anarcho-syndicalisme' instigated, in his view, by imperialist powers determined to divide Africa's forces through a multitude of political and unionist affiliations.[9] The most notable of those unions were the Teachers' Union headed by Koumandian Kéita and the African Confederation of Christian Workers (CATC) headed by David Soumah.

A second reason was that Touré had formed a coalition with Diawadou Barry of the BAG and Ibrahima Barry Alias Barry III of the DSG in the last weeks leading to the September 1958 referendum and, as a result, the latter two leaders joined the first government of independent Guinea under the hegemony of Touré's party. This move had angered many leaders and members of the African Reassembly Party (PRA) of which both the BAG and DSG were founding members. In fact, the Touré-Barry-Barry coalition had consecrated the merger of the BAG and DSG into the PDG for the purpose of promoting the 'No' vote which Guineans ended up casting overwhelmingly on 28 September, thereby bringing about Guinea's independence.

This leads us to the third reason, namely the de facto segmentation of UGTAN which Cooper summarizes as follows: 'One of the casualties of the push for political power which UGTAN had encouraged was UGTAN itself: as the territorial governments became the relevant units of political action, it broke (by 1959) into territorial units. The dream of

9 Touré (1963), *La révolution guinéenne*, 272.

African trade union solidarity faded along with it'.[10] Suret-Canale places the deterioration of UGTAN in the context of what he calls the rapid succession of political circumstances in 1958, beginning with General de Gaulle's return to power in France, due to which the UGTAN Congress scheduled for September 1958 was postponed in favour of de Gaulle's constitutional referendum. Then political circumstances changed abruptly with Guinea's advent to independence under Touré, so that when the Congress was finally held in January 1959, it was in the capital of independent Guinea and the leader it elected was now the head of a sovereign state: President Sékou Touré of the Republic of Guinea. It is, therefore, not too surprising that the apotheosis of Touré's plebiscite was short-lived, as Suret-Canale put it: 'the Governments that had come into being as a result of the balkanisation [of the French West Africa Federation] could not tolerate the existence of a Pan-African confederation headed by a foreign head of state considered to be a revolutionary agitator; thus, they put in place, more or less rapidly, "autonomous" national union alliances.'[11] One is inclined to suggest that soon after the Conakry Congress Touré understood that the dream of Pan-West African trade unionism was evaporating and began to focus more forcefully on the reconstitution of Guinea's labour movement under the authority of his party. Another difficulty relating to the creation of one national labour organization was that the still assertive Teachers' Union had ties with the Federation of Black African Students in France (FEANF) which, in turn, was strongly connected throughout French Africa from which Guinea was being increasingly isolated for having rejected the Franco-African Union.

This latter point is of particular relevance because the Teachers' Union was the only national labour organisation that openly challenged the PDG at this delicate juncture of the struggle for political dominance. The event took place in 1961 and entered the PDG lexicon as 'teachers' plot'. Pending further research on this and other 'plots' that goes beyond the unchecked accounts by former PDG members/supporters and former opponents to

10 Cooper (1997), 'UGTAN, the Loi-cadre and the Breakup of l'AOF'.
11 Suret-Canale (2007), 'Les syndicats confédérés (CGT) en AOF'.

the regime, it is fair to infer from the available literature that the confrontation between the PDG and the Teachers' Union began with a perfectly legitimate procedure launched within the boundaries of the Constitution. According to narratives reported by Claude Abou Diakité,[12] Almamy Fodé Sylla,[13] Ibrahima Baba Kaké,[14] Raymond-Marie Tchidimbo,[15] and Mahmoud Bah,[16] the process began with a memorandum to the government from the Union pointing out the inadequate compensation regime under which Guinea's teachers had been working, and demanding a meaningful adjustment of their salaries and benefits. Between April and October 1961, the Teachers' Union leadership and the government exchanged written and verbal communications, including a letter from Koumandian Kéita to Sékou Touré in which union leaders attempted to appeal to Touré's Marxist sense of social justice. Based on this reference to Marxism, Touré labelled the agitation a 'communist plot', accusing the USSR of being behind the widespread student riots which followed the arrests of prominent teachers and union leaders, including Koumandian Kéita, Mamdou Traoré Alias Ray Autra, Djibril Tamsir Niane, and Ibrahima Kaba Bah. The teachers were expeditiously sentenced to long prison terms by the High Court of Justice in November 1961. More arrests followed in Conakry, Kindia, and Labé, including those of leaders of the Civil Servants' Union who had demanded justice for their colleagues.[17]

As a result of these confrontations, the government, having interpreted the events as an attempt to destabilise the regime, moved more decisively to bring all the existing trade unions under the CNTG and to make the latter, once and for all, the third institutional organ of the PDG. Henceforth, as shown on the table opposite, the national labour movement was structured alongside the party-state's bottom-up political organisation, thus effectively integrating industrial labour into the party's apparatus.

12 Diakité (1972), *Guinée enchaînée ou le livre noir de Sékou Touré.*

13 Sylla (1985), *L'itinéraire sanglant.*

14 Kaké (1987), *Sékou Touré le héros et le tyran.*

15 Tchidimbo (1987), *Noviciat d'un évêque.*

16 Bah (1990), *Construire la Guinée après Sékou Touré.*

17 Kaké (1987), *Sékou Touré*, 98–99; Bah (1990), *Construire la Guinée*, 54–55.

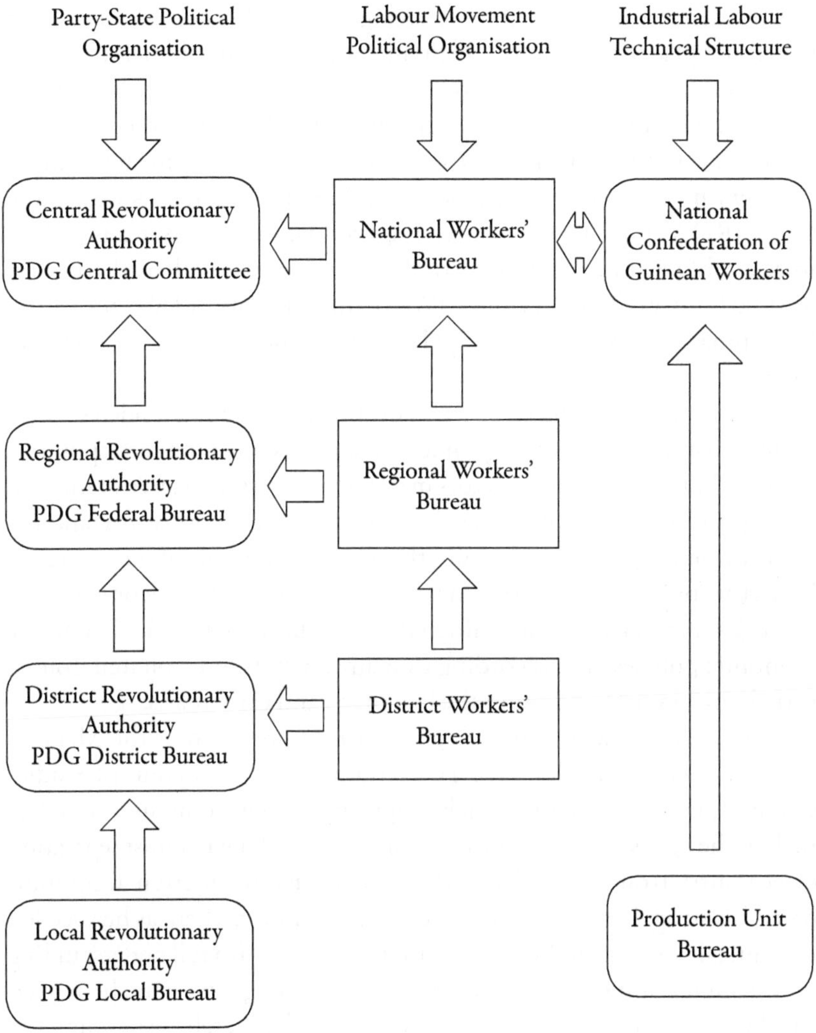
Party-State Political Organisation
Labour Movement Political Organisation
Industrial Labour Technical Structure
Central Revolutionary Authority PDG Central Committee
National Workers' Bureau
National Confederation of Guinean Workers
Regional Revolutionary Authority PDG Federal Bureau
Regional Workers' Bureau
District Revolutionary Authority PDG District Bureau
District Workers' Bureau
Local Revolutionary Authority PDG Local Bureau
Production Unit Bureau

This party-state hierarchy was consolidated during the first decade of independence, the rudiments of it having been established as early as 1957 in lieu and place of the canton chieftaincies and related colonial structures. Through a mechanism known as 'democratic centralism', members of the so-called working class elected their representatives to workers' bureaus at each level of the hierarchy. The top official of each bureau became a statutory member of the corresponding PDG bureau, just as were those of the JRDA and URFG bureaus. The Production Unit Bureaus (CUP) were established in actual industrial establishments such as the ENTA tobacco factory of Conakry, the SIPAR perfume factory of Labé, the Patrice Lumumba Government Printing House, the Sanoyah textile factory, and so on.

The peculiarity of this political-industrial arrangement resided in three points. First, though politically under the supervision of the corresponding workers' bureau, particular sectors maintained a certain degree of internal managerial autonomy. Such was the case of the transport sector, and the market women's guild. Incidentally, the relative autonomy of these particular sectors played a crucial role in the success of the market women's riots of August 1977, an event that inflicted a severe blow on the PDG domestic economic policies and, according to many analysts, precipitated Touré's turnabout toward the West in the late 1970s and early 1980s.

Second, it reflected Touré's peculiar interpretation of the Marxian doctrine of class struggle. Having been trained in the Communist Studies Group (GEC) set up in the French Empire by French Communist intellectuals in the 1940s, the Guinean leader first espoused the Leninist separation of peasantry from industrial workers when such distinction accommodated his struggle for power between 1947 and 1957. Then, as he acceded to political power at the head of the PDG regime with a full understanding of the ability of industrial trade unions to challenge the state, he moved to adopt a Maoist approach to the class struggle, thereby expanding the notion of productive forces beyond the confines of wage-earners. Here, Touré appropriated the Marxist definition of 'working class' as consisting 'of all the forces of production dominated and exploited by the holders of instruments of production; thus, it plays a major rôle (sic) in the nation's economy and the nature of its social relations. This definition covers, besides the industrial workers, the agricultural labourers and the wage-earning categories exploited by a class of employers who are the owners of the instruments of production'.[18] This conception was in perfect harmony with the PDG which, by design, was a mass party akin to the Maoist model.

Third, through this political-industrial arrangement the party-state was able to influence the Guinean labour force in foreign-run industries such as the bauxite mining companies of OFAB/CBG of Boké (dominated by the American HALCO Mining and the Canadian ALCAN), OBK of Kindia (dominated by the Soviets), and FRIGUIA of Fria (dominated by the French Pecheney). The influence that the government managed to wield in these industrial establishments gave the party-state a powerful political and economic leverage in its dealings with the foreign partners operating them. This, in itself was a great deal since the bauxite industry represented about 93 per cent of the country's principal source of national revenue.

The question to be addressed at this point of the discussion is: How did Touré's conception of the interrelation of trade unionism, party politics, and state authority influence Guineans' perception of these three spheres of power, and to what extent has this conception survived his regime? The first portion of the question can be addressed on two levels. In the first place, the implementation of the said conception caused the transformation of the hitherto democratic and powerful labour movement of Guinea – the same force that spearheaded the struggle for emancipation and equality in the turbulent decade post World War II – into an echo chamber for the state. By the same token, the state was reduced to an executive tool for the party whereas the latter was conceptualised as the most authentic embodiment of the people's political will.

On another level, Touré's political philosophy also the political doctrine of the PDG generated a virtual square inside which the relations between government and the governed were profoundly altered, making the political superstructure of democratic centralism a laboratory of mass conformism and personality cult. Because the state was subordinated to the party, Guineans were technically ruled in accordance with the statutes of

18 Touré (1977), *Africa on the Move*, 244.

the PDG more than they were governed in accordance with the country's Constitution. This is to say that party membership took precedence over citizenship. The compact called 'people' was presented as 'the sole legal and legitimate source of revolutionary power' and strategically identified with the party; hence the source of mass conformism. Both the party and the state were identified with Touré in his quadruple capacity of secretary general of the party, head of state, head of government, and Supreme Leader of the Revolution; hence the roots of the cult of the leader. This ideological equation made the question of patriotism and political loyalty a slippery slope: disagreeing with Touré became synonymous with challenging the state; and since that was de facto synonymous with being unfaithful to the party, the line between voicing a constructive disagreement and being labelled counter-revolutionary and enemy of the people was too often blurred.

In retrospect, it is unclear whether this perverse interpretation of dissent was an actual component of Touré's political philosophy or a self-serving anomaly entertained by members of his inner circle. Former members of the PDG establishment have been at variance with one another on this issue. Some argue that it was an anomaly citing instances in which Touré brought into the government individuals known to have harboured resounding dissent toward him personally or toward some of his policies. Such accounts have come from former dignitaries like Galéma Guilavogui,[19] Sikhé Camara,[20] Bobo Dieng,[21] and Baïlo Téliwel Diallo.[22] Other former PDG dignitaries such as Sékou Kaba,[23] Fodé Cissé,[24] Kandas Condé,[25] and

19 Camara (2007), *Le pouvoir politique*, 67–97.

20 Ibid., 165–189.

21 Ibid., 213–236.

22 Ibid., 237–257.

23 Ibid., 192–211.

24 Fodé Cissé was a journalist for the National Radio Network of Guinea. He also served as ambassador, and director of the same network. Interviewed by the author in Conakry (August 1992).

25 Kandas Condé served as member of the CNTG Executive Bureau. Personal communication with the author in Conakry (September 1994).

Fatou Diarra[26] suggested that the de facto intolerance for dissent was both couched in Touré's own conception of power and pushed to the extreme limit by members of his entourage. Both Kaba and Diarra supported this point of view by arguing that intolerance for, and outright suppression of dissent is a universal feature of single-party regimes. Justin Morel Junior[27] and Dorank Assifat Diassény[28] offered more nuanced views arguing that one must distinguish the political behaviour of party-state officials on the ground from Touré's official philosophy of political power as expounded in his speeches and writings.

Each of these views reveals serious flaws in the PDG theory and practice of democratic centralism. The only acceptable scenario of democratic debate in that system was intra-party 'criticism and self-criticism' wherein party members were to resort to collective political introspection in the hope of generating objective and constructive criticism of the workings of the party-state. A daunting problem with this was that although ordinary citizens took advantage of the town halls invariably presided over by President Touré to voice their concerns and ask pointed questions, the only behaviour of party leaders that resembled 'criticism and self-criticism' was their acquiescence to whatever opinions Touré expressed. This, once more, brings the issue of intolerance for dissent to the fore.

It must be added, nevertheless, that due to the political co-optation discussed earlier, the CNTG was actively involved in the formulation of the party-state's labour policies, including those dealing with employment,

26 Fatou Diarra was a businesswoman. She served as ambassador and member of the URFG Executive Bureau. Personal communications in Conakry and Manéyah (May 1994 and February 1995).

27 Justin Morel Junior was a journalist for the National Radio Television of Guinea under Touré. He also served as national director of the network, and minister of Information under Conté, director of Information and Communication for the UNICEF Conakry bureau, and is currently minister of Information under the regime of Captain Moussa Dadis Camara. Interviewed in Conakry (December 1992).

28 Dorank Assifat Diasseny was professor of philosophy at the University of Conakry. He served as national party inspector, and director of the Presidential Press Bureau under Touré. He also served as minister in a number of departments under Conté. Personal communication in Conakry (September 1992, March 1994, and June 1995).

salary, pension, health care, retirement, and so on. Thus, for example, thanks in part to CNTG input, argues El Hadj A.L. Diallo,[29] graduates of Guinea's National University and vocational schools were guaranteed employment by the state. Again, the CNTG was an integral component of the party-state apparatus and its constituents were fully aware of this. Hence, when different segments of the country's labour force paraded behind revolutionary banderols to celebrate Independence Day or the 14th of May (the anniversary of the PDG), they were consciously expressing a adherence to the principles of the party-state and the ideals of its revolution.

Trade Unionism and the Revival of Pluralism in the Post-Sékou Touré Era

The establishment of democratic institutions and a culture of good governance has been the paramount objective of Africa's trade unions and related civil society organisations (CSOs) in the struggles launched in the mid 1980s. Pro-democracy forces across the continent no longer were inclined to accept or appease single-party regimes and military autocracies in the name of preserving national unity. In Guinea, the onset of the struggle required a major turnabout if the negative aspects of the PDG legacy discussed above were to be shaken off and if the intransigency of Conté's military autocracy was to be braved. However, to the extent that it typifies the rhetoric according to which the chaotic socio-political climate created under Conté is a logical outcome of Touré's regime, the notion that the January 2007 strike marked the 'death of Sékou Touré'[30] is a far-fetched

29 El Hadj Abdoulaye Lélouma Diallo is a retired ILO administrator. He also served as ranking CNTG officer, and as Guinea's representative to the Organization of African Labour Unity (OUSA) in Accra, Ghana. Interviewed in Boston (August 2006); personal communications in Geneva (May 2009).

30 McGovern 'Janvier 2007 – Sékou Touré est mort', 125–145.

argument. The notion is, at best, a misleading interpretation of Guinea's recent history and, at worst, a statist view that tends to suggest that the country had been frozen in some twilight abyss.

Nothing is further from the truth. In effect, Conté's military junta came to power under the Military Committee for National Redemption (CMRN) promising to correct the wrongdoings of the Touré regime, hence the term 'Redemption'. Accordingly, in addition to the automatic suspension of the Constitution and the immediate disbanding of the PDG and its mass organizations, the new regime 'rushed to the IMF and World Bank's school of shock therapy hoping to salvage Guinea's ailing national economy with their one-fit-all remedy', indicate Diallo et al.[31] In a speech delivered on 22 December 2009 under a thick cloud of tension and anxiety, President Conté announced a new policy of economic liberalization, the framework of which had been outlined a few months earlier in a program known as 'Interim Plan for National Relief' (PIRN).

The PIRN later proved to be nothing less than the entry point of the infamous Structural Adjustment Programs (SAPs) a full understanding of whose socio-economic effects requires further research. The plan comprised five main components: monetary reform; privatization of the banking and credit institutions; reduction of the civil service personnel; privatization or elimination of state-run companies and promotion of private enterprise, and liberalization of prices and the market. Thus, for instance, the civil service personnel were cut down from 90,300 employees in 1985 to 51,588 in 1990, without a viable plan to ensure a manageable transition for the laid-off employees and their families. Also, the ill-prepared monetary reform from the syli in existence since October 1972 to the Guinean franc and the concomitant stiff devaluation of the new currency, coupled with the failure of similar measures, resulted in a free-fall of the new currency. The Guinean franc (GNF) fell from 335 GNF/USD1 in 1986 to 750 GNF/USD1 in 1990 and to 850 GNF/USD1 in 1992. Unemployment rose incrementally due to the lay-offs and the non-employment of most of the college graduates flocking the job market year after year. With that and

31 Diallo, Dopovogui et Kester, *Guinée*, 18.

the weakening of the purchasing power of those still employed it became increasingly evident to the country's predominantly urban-based blue- and white-collar workers that the regime's promises of '*redressement national*' had become empty slogans.

These developments coincided with the end of the Cold War and the emergence of pro-democratic movements across Africa. Trade unions, student and religious organizations, and the like demanded nothing short of systematic changes in the ways in which their countries had been governed. And it is in this context that the rebirth of pluralism in Guinea's trade unionism must be tackled in order to adequately understand the full historical meaning of the strike of January 2007 and the ones that preceded it.

The new CNTG and the Labour Alliance of Guinean Workers (USTG) that spearheaded the first far-reaching of these strikes in June 2006 epitomize a dialectic process of continuity and change in the political culture of Guinea. The process has marked the country's recent history by posing an unprecedented challenge to the traditionally accepted notion of the unquestioned centrality of the state. It began with the 'return' of the CNTG in 1985, after it had been forced into retreat during the first months of the CMRN regime. The return was sanctioned by Presidential Decree No 231 PRG of 24 September 1984 and put in effect by Decision No 4592/MTFP of 21 December 1984 of the minister of Labour. It was also marked by the resumption, in 1985, of a program called African Program for the Development of Workers Participation (PADEP) in collaboration with the Organisation of African Labour Unity (OUSA), the Federation of Netherlands Trade Unions (FNV), and the Netherlands Institute for Social Studies (ISS). The program was launched in 1981 and during the Pan-African labour conference held in Nairobi in 1982, and subsequent workshops in eleven countries, including Guinea (1983). It has mainly revolved around labour research and education toward democratic participation.[32]

Through this and similar activities the CNTG reinforced and expanded its international affiliations, the sustained development of which had been a focal point for the PDG regime, albeit from an entirely different political

32 Idem, 13–14.

and ideological standpoint. In fact, in the earlier stages of the PADEP (1981–84), the CNTG had closely collaborated with then likeminded labour organisations of socialist countries such as the USSR, Hungary, Bulgaria, Romania, China, Czechoslovakia, East Germany, and so on.

While reinforcing and expanding these affiliations, which will play a pivotal part in the success of the strikes of 2006 and 2007, the new CNTG was by the same token laying the foundation for a new, pluralistic and democratic national trade unionism, without sacrificing the positive organisational aspects of the PDG legacy. One such aspect upon which the new labour movement has capitalized is the organic vertical decentralisation of its national organisations to which has been added a lateral network of professional federations. The number of national federations started up at seventeen in 1985 and stabilised at sixteen in the following years with the federations of National Education, Public Health, Mining, and Rural Development leading the flock in terms of membership and organisational dynamism.[33]

The adoption of a new Constitution consecrating political and media liberalisation in 1990 brought about new possibilities for trade unionism to flourish. However, the economic conditions of the working class kept deteriorating and it was at this crucial juncture that the Conté regime began to feel encroached by the fast-paced political and unionist liberalisation. This was so because both political parties and trade unions had begun to organise and/or support rallies and self-imposed diurnal curfews known as 'opérations ville morte' in efforts to sway the government to relax its rigid concept of state centrality. The regime complicated matters even further by adopting an openly contemptuous attitude toward the political parties and an implicitly exclusionary one toward the unions. On this latter aspect the Conté regime stood in contradistinction with its predecessor: whereas Touré's regime weakened trade unionism through political co-optation, in a perverse way Conté's lent power and freedom to the labour force by ostracising the unions.

33 Ibid, 41–42.

This contradistinction refutes the notion that the actions of the unions in 2006 and 2007 were still aimed at inflicting a last blow on the PDG legacy. It refutes, for instance, the implication which McGovern and others seem to make that Guineans are still stuck in the jaws of the PDG mainly because 'Sékou Touré's regime has survived him both in symbolic and rhetorical terms as it has been the case in other countries'.[34] Historically, McGovern is correct, though, when he states that the terms 'Sékou Touré era' or 'Sékou Touré regime' do not solely refer to Sékou Touré's words, despite the fact that he attempted to monopolise the discourse and that his writings are still present in the country. He is also correct when he specifies: 'That regime was also a discursive and symbolist one which rested on a shared language in which participated the Guinean people, not only as an audience, but also as producers of the same language'.[35]

What McGovern and some of the authors cited in his article do not fully explain is that the discursive and symbolist communion that Touré and the Guinean people constructed while producing the national language that fuelled the PDG ideological discourse was not a mere regime, in the classic sense of the term. The construct had indeed matured into a full-blown political culture which, ultimately, contained and nurtured the regime itself. Like any other ideological single-party system of its kind, the PDG relied heavily upon a populist symbolism to garner the nationalistic predispositions of the Guinean people. The failure to understanding this pivotal aspect of the political history of Guinea has caused many to mistake the survival of major aspects of the political culture built during the PDG era for that of the regime itself.

In any case, the exclusionary policy that the Conté regime maintained toward the trade unions, even in the face of the rapid deterioration of the living and working conditions of the salaried labour force, was among the underlying causes of the crisis which began in March 2006 and culminated in January–February 2007, as El Hadj A.L. Diallo has indicated.[36] Diallo

34 McGovern (2007), 'Janvier 2007 – Sékou Touré est mort', 133.

35 Ibid., 133.

36 El Hadj Abdoulaye Lélouma Diallo, interview, Boston, 2006.

is quick to underscore the depth and width of the crisis by to enumerating an additional set of factors which other union leaders have corroborated.[37] One such factor was the deficit of accountability closely linked to the degeneration of the Conté administration into an arena of factional rivalries among the financial oligarchy, and the political and biological clans surrounding the ailing president.

In hindsight, it is not an exaggeration to say that the administration had hardly functioned as a legitimate state in the five years or so leading to the crisis of May–June 2006. In effect, even around the presidential elections of 2003, it had become apparent that President Conté's rapidly deteriorating health had made him physically and mentally unfit to govern. As a result, a spiral of cabinet reshufflings ensued at the whim of a few barons upon whom the incapacitated general had come to rely for the survival of his regime. The National Assembly, which has been heavily dominated by the ruling PUP party since inception in 1995, had merely served as a rubber stamp for those barons and their concentric predatory alliances. The upper echelons of the armed forces had joined the praxis of state predation as well, thus creating a rift between the officer corps and the troops. Lastly, the education sector had been grossly neglected and this had made high schools and colleges easy preys of both pro-government and opposition forces in their struggle for power.

It was in the midst of this chaotic situation that the police arrested two of President Conté's closest financial allies on 7 December 2006 for bank fraud. These were Mamadou Sylla, a telecommunication baron, and Fodé Soumah, the former vice governor of the Central Bank. When the president injected himself in the case by personally going to the jail, demanding the release of the two men, and uttering to penitentiary officials 'I am the law', the union leadership cried foul and decided to resume the 2006 general strike. Officially, that strike had only been *suspended* under the agreements signed by the unions, the government and the bureau of employers in June of that year. This egregious disregard for the law by the president

37 Ibrahima Fofana is the secretary general of the USTG. Personal communications in Atlanta (August 2006).

triggered the January 2007 general strike which is viewed as the largest movement of its kind in Guinea since the early 1960s. As early as August 2006, however, USTG secretary general Ibrahima Fofana had hinted that unless the government implemented earnestly all the points contained in the June agreements 'further action will be taken soon to resolve once and for all this lingering crisis'.[38] But it was the December developments that prompted the leaders of the January 2007 strike to expand the demands beyond salary increase, the reduction of the prices of gasoline, rice, and the like, and to thenceforth include the formation of an inclusive government under a prime minister to be appointed with the concurrence of the pro-democratic forces.

As the culmination of a gradual process of empowerment of trade unionism and civil society, the 2007 strike marked the recent history of Guinea in several ways. Apart from the 'mini regime change' discussed earlier, the tenacity of its leadership earned the country's labour movement widespread support and respect. The support came from national and international labour and civil society organizations in Africa and other continents, as well as from ECOWAS, the African Union, and the UN.

Also, Rabiatou Sèrah Diallo, the secretary general of the CNTG, was hailed as the 'iron lady of Guinea', 'a heroine through whose capable leadership the women of Guinea and Africa have earned renewed recognition comparable only to the one generated by the works of Wangari Maathai of Kenya and President Ellen Johnson-Sirleaf of Liberia', as Nadine Koné of Open Society Initiative for West Africa (OSIWA) has argued.[39] In fact, Diallo has been a member of the ILO Executive Board since 2005, a position which she is the first African women to hold.

Moreover, the fact that the resolution of the crisis involved sustained diplomatic efforts on the part of individual African and foreign governments, the ECOWAS Commission, the African Union Commission, the ILO, the International Organization of Francophony (OIF) and the UN,

38 Ibid.

39 Nadine Koné is a program assistant in the OSIWA Governance & Economic Governance Program. Personal communications in Dakar (July 2009).

lent greater moral capital to Guinea's labour movement. Lastly, the measured manner in which the *Intercentrale syndicale* (i.e., the coalition of trade unions that led the strike) challenged the government without succumbing to political temptations earned it further moral and social capital among Guinea's labour force.

Notwithstanding these gains, the 2007 strike and its aftermath revealed serious weaknesses inside the labour movement which must be addressed in earnest if the unions are to live up to the hopes and expectations of the Guinean people, which *Le Diplomate* summed up under the telling title 'Labour Movement: The Sole Hope of the Guinean People':

> In their quest for a lasting solution to the many crises that have been tormenting the country for years, the Guinean people have vested their trust and reliance upon the labour movement due to the latter's proven determination to bring about such solutions. In two largely successful strikes the movement has marked the collective conscience of Guineans as the powerful force which, at any time, is willing and able to twist the neck of the minority that unscrupulously exploits the overwhelming majority in this country. Hence, it has become the only force capable of commanding respect from the government [...] This movement which encompasses the labour forces of the public, private, and mix sectors is today in the eyes of most fellow citizens more credible than the political class.[40]

The weaknesses include communicational and organizational disconnects between the leadership and the base which became evident during the 2007 strike and allowed needless destruction of public and private property to occur in the countryside. They also include little known adverse effects of some of the unions' activities on vulnerable segments of the population. An example of this was that the deliberate scheduling of the 2006 strike during the period of annual exams compromised the academic year for most schools and colleges in the country, thus making students the ultimate victims of the strike.

Another weakness has been the inability of the movement to judiciously engage the rest of civil society and the political class for the preservation and deepening of the governmental reforms brought about by

40 Condé (2006), 'Le mouvement syndical: L'unique espoir des Guinéens'.

the strike. To be sure, soon after the appointment of Lansana Kouyaté as prime minister and the forming of his government, the entire movement lost its guard and fell in a state of complacency. This gave the Conté camp the opportunity to undermine the actions of Kouyaté's government and render it incapable of adequately addressing the pressing needs of the population. As a result, the government saw its legitimacy and political capital erode until it could no longer withstand the president's manoeuvres. Ultimately, Conté a decree sacking Kouyaté and repealing much of the progress made since March 2007. Consequently, by the death of President Conté in December 2008, the country had practically reached the level of political despair in which it was in the eve of Sékou Touré's death in March 1984. Hence, the ease with which the junta of the National Council for Development and Development (CNDD) took over under Captain Moussa Dadis Camara and rolled back the so-called constitutional order for the restoration of which the international community has been calling.

Conclusion

In 2008 the fiftieth anniversary of Guinea's independence was celebrated in the midst of one of the profoundest crises in the country's recent history. What had been expected to be a moment of collective consultation and preparation toward a better future gave way to a heated exchange of accusations and counter-accusations, thus denoting an ever widening generational, political, philosophical, ethnic and regional gap. However cynical, and most are, these accusations and counter-accusations were meant not to disparage the 'No' vote which resulted in Guinea gaining independence, but to fustigate what many have considered to be a gross mismanagement of the country's independence. Therefore, although some have gone as far as to lament the 'wasted fifty years' or 'the undeserved plunder of a nation's soul' or else 'the unpatriotic behaviour of the successive regimes that have ruled independent Guinea', the cynicism thus expressed towards the missed opportunities of the past fifty years attests to one crucial aspect of Guinea's political culture. That is irrespective of their generation, political sensibility, philosophical persuasion, ethnic and regional background, Guineans as a whole are deeply proud of their independence and, by the same token, cognizant of the historic value of the 'No' vote and the struggle that resulted in that vote. Hence, the cynicism with which many have lamented the non-materialization of the hopes and expectations originally associated with their forefathers' heroic rejection of colonialism is reflective of a high degree of nationalism which, in turn, is one of the most critical facets of Guinea's political culture.

This chapter has sought to place the latest manifestations of that political culture in the context of Guinea's successive historical transitions. In little over a half a century, the country have gone from a the status of a colony with limited political pluralism to that of a sovereign nation-state under a regime of party-state; from military rule to post-Cold War political liberalism, and to yet another military rule. With this latter's true intentions regarding the future of the interrupted democratization process still being anyone's guess, it is fair to conclude that the work of the labour movement studied in the chapter is as crucial today as it was under UGTAN. This is so, especially in view of the Pan-African solidarity which trade unions and other civil society organizations recreated in the last decade of the Cold War in their struggle for democratic governance.

The chapter has demonstrated that confusing the continuity of this political culture with a survival of the PDG regime decades after Touré's death is a historical fallacy couched in a greater cognitive problem. That problem is a failure to comprehend the fundamental fact that modern African political cultures are deeply rooted in the collective conscience and collective memories of the first generations of post-colonial Africans and that they do not evaporate with the regimes that fostered them. Hence, the root causes of the resilience of this particular breed of political cultures are to be sought in the ability of the same collective conscience and collective memories to transcend political conjunctures and generational biases. It is a regrettable fact that many authors have rather endeavoured to seek the causes merely in the nostalgic palliations that a handful of surviving former members of the defunct regimes may want to offer.

Lastly, the chapter has sought to establish that trade unionism has contributed to the preservation of a particularly potent set of values which, having thus endured under the harshest political conditions, resurge whenever the situation warrants and provide a badly needed guiding light as the political class fails to adequately play its role. In the process, trade unionism has exhibited flaws, both strategic and tactical. Unless these are remedied, the hopes and expectations elicited during the nation-wide strikes of 2006 and 2007 run the risk of being replaced by deception and disillusionment. Although it may be too early to draw conclusions from the struggle for the return to constitutionality from the current military rule of the CNDD, one cannot ignore the recent decision of the *Forces vives* to get rid of Rabiatou Sèrah Diallo, along with opposition leader Jean Marie Doré, as their spokespersons. This is of great significance not only because the *Forces vives* are a large coalition of CSOs and political parties that have led the struggle against the military rule of both General Conté and now Captain Camara, but also because they no longer trust Diallo and Doré as their spokespersons. Only time will tell if this is only a temporary amendatory measure or an actual fall from grace for the 'iron lady' of the CNTG and an outright vote of no confidence against the trade unions for their inability to capitalize on the socio-political gains discussed in this chapter.

References

Bah, M. (1990) *Construire la Guinée après Sékou Touré*, Paris: L'Harmattan.

Camara, M.S. (2007) *Le pouvoir politique en Guinée*, Paris: L'Harmattan.

Condé, M. (2006) 'Le mouvement syndical: L'unique espoir des Guinéens', *Le Diplomate*, retrieved February 2007 from www.lediplomateguinee.info/news131.htm.

Cooper, F. (1997) 'UGTAN, the Loi-cadre, and the Break-up of AOF', in C. Becker, S. Mbaye, I. Thioub (eds), *AOF: réalités et héritages. Sociétés ouest- africaines et ordre colonial, 1895–1960*, tome 2, Dakar, Direction des Archives du Sénégal.

Diakité, C.A. (1972) *Guinée enchaînée ou le livre noir de Sékou Touré*, Paris: D.A.C.

Kaké, I.B. (1987) *Sékou Touré le héros et le tyran*, Paris: Jeune Afrique Livres.

McGovern, M. (2007) 'Janvier 2007 – Sékou Touré est mort', *Politique africaine*, 107, 125–145.

Suret-Canale, J. (2007) 'Les syndicats confédérés (CGT) en AOF, 1943–1957. Quelques problèmes d'interprétation', retrieved 13 April 2009 from htpp://tekrur-acad.refer.sn/IMG/pdf/07S2SURETC.pdf

Sylla, A.F. (1985) *L'itinéraire sanglant*, Paris: ERTI.

Tchidimbo, R.-M. (1987) *Noviciat d'un évêque*, Paris: Fayard.

Touré, A.S. (1963) *La révolution guinéenne et le progrès social*, Conakry: Imprimerie Nationale 'Patrice Lumumba'.

Touré, A.S. (1967) *The Doctrine and Methods of the Democratic Party of Guinea*, Conakry: Imprimerie Nationale 'Patrice Lumumba'.

Touré, A.S. (1977) *Africa on the Move*, Conakry: Imprimerie Nationale 'Patrice Lumumba'.

GEORGES MINET

On Social Partnership in West Africa

Introduction

In the standard ILO definition, social dialogue consists of 'all types of negotiation, consultation or simply exchange of information between, or among, representatives of governments, employers and workers, on issues of common interest relating to economic and social policy'.[1] There is wide agreement, at least on paper, that 'social dialogue is an important component of good governance, and an instrument for participation and accountability',[2] with the ILO holding that 'a basic requirement of good governance is that there should be institutions that provide for the effective participation of interest groups in the formulation and implementation of policies that affect them'.[3]

While a recent ILO African meeting stressed that 'effective tripartism is a mechanism of governance that enables labour markets to function efficiently and equitably',[4] not everyone is convinced, however, of the benefits of social dialogue, either within or outside African polities. Within, promoters of the concept include labour and social affairs ministries, labour unions – as well as some, but not all, other components of

1 ILO (1996), *Conclusions concerning Tripartite Consultation*; ILO (2002) *Resolution on Tripartism and Social Dialogue*.

2 World Commission on the Social Dimension of Globalization (2004), *A Fair Globalization*, paragraph 240.

3 ILO Governing Body document (2003), GB.286/WP/SDG/3, paragraph 6.

4 ILO (2007), *Conclusions of the Eleventh African Regional Meeting* (Addis Ababa, 24–27 April), paragraph 21 (doc. AfRM/XI/D.3 (Rev.)).

civil society – and employers' organizations. Outside, the main advocate of the virtues of social dialogue is a UN specialized agency, the International Labour Organisation, whose mandate binds it to relentlessly plead for an enlargement of the scope of a collectively-regulated regime of labour conditions worldwide. The United Nations itself, through the cycle of conference summits it gathered during the 1990s, tried to give emphasis to the issue of labour rights in the context of the democratization ethos. The European Union, which has endorsed the ILO's 'Decent Work Agenda' – a twenty-first century repackaging of that organisation's time-honoured policies – has evolved into a close ally, with the EU Commission and especially the European Economic and Social Committee bringing their support to ILO endeavours in developing countries. As regards French-speaking Africa, individual EU member-states, such as Belgium and, to a lesser degree, France are also committed to sponsor ILO-executed programmes on top of their own. Lastly, Belgian and French trade-union confederations, as well as the German Friedrich-Ebert Foundation, have brought their expertise to assist their African counterparts.

However, if social dialogue counts a host of active, if predictable, supporters, it also faces a motley crowd of detractors. On the domestic front, Treasuries are perhaps the most formidable of those, although advisors at presidential level did similarly figure as powerful brakes on the design of any progressive labour agenda at the height of the implementation of structural adjustment. Their brief was hardly distinguishable from the recipes pushed by the Washington-based international financial institutions, the IMF and the World Bank Group which, while part of the UN System to which also belongs the ILO, gave short-shrift to labour concerns about workers' rights and meaningful collective negotiation of working conditions. The UN Regional Development Banks have nevertheless been characteristically less sanguine in their 'neo-liberal' policy advice, even though the African Development Bank moved from a rather independent African stance under Adebayo Adedeji to more conformist views under the World Bank-trained K.Y. Amoako.

One should not forget either that a whole crop of Third World economists remains highly dubious about the blanket relevance of the social dialogue mantra, if not plainly critical as to its impact on the growth of developing economies. Also, the ideologically motivated semantic shift from the traditional concept of 'industrial relations' to that of 'social dialogue' has justly attracted the remark that the latter had all the trappings of 'a supremely vague ... if not vacuous term'.[5] In any case, there is no contesting the political legitimacy of the social dialogue agenda in the face of its constant restatement by the tripartite delegations at the yearly gatherings of the International Labour Conference, and its formal endorsement by countless resolutions of various UN organs. And the effectiveness of strong tripartite social dialogue in counteracting harmful economic agendas over the last two decades has been repeatedly documented.[6] What must interest us now is the ways in which this international commitment actually mirrors the living reality of West African situations.

Social Dialogue in West Africa: The National Level

Social dialogue at the national level was deemed by the turn of the millennium to have 'become an important component of good governance in many countries'.[7] In Africa, as elsewhere in the so-called developing world, it was purported that 'there is increasing recognition, particularly in government circles, that in order to effectively address the challenge of globalization and the new economic realities it is no longer the case that government must retain exclusive authority over policy formulation'.[8] This trend appeared evident in the African case from the number of tripartite

5 Standing (2008), 'The ILO: An Agency for Globalisation?', 371, 373.
6 For a recent assessment of the impact of tripartism in selected countries, see Frayle (2010), *Blunting Neoliberalism, Tripartism and Economic Reforms in the Developing World.*
7 Ishikawa (2003), *Key Features of National Social Dialogue*, 1.
8 Fashoyin (2001), 'Industrial Relations in Developing Countries', 42.

institutions that have been set up or resuscitated throughout the continent, especially in francophone Central and West Africa.[9]

Listed as one of the internal factors of the crisis of African states, along with problems of leadership and elite, is 'disempowered society, which finds it difficult if not impossible to defend its interest collectively or influence governance'.[10] Social dialogue may prove a remedy as long as various challenges associated with its operation can be met. It is based on respect for democratic principles, workers' rights, and the independence of employers' and workers' organizations. The legal framework is founded on the principles of freedom of association and the right to collective bargaining and reinforced by ratification and effective implementation of various relevant instruments.[11] The often neglected role of labour administration, labour courts, tripartite and dispute settlement bodies is crucial, as is the function of international labour standards and national labour laws. Enforcement of protective regulations is patently problematic and patchy.[12] Although almost all countries in Africa have ratified the fundamental ILO Conventions,[13] their effective implementation obviously remains far from being achieved. Thus, in some countries, large groups of workers, in particular public service employees and agricultural workers are denied the right to meet and organize. This exclusion of such a large proportion contributes to narrowing down the coverage of social dialogue.

9 As documented in the ILO/PRODIAF national studies listed at http://prodiaf.org.

10 Berhe (2004), *Supporting Africa's Efforts*, 33.

11 Relevant ILO Conventions are: Labour Administration, 1978 (No. 150); Labour Relations (Public Service), 1978 (No. 151); Workers' Representatives, 1971 (No. 135); Tripartite Consultation (International Labour Standards), 1976 (No. 144); Collective Bargaining, 1981 (No. 154).

12 Filali Meknassi, R. (2010), 'The Effectiveness of Labour Law'.

13 ILO Conventions on: Forced Labour, 1930 (No. 29); Abolition of Forced Labour, 1957 (No. 105); Freedom of Association and Protection of the Right to Organise, 1948 (No. 87); Right to Organise and Collective Bargaining, 1949 (No. 98); Equal Remuneration, 1951(No. 100); Discrimination (Employment and Occupation) 1958 (No. 111); Minimum Age, 1973 (No. 138); Worst Forms of Child Labour, 1999 (No. 182).

End of the 1990s assessments offer the picture of a 'labour relations crisis' in francophone Africa, as 'rules of the game' were changing across the continent, 'from protection-seeking public interventions, often characterized by low productivity, towards systems of regulation which enhance competitiveness'.[14] Accordingly, 'a new type of industrial relations' was then judged necessary 'to provide an effective framework for the interaction of social partners that is required for sustainable economic growth'. It was observed that, in the context of structural adjustment, 'workers and their trade unions anxiously seek dialogue to participate in a process which has a direct impact on their lives, yet there are few functioning national policy-making bodies involving the social partners that make effective contributions today'.[15]

A 1991 review of the patterns of industrial relations and tripartite relationships across fourteen francophone African countries had posited that 'tripartism in French-speaking Africa has all but disappeared as an active part of industrial relations'.[16] A few years later, an ILO study contrasted the frequent recourse to national tripartite agreements in transition and Latin American countries with the general absence of participatory handling of economic adjustments in Africa, noting that existing bodies for consultation on social issues had mostly been ineffective in such context: in francophone countries in particular, there was 'a formal and fairly elaborate structure of industrial relations, but it (was) little used in practice'.[17] A decade further, in 2007, the ILO was still recording on a wide scale an 'absence of strong tripartite institutions' in African countries.[18] However, it also appeared rather confident that a right turn was at last being taken, with a fresh political recognition that the role of 'social partnership' played a meaningful role in crafting employment-friendly economic policy.

14 van der Geest and van der Hoeven (1999), *Adjustment, Employment and Missing Institutions*, 67.

15 Martens (1991), 'French-speaking Africa', 298.

16 Ibid., 329.

17 ILO (1997), *World Labour Report 1997–98*, 170, 172.

18 ILO (2007), *The Decent Work Agenda in Africa 2007–2015*, paragraph 267.

Today, the picture of labour relations in francophone Africa is mixed. On the one hand, collective bargaining faces considerable challenges, with persistent decline in both trade union and density and collective bargaining coverage across the continent. The high prevalence of the informal economy, low levels of formal wage employment, shift to atypical employment, and difficulties in organizing workers in small and micro enterprises and in rural areas, are among the main factor accounting for these low rates.[19] These problems have been exacerbated by structural adjustment and economic and public sector reforms pursued in the 80s and 90s, which further reduced levels of formal, non-agricultural wage employment, a significant source of traditional trade union membership, while generally forcing unions onto the defensive.[20]

On the other hand, a new positive trend across the continent has been the negotiation of tripartite 'social pacts' or 'partnership agreements'. While these national-level accords are often negotiated as a way out of civil or economic crisis, they also can serve as the basis for a resurgence of collective bargaining. Economic and social pacts make for a popular formula today in West Africa, and their results are inspiring for post-crisis countries, or for countries where consolidation of the social peace is at stake. Thus, Senegal adopted in 2002 a National Charter on Social Dialogue with a view to upgrade the institutional framework for social dialogue between the State, private sector employers and workers. The Charter, which was signed by all employers' organisations and the major unions and became effective in March 2003, applies broadly to all sectors of economy, including the public and the private sectors as well as the informal sector. It embodies a commitment to the principles of partnership, good faith, mutual respect and willingness to be faithful to agreements, and for the state and employers to guarantee the freedom of association of workers. The Charter lays down a set of respective rules of conduct for each of the three partners, acknowledging in particular labour's stake in and contribution to business

19 See Alby et al. (2005), *Labor Institutions, Labor-Management Relations and Social Dialogue*; Nhlapo (2007), 'Building Sustainable Unions in Africa'.

20 Wood and Brewster (2007), *Industrial Relations in Africa*, 6.

performance, and establishes an institutional framework for dialogue at each of the national, sectoral and enterprise levels. A tripartite National Social Dialogue Committee is entrusted with tasks of conflict prevention and resolution, the encouragement and monitoring of collective agreements and research on ways and means to improve the business environment, without neglecting the improvement of terms and conditions of work. Alongside this national body, bipartite social dialogue committees are to be set up at the sectoral and the enterprise levels. The Charter was designed as a tool to improve labour-management cooperation in Senegal by providing the right setting to process disputes and build faith among the three concerned parties. A recent assessment holds that 'cooperation between the various trade union groups and tendencies has been quite positive in this context'[21] – although, to be more effective, this body would benefit from a better sense of commitment from the government and the employers' sides: in the unions' view, it has 'not yet succeeded in bringing an adequate response to workers' demands'.[22] There is no doubt that the CNDS has built since its inception a convincing track record, through the expertise of its active Commission de médiation sociale, which had succeeded by 2008 in solving three-quarters of the cases submitted to it, while also facilitating the conclusion of important agreements on the age of retirement at the national and sector levels. In any case, plans are underway to strengthen the CNDS mechanism.[23]

In another country, Mali, the 2001 partnership agreement[24] committed the government and the social partners (with the exception of one trade union) to promote a 'responsible social dialogue with the aim

21 Laurijssen (2010), *Trade Union Pluralism and Proliferation in French-speaking Africa*.

22 ITUC (2009), *Annual Survey of Violations of Trade Union Rights*, at www.ituc-csi.org.

23 PRODIAF/BIT (2008), *Dialogue social en Afrique, Pratiques et expériences*, 11–41, at www.cnds.org.

24 The *Pacte de solidarité pour la croissance et le développement* was signed by the government and the social partners in August 2001, and succeeds an earlier agreement, the *pacte social* of 1992.

of encouraging social conditions conducive to economic development'. Concertation takes place on a yearly basis through an ad hoc tripartite committee to review the implementation of the agenda. Conceived as a broad policy agenda, it lists a series of measures to improve private sector development and job creation, as well as the lot of public sector employees. So far, it appears to have generated negotiations on wages and working conditions.

Other examples of revamped collaborative frameworks for labour relations in the region include Benin (Conseil National du Travail), Burkina Faso (Commission Consultative du Travail), Niger (Commission nationale de dialogue social) and Togo (Conseil National du Dialogue Social). A recent summing-up of experiments in Niger and Togo suggests that their new-fangled institutions are set to perform a useful function.[25] But the picture remains mixed, as their position is clearly fragile and permanently challenged. The Niger CNDS, whose atypical quadripartite composition makes room for civil society organisations, has managed to bring various collective disputes to an end and deflate a number of strike threats in the past years.[26] In Togo, however, the unions have pointed out 'the absence of social dialogue' after the creation of the new Council in 2007.[27]

To sum up the performance of the multi-stakeholder frameworks for social dialogue in the region, a distinction should perhaps be made depending on the sort of issues included in their missions. While their record in matters of dispute prevention and settlement undeniably embodies many success stories,[28] proving that theirs is not a pro forma framework, their effectiveness in influencing national socio-economic policy can hardly be taken for granted. Not that these countries are alone in such respect, as illustrated by the ongoing debate in South Africa regarding the suitability and need for improvement of its National Economic Development and Labour Council. The rating of the role played by Niger's CNDS in public

25 PRODIAF/BIT (2008), *Dialogue social en Afrique.*

26 Ibid., 61–76.

27 ITUC (2009), *Annual Survey.*

28 The achievements of the 'médiation sociale' in the public service are worth mentioning here; see www.ofpa.net/activit/medsoci.htm.

policy formulation as 'marginal' probably applies to most of the institutions mentioned here.[29] ILO African delegates stressed accordingly in 2007 the need that new or existing dialogue mechanisms should become 'fully utilized by governments' in the preparation and implementation of national development strategies.[30]

By contrast, their eminently useful economic function in providing the means to nurture a positive social climate – the 'social and civil peace' crucial for national development – must today be acknowledged beyond any doubt. Also, national trade union movements, through their involvement in the operation of these mechanisms, have found new ways of enlarging their agendas to subsume broader swaths of 'participatory governance', thus becoming more reliable partners in the building of national consensus.

To ensure that the achievements so far prove sustainable, a variety of challenges must however still be met and many weaknesses be corrected. Beyond the obvious prerequisite of political will, concerns range from a persistent lack of appropriate financial and human means to improving the legitimacy of the outcomes of dialogue through overdue reforms to ensure the representativeness of the participants in dialogue processes. Of course, one will remember that, a decade ago already, worldwide data on average union density and bargaining coverage showed clearly enough that 'only a minority of the world's population enjoys the right to social dialogue via tripartism or bipartism'.[31] Indeed, West African realities only manifest with peculiar sharpness a situation where strong and effective democracy at work is the exception rather than the rule in most parts of the world. A major challenge remains that of ensuring that the most representative unions are assigned pride of place in the dialogue structures, whose own legitimacy depends on the proper determination of these organisations.[32] A recently developed 'Voice Representation Security Index' ranks four West African

29 PRODIAF/BIT (2008), *Dialogue social en Afrique*, 72.

30 ILO (2007), *Decent Work Agenda*, paragraph 22.

31 Kuruvilla (2006), 'Social Dialogue for Decent Work', 179.

32 See, for example, Oumarou (2002),'Niger', 47–55.

countries among those that, 'apparently convinced of the need for voice, have taken steps to secure it, without succeeding so far'.[33]

Trade union proliferation and fragmentation in the region, stemming from an abuse of the healthy principle of union pluralism, has 'considerably weakened the efficiency and the credibility of the trade union movement', leading in particular to a widespread collapse of collective bargaining.[34] Among its causes, government interference, employer hostility and partisan politics all compounded the inadequacies of the legal framework to result in the workers' frustration in the face of unfair and undemocratic practices. Such dire situation has by now generated a promising process of building national trade union unification agendas, with help from the ITUC African Regional Organisation. While some labour unions, such as those in Benin and Burkina Faso, can boast a record of unity in action, others, such as the two Mali confederations, show no willingness to cooperate. The experience of Senegal, where a reduction of the number of national trade union centres from eighteen to three or four could probably be set as a unification objective under an agenda de rapprochement, suggests that social dialogue institutions – in this instance the CNDS – offer a conducive framework for cooperative and unification efforts. Burkina Faso, with its six national centres collaborating by way of an *Intersyndicale*, makes for 'one of the more positive examples in the region of trade union unity in action, in the absence of structural unity',[35] a situation that is beneficial to the running of the tripartite mechanisms. The prospect for addressing the whole issue of unification were heightened in October 2009 by the *Appel de Lomé sur la liberté syndicale et les défis de l'unité du mouvement syndical en Afrique*, issued by the trade union leaders of Benin, Burkina Faso, Cameroun, RD Congo, Sénégal and Togo with a view to increase the upgrade the relevance and efficacy of trade union action through the promotion of a general

33 The countries are Benin, Burkina Faso, Ivory Coast and Senegal; see ILO (2004), *Economic Security for a Better World*, 272.

34 An up-to-date comprehensive picture in this regard is that of Laurijssen (2010), *Trade Union Pluralism*; see also Fonteneau et al (2004) *Histoire du syndicalisme en Afrique*.

35 Laurijssen (2010), *Trade Union Pluralism*.

process of unification. This recognition of the urgency of taking a host of initiatives to overcome at last the fragmentation problem at all levels of the union movement augurs well for the effective functioning of social dialogue structures throughout the region.

But there are other, persistent, obstacles to conquer in order to make such structures truly robust. For decades now, the ritual observation has been voiced that labour administrations in the developing world are under-resourced and lack authority, especially when compared with their economic and financial counterparts.[36] ILO tripartite African gatherings have ceaselessly complained about the marginalisation or utter absence from strategic social and economic policymaking of labour ministries, which also acts as a significant constraint on the workings of social dialogue. The somewhat quixotic quest for upgrading their influence within the government machinery and improving their 'Cinderella' status continues then unabated, with ILO support anchored in the topical international convention (number 150 of 1978) on Labour Administration, and in a renewed sense that stronger labour departments are essential to the success of any social dialogue agenda.

Lastly, although there cannot be here any pretention to thoroughness in the listing of the pitfalls facing this agenda, the Bretton-Woods push for labour market deregulation in Africa as elsewhere has naturally led its mark on the potential for dialogue. Under the guise of creating a 'better business environment', a general attack was performed on labour standards as enemies of market-friendly policies and ultimately of economic development, notably via the *Doing Business Index* of the World Bank.[37]

36 The situation is not peculiar to poor countries: an ex-US Labor Secretary had occasion to assert that both fiscal and monetary policy are 'not solely the province of the Financial Ministers (and) the central bankers', since they are 'centre-pieces of social policy' (R. Reich, *Global Employment Forum*, ILO, Geneva, 1 November 2001).

37 See Bakvis, P. (2006), *How the World Bank and IMF use the Doing Business Report*; Cazes and Berg (2007) *The Doing Business Indicators*.

Regional Social Dialogue

A typical list of concerns associated with the social dimension of integration will include its impact on employment, uneven distribution of benefits among the member countries, regulatory competition between them, and uneven bargaining power between mobile capital and immobile labour.[38] There is by now a good measure of political recognition that social dialogue has a role to play in developing the social content of Africa's engagement in the regional and global economy, both at the sub-regional and continental levels. The challenge is for African governments, employers and trade unions to better explore the scope for influencing the regional economic communities (RECs) and other relevant groupings such as the Organization for the Harmonisation of Business Law in Africa (OHADA), from the perspective of promoting social dialogue. Apart from ECOWAS and WAEMU in West Africa,[39] efforts to that end are made in the Southern African Development Community (SADC), the Economic Community of the Great Lakes Countries (CEPGL), the Central Africa Economic and Monetary Community (CEMAC) and the East African Community (EAC). Regional social dialogue is thus slowly emerging within economic communities in Africa, with SADC and UEMOA showing the way. At the continental level, the African Union has also institutionalised consultation with the social partners through its Labour and Social Affairs Commission and the recently launched Economic, Social and Cultural Council.

At the outset, one should be aware of the limitations of the African RECs. As the then head of ECA observed in 2004, in the absence of strong institutions to implement the regional integration objectives, 'you are not going to make much progress ... Our institutions have not been strong

38 See, for example, van Liemt (2004), *The Social Dimension of Trade in ASEAN*.

39 The WAEMU members are: Benin, Burkina Faso, Côte d'Ivoire, Guinea-Bissau, Mali, Niger, Senegal and Togo. The other members of ECOWAS are: Cape Verde, Ghana, Guinea, Liberia, Nigeria, Sierra Leone and The Gambia. The combined population of ECOWAS is 260.3 million (Buthelezi (2006), *Regional Integration in Africa*).

enough and they lack resources, both human and financial.'[40] However, the 2004 ARIA report, which placed the RECs into five categories based on their performance, rated as strong performers, 'above average,' ECOWAS and WAEMU – along with SADC (while CEMAC was only average). But a host of factors account for the slow pace at which the African ideal of integration is moving, e.g. the overlapping regional membership, the failure of countries to translate regional decisions into national practice and the almost complete absence of popular participation in the processes of integration.

This last obstacle poses a particular threat to the advancement of the social dimension of regional integration in Africa where social and civil dialogue has so far been either ineffective or non-existent at the regional level. Instead, dialogue on African integration has been historically 'monopolized by governments and intergovernmental organizations'[41] with only a marginal role given to other stakeholders, in particular workers' and employers' organisations. Only a third of African countries have national regulations or policies for involving civil society in deliberations over regional policies. As the Economic Commission for Africa and the African Union have asserted, 'unless the people are aware of regional integration and interested in its success, the current state of African regional economic communities is unlikely to change' – which makes highly desirable civil society involvement in their rationalisation.[42]

African leaders are nonetheless politically committed to prioritising the socio-labour dimension of economic integration and securing a measure of civil society involvement in the integration process, as shown at a 2004 ILO-sponsored summit by their emphasis on the need to further social dialogue at all levels of governance including the regional level.[43] A 2005 follow-up meeting between the AU, the RECs and the ILO demonstrated

40 *Africa Renewal* 18(3) (October 2004): 23.

41 ECA/AU (2006), *Assessing Regional Integration in Africa II*, 88.

42 Ibid.

43 ILO/AU (2004), *Outcome Documents of the Extraordinary Summit of Heads of State and Government of the African Union on Employment and Poverty Alleviation in Africa* (Ouagadougou, September).

that most regional communities did not fully include labour and employment issues into their integration programmes, and identified the need to increase the capacity of the RECs to address them. Subsequent sub-regional gatherings convened by the AU saw the adoption of Regional Frameworks for Integrated Employment Policies, to serve as guides in the formulation of national employment policies – with the ultimate aim to hold a Pan-African employment policy forum that could craft an employment policy framework at continental scale.

Strong political commitment of member states to promote social dialogue at community level should be seen as a way to measure their degree of concrete implication in their relevant community, but other prerequisites are identical to those earlier mentioned in any national setting, such as the representativeness and capacity of the social partners, both crucial to ensure the quality and credibility of a regional dialogue mechanism. Of concern is that several employers and workers organizations at sub-regional level are not operational due to lack of funds,[44] and that it remains unclear how they will develop into supranational actors in their own right and wield influence on the RECs policy making without being able to deepen their cooperation. Also essential is for participants to engage in substantive, rather than formal, exchange, thus warding off the risk of transforming the dialogue structure into a mere 'alibi'.[45] But support is general for building social dialogue in the African RECs, with a consensus in the ILO that 'there should be effective institutionalized dialogue at the regional level' and that the status of employers and workers organizations need to be upgraded in that context,[46] a specific application of the view that 'putting in place the conditions that permit the potential of social partnership to be realized is part and parcel of good governance'.[47]

Turning first to the employers' constituency, in addition to the Pan-African Employers' Confederation, West African employers, members of

44 ILO (2007), *The Decent Work Agenda in Africa 2007–2015*, paragraph 115.

45 Niango (2007), *Dialogue social et intégration régionale*.

46 ILO (2007), GB.300/6, *Report and conclusions of the Eleventh African Regional Meeting* (Addis-Ababa, 24–27 April 2007), paragraphs 112, 113, 115.

47 ILO (2003), GB.288/WP/SDG/2, paragraph 57.

the Fédération des Organisations Patronales d'Afrique de l'Ouest (FOPAO), have made known on various occasions their support for, and concerns vis-à-vis the integration process. In 2003, the employers' organisations of ECOWAS defined their role in furthering West African integration,[48] agreeing in particular on a series of initiatives to reinforce their position, including the creation of a federative structure regrouping the employers' organizations of the fifteen ECOWAS countries, with a view to play a more active role in clarifying West African integration strategies.

As to trade unions, the slogan 'no integration without social dimension' captures both the rejection by labour movements worldwide of trading pacts without a human face and their conviction that integration cannot successfully proceed in the absence of a substantive labour content. At the international level, the labour movement has been consistently supportive of regional arrangements. African unions endorse regional integration and want it to accelerate.[49] Stressing their concern that it has 'mainly concentrated on capital and natural resource mobilisation and tended to ignore the critical role of human resource mobilisation and other social aspects', they have consistently maintained that, 'for integration to be successful, the stakeholders, of whom workers and their organisations are a major component, must be involved in the design process, decision making machineries and implementation of all programmes and project activities. Social aspects such as poverty eradication, human and trade union rights, the creation of decent jobs and the observance of international labour standards, should always be among the main priorities'.[50]

48 Conclusions of the Sub-regional workshop on 'Regional Integration and International Cooperation in the ECOWAS: The Role of Employers' Organizations', Ouagadougou, 25–26 February 2003, at http://www.ilo.org/public/english/dialogue/actemp/conf/2003/ouagadougou.pdf.

49 ITUC-Africa was founded in 2007 through the merging of ICFTU-AFRO and DOAWTU, while OATUU affiliated with the WFTU. On the latter's lack of influence within ECOWAS, see Robert (2005), *The Social Dimension of Regional Integration in ECOWAS*, 26–28.

50 ICFTU-AFRO (2005), *A Trade-Union Vision for Africa towards Challenges of Development, Organizing and Social Justice*, paragraphs 67–70, at www.icftuafro.org.

The General Secretary of the Organization of African Trade Union Unity (OATUU) spoke for many beyond his own constituency when he stated that 'liberalisation in the neo-liberal sense is what we don't want ... liberalisation that destroys infant industries in Africa, that does not even promote intra-African trade, and that lessens the proportion of Africa's trade with the rest of the world, that's not our idea'. He also reiterated a main demand: 'our role, as an African trade union organization, is to push the integration of civil society into the process of building the RECs ... We need to push the involvement of African civil society in each of the five sub-regions in order to speed up the process. Otherwise it will take a long, long time. We don't want the regional economic communities to be bureaucratic'.[51] Stating that 'the structure of African economies vis-à-vis globalization makes it imperative to devote attention to sub-regional and regional integration', African unions called in 2002 for 'the establishment of a formal structure within NEPAD to address trade, development and core labour standards' with full trade-union participation.[52] In a similar vein, the 'West African Trade Union Working Group on International Trade and Regional Integration', born in Cotonou in 2005, adopted at Bamako in 2006 a 'Position of the West African trade-unions on regional integration' which, while endorsing the regional project, criticized its slow pace and demanded, *inter alia*, a reform of the regional bodies to ensure trade union participation to the integration process, the strengthening of the powers of ECOWAS and WAEMU to enforce their decisions, a stable funding of the communities' institutions, improved freedom of movement of people and goods, compliance with fundamental ILO standards, and the promotion of corporate social responsibility.

Bilateral trade union relations are also useful in building the workers' regional agenda. Thus, the ITUC-sponsored trade union partnership agreement signed in 2006 between the Confédération nationale des travailleurs

51 *Africa Recovery* 16(2–3) (September 2002): 18.

52 'Declaration of the African Trade Union Conference on the role of African Workers and Trade Unions in the NEPAD, Dakar, 20 February 2002', in P. Bond (2002), *Fanon's Warning*, 39–42.

du Sénégal (CNTS) and the Confédération générale des travailleurs du Mauritanie (CGTM) sought to enable the unions 'to get more involved in managing migratory flows, whilst developing our expertise in helping migrants and not leaving everything to our governments'.[53]

Finally, the broad union agenda established ten years ago thus remains relevant, which insisted that 'labour and other social issues take centre stage, as there cannot be any economic development devoid of a social dimension', and singled out the need for organised labour to be 'involved in the design stages of any regional integration effort' and to demand from 'governments the right to be involved and consulted, together with other stakeholders, on all matters of regional concern'.[54]

Architecture for Regional Social Dialogue in West Africa

Far from being reduced to an association of states, the new regional reality has come to embody the interplay of intergovernmental processes with corporate and civil society agendas, so that an analysis that would limit regional arrangements to an intergovernmental, state-led logic has lost its accuracy. Hence the coining of the concept of 'participatory regionalism'[55] and the shift of focus adopted by the so-called 'new regionalism approach' which, 'while taking account of old, formal, top-down regionalisms that are concerned with unidimensional and/or nation-centric processes', such as trade or market integration, 'acknowledges the importance of movements in civil societies for emancipation, democratisation, material opportunity

53 'Spotlight on Mody Guiro (CNTS-Senegal) and Mamadou Niang (CGTM-Mauritania)', Brussels, 14 May 2007, at www.ituc-csi.org.

54 Mwamadzingo (2001), 'Regional Integration in Africa: Getting It Right', 12.

55 Acharya (2003), 'Democratisation and the Prospects for Participatory Regionalism in Southeast Asia', 382.

and/or survival'.[56] Obviously, such a transformation in outlook seems bound to improve the conditions for the participation of the social partners in crafting regional policies. It is within the sub-regions, rather than at the continental African Union level, that one can find proof of progress in this regard.[57]

While ECOWAS members committed themselves in 2009 to set up a 'Social dialogue Forum',[58] it is the WAEMU which has the most sophisticated experience of the travails involved in creating a dialogue structure after a ten-year long process. The WAEMU Commission[59] had supported early on initiatives aimed at promoting social dialogue in the Union. Various advantages were identified in that respect: the Union's endeavours would enjoy greater visibility, the social partners would develop a stake in the integration project, conflict prevention and the furtherance of social peace would be enhanced. However, institutionalization of social dialogue raised a difficulty, as the WAEMU's Revised Treaty had made no provision for a framework to that effect.

56 MacLean, S.J. (1999), 'Peacebuilding and the New Regionalism in Southern Africa', 944.

57 The AU Labour and Social Affairs Commission recommended in the Fall 2009 that guidelines of good practices of social dialogue in Africa be elaborated in collaboration with the ILO, but ITUC-Africa complained in February 2010 about the attitude of African Labour Ministers in the Commission, judging that it was in need of moving 'towards strengthening its tripartite character' (see at www.ituc-csi.org).

58 The promises of social dialogue within ECOWAS were explored in Robert (2005), *The Social Dimension of Regional Integration in ECOWAS*. In Articles 81 and 82 of the Revised Treaty, ECOWAS commits to setting up mechanisms for consultation with non-governmental and socio-economic organizations, and refers to workers and employers among those whose involvement in the integration process should be encouraged.

59 In the Commission's Secretariat, a Labour Programmes Unit (part of the Social Affairs Division of the Department of Humanitarian and Social Affairs under the Commissioner for Human Development and Gender) is 'involved in harmonizing labour laws for the purpose of creating industrial peace in the region; promoting the welfare and security of workers for the purpose of regional integration and development; revitalizing the labour sector to make it proactive in the regional integration process'.

Consultations held from 1999 between the Commission and the Labour Ministers and social partners of the member states were to figure as the first concrete example of social dialogue in the Union, yielding in 2005 a common commitment to establish a permanent tripartite structure, after a painstaking process ably driven by the Labour Minister of Burkina Faso and the Commission. The final proposal reflected a compromise: while the social partners, especially the trade unions, had advocated a tripartite structure with decision-making power, the Commission held that, as such an option would necessarily entail modifying the Treaty, it had but little chance to win the day. The formula of a consultative organ was thus finally retained, as it merely necessitated the adoption of an Additional Act by the Conference of the Heads of State.

Four major reasons for creating the framework had been listed by the Commission.[60] First, WAEMU could not ignore the worldwide recognition that globalisation must incorporate a social dimension. Secondly, the experience of similar regional groupings in other parts of the world suggested that social dialogue was a plus to secure their efficient functioning, while its absence could thwart the adoption of policy decisions. Thirdly, the social partners had made quite clear their wish to be involved in the Union's decision-making process. Finally, the social crises experienced in some member countries highlighted the need and urgency of making available dialogue and conflict prevention devices. As a matter of fact, the context was deemed propitious by the Commission, as there appeared to be a growing recognition that some kind of participatory device was needed to develop public goodwill towards integration. Of concern were events such as the negative reactions to the extension of the VAT Directive, as well as the fierce opposition of West African civil society to the conclusion of an EPA with the European Union. If, by nature, labour relations are a principal domain for conflict prevention and resolution, social dialogue is also seen as beneficial to political stability. An illustration is that of the Ivorian crisis, diagnosed as evidence of the dire consequences of a lack of national social dialogue: remedies to that situation were sought in that

60 Niango (2007), *Dialogue social et intégration régionale.*

instance through borrowing from the experience of neighbouring countries, such as Mali and Niger, in implementing social dialogue.

At long last, the *Acte additionnel portant création et organisation du Conseil du travail et du dialogue social de l'UEMOA* was signed and entered in force on 17 March 2009.[61] The *Conseil*, a permanent consultative organ of the Union with its own Secretariat, funded through its budget, is given the notably broad mandate of securing the 'effective involvement of all non-state actors in the WAEMU's integration process, in particular through examining and assessing any topic likely to have a social impact within the Union; strengthening consultation and tripartite cooperation mechanisms within the Union; supporting the consolidation of social dialogue processes and structures in member countries' (Article 3 of the *Acte*). Each country sends a nine-members delegation composed of three government representatives, two employers' and two workers' and two civil society representatives (Art. 5), who make up the Council's General Assembly (Art. 7).

The rationale for the new construct, as expressed in the *Acte*'s Preamble, embodies the sense that building a 'strong social consensus' around the stakes, aims, policies and reforms inherent in the economic and monetary integration conditions its success. By contrast, an experiment such as the drafting of uniform labour regulations for the very same countries by the OHADA has not elicited an invocation of, much less a substantial recourse to, the benefits of a standing dialogue framework. Presented as an integrative tool in the legal sphere rather than another integration grouping, the OHADA – whose governance is driven by Justice and Finance Ministers – is mandated to address the area of labour law, subsumed under business law, though an eminently political one – with the effect that it may well have bit more than it could chew, given its raison d'être, i.e. the securing of a propitious business investment climate. Although the feasibility of crafting a useful uniform set of labour regulations for the concerned countries

61 Kone and Soulama (2005), *Etude sur la mise en place d'un cadre tripartite de dialogue social au sein de l'UEMOA*; see also *Acte additionnel N° 02/2009/CCGE/UEMOA portant création et organisation du Conseil du travail et du dialogue social de l'UEMOA*, at http://prodiaf.org.

has been well asserted,[62] the organisation itself has, unsurprisingly, been portrayed as a conduit for neo-liberal globalization policies rather than a symbol of a genuine attempt to shape a regional legal system.[63] Even though the principle of their involvement has been formally acknowledged by the OHADA governing organ,[64] Labour Ministers and the social partners in its member countries have repeatedly complained about the conditions under which the formulation of a draft labour Uniform Act, whose clauses would automatically rescind national labour codes, has been underway. This example suggests that asymmetry, not coherence, remains prevalent between the economic and social contents of African integration.

Conclusion

Rather like a phoenix, the web of tripartite institutions throughout francophone Africa has emerged from its moribund state to a new life over the last decade or so, riding on the last wave of political democratisation worldwide. Can the recorded achievements prove meaningful enough to warrant the hope of progress on the substance of social and labour policies?

Firstly, the success stories suggest a genuine coming back of the social agenda[65] and, at the very least, a sharper awareness that the liberalisation doxa has proven self-destructive. At the same time, in a context of a so-called de-politicisation of development, 'demands for democratisation cannot be confined to the sphere of civil and political rights. A much wider range of demands, including redistributive policies to ensure a minimum level of

62 Béraud, J.M. (2001), *Etude préalable à l'adoption d'un Acte uniforme en Droit du Travail.*

63 Mohamed Salah, M. (2002), *Les contradictions du droit mondialisé*, 122; Akumbu M'Oluna (2008) *Libres propos sur les réformes juridiques au Gabon.*

64 Minet and Vargha (2006), 'The Outlook for African Labour Law'.

65 Yeates, N. (2005), *'Globalization' and Social Policy.*

economic and social rights, is also on the agenda, particularly for workers and the peasantry'.[66]

However, concomitant with the democratisation phase, and really a part of it, an assault unfolded against domestic and international labour standards, as the 'Development Politburo'[67] set about the task of recrafting labour codes under the guise of 'law reform' exercises understood as the supply of 'market-friendly' laws. Rankings of countries found to have anti-employment regulations started appearing,[68] and an Economic Commission for Africa-World Bank report was to hold that 'worker protection laws – minimum wages or hire-and-fire regulations – have to be carefully designed and regularly revised to minimize any adverse effects on business growth and labour demand'.[69] Fantasies about the supposed adverse impact of francophone Africa's legal tradition on efficiency and growth were even uttered, to the scandal of its practitioners.[70] As a matter of fact, the resilience of the 'essentially French model of social relations' characteristic of the sub-region was put to the test'.[71]

Against this offensive, 'institutions of democracy' such as the national tripartite bodies truly had to regain enough vitality to display their concern, and not appear as some sort of merely formal devices characteristic of a form of 'low-intensity democracy'.[72] For sure, tripartite influence on policy-making has remained limited so far,[73] but social dialogue structures are allowing their members to become less defensive. Multilateral (ILO) and

66 Hintjens, H. (1999), 'The Emperor's New Clothes', 391.

67 Easterly, W. (2007), 'The Ideology of Development'.

68 See, for instance, *Doing Business 2007: How to Reform*, 19, Table 4.1, listing 10 such most 'difficult' countries, among which is Niger.

69 *Economic Report on Africa 2005 – Meeting the Challenges of Unemployment and Poverty in Africa*, 273.

70 See references in Kayizzi-Mugerwa (2003), *Reforming Africa's Institutions*, 119; and the rebuttal of Association Henri Capitant (2006), *Les droits de tradition civiliste en question. A propos des rapports Doing Business de la Banque Mondiale.*

71 Croucher (2007), 'Industrial Relations in Francophone Africa – the Case of Niger'.

72 See Evans, T. (2001), 'If Democracy, Then Human Rights?', 629.

73 Ghai, D. (2005), *ILO Participation in PRSPs*.

regional (EU[74]) advice have been helpful in this regard, but ultimately it is up to the forces driving those revamped institutions to show the geniality that will make them into a central force in the region's political and economic landscape. To do so, they will have to go beyond the 'borrowing and bending' characteristic of too many legislative labour reforms in Africa,[75] a necessity that will be met all the more easily when, while making sure that tripartism remains the foundation of social dialogue, they secure – as have Niger and the WAEMU – the proper participation of the whole gamut of stakeholders in socio-economic reforms. What is at stake in the building of African regionalism is the design of a convincing 'social model', with effective standards of labour and social protection. 'Restoring the social question in African policymaking'[76] requires then addressing relations of power, rather than empowering technocracies, and the new availability of visible dedicated means to that end offers some hope that the so-called 'third wave' of democratisation might not be the last.

References

Acharya, A. (2003) 'Democratisation and the Prospects for Participatory Regionalism in Southeast Asia', *Third World Quarterly* 24(2).

Akumbu M'Oluna, J.P. (2008) *Libres propos sur les réformes juridiques au Gabon*, Paris: L'Harmattan.

74 In 2006 at Bamako, the ACP-EU economic and social interest groups highlighted the importance of social dialogue at all levels, and called for an extension of 'the ILO-WAEMU programme for the promotion of tripartite social dialogue' to all ECOWAS countries and ultimately to the whole English- and Portuguese-speaking Africa. The EU European Economic and Social Committee also mentioned then the desirability of enlarging the composition of the regional structure to other interest groups relevant to the social dimension of regional integration, such as peasant associations and cooperatives.

75 Kalula (2003), 'Present at the creation or another false start in Africa?'.

76 Olukoshi (2007), 'Africa: Bringing the Social Back In', 95.

Alby, P. et al. (2005) *Labor Institutions, Labor-Management Relations and Social Dialogue*, New York: World Bank.

Association Henri Capitant (2006) *Les droits de tradition civiliste en question. A propos des rapports Doing Business de la Banque Mondiale*, Paris: Société de législation comparée.

Bakvis, P. (2006) *How the World Bank and IMF use the Doing Business Report to Promote Labour Market Deregulation in Developing Countries*, Brussels: ICFTU/Global Unions

Berhe, A. (ed.) (2004) *Supporting Africa's Efforts to Achieve Sustainable Development, Dialogues at the Economic and Social Council*, New York: United Nations.

Béraud, J.M. (2001) *Etude préalable à l'adoption d'un Acte uniforme en Droit du Travail dans le cadre de l'OHADA*, Dakar: BIT.

Bond, P. (2002) *Fanon's Warning:* A Civil Society Reader on Nepad, Trenton NJ: Africa World Press.

Buthelezi, S. (2006) *Regional Integration in Africa: Prospects and Challenges for the 21st Century*, Capte Town: Ikhwezi.

Cazes, S. and Berg, J. (2007) *The Doing Business Indicators: Measurement Issues and Political Implications*, Geneva: ILO.

Croucher, R. (2007), 'Industrial Relations in Francophone Africa – the Case of Niger', in G. Wood and C. Brewster(eds) (2007) *Industrial Relations in Africa*, Basingstoke: Palgrave Macmillan.

Easterly, W. (2007) 'The Ideology of Development', *Foreign Policy*, July/August.

ECA/AU (2006) *Assessing Regional Integration in Africa II*, Addis Ababa: ECU and AU.

Evans, T. (2001) 'If Democracy, Then Human Rights?', *Third World Quarterly*, 22(4).

Fashoyin (2001) 'Industrial Relations in Developing Countries', in R. Blanpain and C. Engels (eds), *The ILO and the Social Challenges of the 21st Century*, Leiden: Kleuwer Law International.

Filali Meknassi, R. (2010) 'The Effectiveness of Labour Law and Decent Work Aspirations in the Developing Countries', in T. Teklè (ed.), *Labour Law and Worker Protection in Developing Countries*, Geneva: ILO.

Fonteneau, G. (2004) *Histoire du Syndicalisme en Afrique*, Paris: Karthala.

Frayle, L. (ed.) (2010) *Blunting Neoliberalism, Tripartism and Economic Reforms in the Developing World*, Basingstoke: Palgrave Macmillan/ILO.

van der Geest, W. and van der Hoeven, R. (eds) (1999) *Adjustment, Employment and Missing Institutions in Africa, The Experience of Eastern and Southern Africa*, London: James Curry.

Ghai, D. (2005) *ILO Participation in PRSPs: An Independent Evaluation*, Geneva: ILO.
Hintjens, H. (1999) 'The Emperor's New Clothes: A Moral Tale for Development Experts?', *Development in Practice* 9(4).
ILO (1996) *Conclusions concerning Tripartite Consultation at the National Level on Economic and Social Policy*, Geneva, ILO.
ILO (1997) *World Labour Report 1997–98: Industrial Relations, Democracy and Social Stability*, Geneva: ILO.
ILO (2002) *Resolution concerning Tripartism and Social Dialogue*, Geneva: ILO.
ILO (2004) *Economic Security for a Better World*, Geneva: ILO.
ILO (2007) *The Decent Work Agenda in Africa 2007–2015*, Geneva: ILO.
Ishikawa, J. (2003) *Key Features of National Social Dialogue*, Geneva: ILO.
Kalula, E. (2003) 'Present at the creation or another false start in Africa?', *Inaugural Lecture*, New Series, No. 229, University of Cape Town.
Kayizzi-Mugerwa, S. (ed.) (2003) *Reforming Africa's Institutions: Ownership, Incentives, and Capabilities*, Tokyo: United Nations University Press.
Kone, Z. and Soulama, T. (2005) *Etude sur la mise en place d'un cadre tripartite de dialogue social au sein de l'UEMOA*, Ouagadougou: UEMOA.
Kuruvilla, S. (2006) 'Social dialogue for decent work', in D. Ghai (ed.) (2006) *Decent Work: Objectives and Strategies*, Geneva: ILO.
Laurijssen, E. (2010) *Trade Union Pluralism and Proliferation in French-speaking Africa*, Geneva: ILO.
van Liemt, G. (2004) *The Social Dimension of Trade in ASEAN, A Preliminary Analysis of the Issues involved*, Geneva: ILO.
MacLean, S.J. (1999) 'Peacebuilding and the New Regionalism in Southern Africa', *Third World Quarterly* 20(5).
Martens, G. (1994) 'French-speaking Africa', in A. Trebilcock et al (eds), *Towards Social Dialogue: Tripartite Cooperation in National Economic and Social Policy-making*. Geneva: ILO.
Minet, G. and Vargha, C. (2006) 'The Outlook for African Labour Law: Between the OHADA Way and the World Bank Recommendations', in: *Labour Law: Its Role, Trends and Potential, Labour Education* 2/3 (143–144).
Mohamed Salah, M. (2002) *Les contradictions du droit mondialisé*, Paris: PUF.
Mwamadzingo, M. (2001) 'Regional Integration in Africa: Getting It Right', in *The Challenge of Globalization in Africa: The Trade Union Response, Labour Education* 2001/2, 123.
Nhlapo, S. (2007) 'Building Sustainable Unions in Africa', *Metal World* 2: 18–21.
Niango, M.A. (2007) *Dialogue social et intégration régionale: le cas de l'UEMOA, Etude pour le dixième anniversaire du PRODIAF*, Ouagadougou: PRODIAF.

Olukoshi, A. (2007) 'Africa: Bringing the Social Back In', *Global Social Policy* 7(1).

Oumarou, M. (2002) 'Niger', in *La représentativité des organisations de travailleurs et d'employeurs en Afrique francophone*, Dakar: BIT.

Robert, R. (2005) *The Social Dimension of Regional Integration in ECOWAS*, Geneva: ILO.

Standing, G. (2008) 'The ILO: An Agency for Globalisation?', *Development and Change*, 39(3).

Wood, G. and Brewster, C. (eds) (2007) *Industrial Relations in Africa*, Basingstoke: Palgrave Macmillan.

World Commission on the Social Dimension of Globalization (2004) *A Fair Globalization: Creating Opportunities for All*, Geneva: ILO.

Yeates, N. (2005) *'Globalization' and Social Policy in a Development Context. Regional Responses*, Geneva: UNRISD.

Notes on Contributors

AKUA BRITWUM is a Research Fellow at the Centre for Development Studies at the University of Cape Coast, Ghana.

MOHAMED SALIOU CAMARA is Assistant Professor of History and International Studies at the Embry-Riddle Aeronautical University in Daytona Beach, USA.

AZIZOU CHABI IMOROU is a researcher at LASDEL (Laboratoire d'Etudes et de Recherche sur les Dynamiques Sociales et le Développement Local) in Benin.

JAMES JONES is Associate Professor of History at West Chester University, USA.

GEORGE MINET has recently retired from the International Labour Organisation (ILO), where he was most recently Director of the Inter-Organization Relations Office (IGOs and NGOs) at ILO headquarters. He also served the ILO as Senior Labour Law Specialist for Francophone Africa and Asia.

KWAMINA PANFORD is Associate Professor and Chair of the Department of African-American Studies at Northeastern University, USA.

DAVID PERFECT works as a researcher for the Equality and Human Rights Commission (UK).

CRAIG PHELAN is editor of the journal *Labor History* and Professor of Modern History at Kingston University London.

ELIZABETH SCHMIDT is Professor of History at Loyola University, Baltimore, USA.

OUSMANE OUMAROU SIDIBE is Dean of Law and Economics at the University of Mali. Between 1993 and 1995 he was Mali's Minister of Labour, and he now holds the position of Director of the Programme for Institutional Development in Mali.

ANNE-CATHERINE WAGNER is Professor of Sociology at l'Université de Paris I.

Index

Trade Unions Past, Present and Future

Edited by Craig Phelan

This series publishes monographs and edited collections on the history, present condition and possible future role of organised labour around the world. Multi-disciplinary in approach, geographically and chronologically diverse, this series is dedicated to the study of trade unionism and the undeniably significant role it has played in modern society. Topics include the historical development of organised labour in a variety of national and regional settings; the political, economic and legal contexts in which trade unionism functions; trade union internationalism past and present; comparative and cross-border studies; trade unions' role in promoting economic equality and social justice; and trade union revitalisation and future prospects. The aims of the series are to promote an appreciation of the diversity of trade union experience worldwide and to provide an international forum for lively debate on all aspects of the subject.

Volume 1 Craig Phelan (ed.): Trade Unionism since 1945: Towards a Global History. Volume 1: Western Europe, Eastern Europe, Africa and the Middle East.
467 pages. 2009. ISBN 978-3-03911-410-8

Volume 2 Craig Phelan (ed.): Trade Unionism since 1945: Towards a Global History. Volume 2: The Americas, Asia and Australia.
364 pages. 2009. ISBN 978-3-03911-950-9

Volume 3 Pablo Ghigliani: The Politics of Privatisation and Trade Union Mobilisation: The Electricity Industry in the UK and Argentina.
293 pages. 2010. ISBN 978-3-03911-961-5

Volume 4 Heather Connolly: Renewal in the French Trade Union Movement: A Grassroots Perspective.
260 pages. 2010. ISBN 978-3-0343-0101-5

Volume 5 Magaly Rodríguez García: Liberal Workers of the World, Unite? The ICFTU and the Defence of Labour Liberalism in Europe and Latin America (1949–1969).
354 pages. 2010. ISBN 978-3-0343-0112-1

Volume 6 Jeffrey Sluyter-Beltrão: Rise and Decline of Brazil's New Unionism: The Politics of the Central Única dos Trabalhadores.
481 pages. 2010. ISBN 978-3-0343-0114-5

Volume 7 Craig Phelan (ed.): Trade Unions in West Africa: Historical and Contemporary Perspectives.
288 pages. 2011. ISBN 978-3-0343-0117-6

Volume 8 Forthcoming.

Volume 9 Tracy Carson: Tomorrow It Could Be You: Strikes and Boycotts in South Africa, 1978–1982.
325 pages. 2011. ISBN 978-3-0343-0119-0

Volume 10 Laura Ariovich: Organizing the Organized: Trade Union Renewal, Organizational Change and Worker Activism in Metropolitan America.
310 pages. 2010. ISBN 978-3-0343-0132-9

Volume 11 Indira Palacios-Valladares: Industrial Relations after Pinochet: Firm Level Unionism and Collective Bargaining Outcomes in Chile.
268 pages. 2011. ISBN 978-3-0343-0136-7

Volume 12 Zhining Ma: The ACFTU and Chinese Industrial Relations.
260 pages. 2011. ISBN 978-3-0343-0205-0

Volume 13 Quenby Olmsted Hughes: "In the Interest of Democracy": The Rise and Fall of the Early Cold War Alliance Between the American Federation of Labor and the Central Intelligence Agency.
218 pages. 2011. ISBN 978-3-0343-0212-8